JORGE LORENZO

JORGE LORENZO
MY STORY SO FAR

ERNEST RIVERAS TOBIA

Translation by Matthew Roberts

Haynes Publishing

The Spanish edition was published in 2008 as *Jorge Lorenzo: Por
Fuera Desde Dentro* by La Esfera de los Libros, S. L., Avenida de
Alfonso XIII, 1 bajos, 28002 Madrid
This English-language edition was published in May 2009 as *Jorge
Lorenzo: My Story So Far* by Haynes Publishing

A catalogue record for this book is available from the British Library

ISBN 978 1 84425 702 7

Library of Congress catalog card no 2008943649

Published by Haynes Publishing,
Sparkford, Yeovil, Somerset BA22 7JJ, UK
Tel: 01963 442030 Fax: 01963 440001
Int.tel: +44 1963 442030 Int.fax: +44 1963 440001
E-mail: sales@haynes.co.uk
Website: www.haynes.co.uk

Haynes North America Inc.,
861 Lawrence Drive, Newbury Park, California 91320, USA

Designed and typeset by Dominic Stickland
Printed and bound in the UK

CONTENTS

Prologue by Jorge Lorenzo 8

Foreword: Forming the grid 10

Introduction: Warm-up lap: entering 'Lorenzo's Land' 15

1. **X-dentro: On the inside** 64
   Jorge Lorenzo, up close and personal

2. **X-fuera: Around the outside** 126
   The family, plus one

3. **Through the chicane** 157
   The fears of a champion

4. **Opening the throttle** 210
   It's 'LorenShow' time

5. **Over the line** 238
   Jorge Lorenzo: a champion in the making

6. **On the podium** 274
   Signing for Yamaha

7. **MotoGP 2008** 282
   Rookie of the Year

Jorge Lorenzo Guerrero Results and statistics 310

Index 316

This book is dedicated to:

You, dear reader, for trying to understand me by buying this book.
María, my mother, for the unconditional love day after day.
'Chicho', my father, for your hard work and the good times together.
My sister Laura, who I see very little but love very much.
José, for showing me how a grandfather should be, and to all my Galician family.
Carmelo Ezpeleta, for his inestimable help.
Giampiero Sacchi, for your faith in the early days.
My sponsors.
Eva, a very special girl.
Lin Jarvis and Yamaha.
Ramón Forcada, Javier Ullate, Valentino Negri, Walter Crippa and Carlo Luzzi, my mechanics in MotoGP.
Ricky Cardús and family.
Sebastián Salvadó, for your love.
Jonathan Susmozas and family.
Juan Llansá, my trusted friend and now the youngest granddad in the paddock.
Carles Pujol from Gym Sants.
Gabriel Roca, for all your support.
Massimo Capanna.
Pep Font.
Marcos Hirsch, my 'Brother', for teaching me and protecting me.
My biographer, Ernest Riveras, a great communicator and even better person.
My fans.

Special thanks

This book could not have been completed without the help of
Natalia Hidalgo and everybody at La Esfera de los Libros; Jaime
Olivares, Emilio Perez de Rosas and Simone Rosa; Miguel Ángel
Violán, Jordi Perez and Älex Rovira. Also special thanks go to those
'guilty' for the Lorenzo menu at the Hotel Barceló-Sants: Juan
Barranco and all the waiters and kitchen staff. Finally, to Pol, Álex
and Gemma. To all of you, thank you.

Ernest Riveras Tobia
Ernest Riveras Tobia is the lead commentator on MotoGP for Spanish national television
network TVE. Ernest has spent over twenty years with TVE, covering no fewer than 25
different sports. He is well known for covering major cycling events, including the Giro
d'Italia, Vuelta de España and Tour de France, and he was the channel's main anchor for
the European and World Athletics Championships from 1999 to 2006 – as well as for the
Olympic Games of Barcelona, Atlanta, Sydney, Athens and Beijing. He is also Sports
Editor of a regional TVE channel, presenter of national sports magazine television show
Estadio 2 and founder of the prominent sports website *Deporte.es*.

Matthew Roberts
Matthew Roberts is one of the leading journalists in the MotoGP paddock. Having earned
a degree in Spanish and Communication Arts in 2000 he moved to Barcelona to work for
Dorna Sports, rights holders to MotoGP, and was the world feed commentator for the
series from 2001 to 2005. In 2006 he went freelance and combined several roles within
the paddock with that of pit-lane reporter for the BBC, as well as commentating on the
Indoor Trial World Championship and European Beach Soccer League. During his time in
Spain he also worked as a correspondent for Reuters news agency and *The Times*
newspaper. Matt returned to the UK in 2007 and now works directly for the BBC,
continuing his prominent role in their MotoGP coverage and making regular
contributions to their football magazine show *Football Focus*.

PROLOGUE

Everything depends on the way you look at it. Twenty-one may seem a young age to be taking time out to take stock of your life and tell your story. In fact, it is. But I also think that the success of a book depends on three main factors: who is writing it, who it is about and, of course, the quality of what is written. That is why I try to look at this from a different angle: here are two decades' worth of experiences – joy, disappointment, victories, failures, opinions, anecdotes, confessions – and it all adds up to create the tip of OUR iceberg. I am a double World Champion and MotoGP Rookie of the Year: that forms the basis of a decent story, don't you think?

I'm a fighter and a perfectionist, as I'm sure you know, and for my first book I wasn't prepared to settle for anything less than the best. Quite the opposite! So I can assure you that by the time you reach the end of this book you won't have turned over the typical three hundred plus superficial and unsentimental pages. I think that if somebody is going to write a book then they have to really take the plunge, tell the whole story (or at least as much of it as they can). That is why I don't see this book merely as the biography of Jorge Lorenzo. Here you will find out the truth about my life. Our truth. For me, reading it for the first time was like looking in the mirror, seeing that most intimate reflection that up to now only I knew. At the end of the day you can always lie to and mislead other people but when you look at yourself in the mirror, you can't lie to yourself.

To be honest, time has passed so quickly that I have barely even noticed. It only feels like a couple of days ago that I was tearing around the wastelands of Mallorca on a minibike and now I am in my second season of MotoGP. Life as a rider goes by too quickly; by the time you stop to think about it another season has gone past, you're already fully immersed in the next one and you can't even remember what happened a year ago. To make sure that didn't happen I put my trust in Ernest Riveras and gave him the keys to open the doors to my past. There turned out to be more doors than even I knew existed.

I was born in Mallorca but I believe my soul is from Sparta. Ever since the day I came into this world I was created and trained for a cause. In the case of the Spartans it was to defend their city and their FREEDOM to the death. Mine is to reach the very pinnacle of motorcycle racing. Spartans lived, ate and breathed for the cause. We fight with our backs to the wall to win our battles. Like the Spartans, I don't like to be beaten but I have to admit that this book has won me over. My dear friend, I hope that it can win you over too, without you barely realising it, but please don't take it as a defeat. We'll meet again, over these pages and in the races that lie before us. For Sparta!

Jorge Lorenzo

FOREWORD

Forming the grid

25 March 2008, 12.00pm
Kinepolis Cinema, Madrid
D-DAY

It had been hard work, not only writing this biography but also making sure that it reached Jorge Lorenzo's high expectations. Jorge had been a perfectionist about its design from the beginning, initially demanding that the front cover feature a photo of him dressed as half rider, half gladiator. The Spanish publishers managed to get that idea out of his head, telling him it would look more like a futuristic comic than the biography of a sportsman. But that was the last concession Lorenzo was willing to make and, instead, he insisted on a mid-shot of him in casual clothes looking up at his 'X-fuera' ['Around the Outside'] logo. The Italian photographer Simone Rosa, who covers the MotoGP World Championship, was given the task of bringing Jorge's idea to life and, luckily for him, he got it right. The photo and cover design of the original Spanish version of this book came directly from Jorge (even the shiny finish!) and even the most sceptical observers were forced to concede that his idea had been good. In fact, he has also overseen the design and the photographs used in this edition. Anyway, the big day finally arrived and the 'book about the life of Jorge Lorenzo' (he still refuses to refer to it as a biography) was launched. The presentation took place in Madrid and it served as confirmation to Jorge that his venture away from his natural habitat was going to be well received by the public. It was something that had really concerned him, but his fears were quickly forgotten, with many journalists and at least twenty photographers there to cover the event.

The day also featured a tour of Spain's main television studios, and it all served to comfort and relax Jorge. Having decided to open the doors to the most intimate side of his life through the writing of the book, its presentation was the moment to bare his soul and he needed to know that everything was perfect – in place, under control, just as he likes things.

Also, let's not forget the 'minor detail' that the 2008 season had fired up two weeks earlier in Qatar, where Jorge Lorenzo made the best premier-class debut since Max Biaggi in 1998, going from pole position to the podium, and that it was the week of the Spanish Grand Prix at Jerez. On top of that, his rivalry with Dani Pedrosa was developing into a matter of national debate, with the pair having declined to shake hands after the opening race. As a result, expectation and success were guaranteed. Jorge Lorenzo had become a true Spanish sports star. The football team had yet to win the European Championship, but along with Pedrosa he now formed part of the country's elite international performers, including the likes of Pau Gasol, Rafa Nadal, Fernando Alonso and Alberto Contador.

The presentation was hosted by one of the most highly respected journalists in the country, Lorenzo Milá, who presents the nine o'clock evening news on TVE. Shortly after the ceremony it dawned on me why both Jorge and I had agreed that the other 'Lorenzo' should be the man in the middle. It wasn't just the coincidence of their names, or that he was a well-known petrolhead. It was because we both knew of his ability to speak with his heart on his sleeve. And that was exactly what Lorenzo Milá did with Jorge Lorenzo as we travelled together in a minibus from the TVE studios to the launch. It was a case of quickly outlining what the rider wanted saying about him and his book. After hesitating slightly, Lorenzo (Milá) said to Lorenzo (Jorge): 'My friend, don't be what other people want you to be, try to always be yourself. Don't try to please. Speak clearly and honestly. If somebody doesn't like you they never will, but don't ever be untrue to yourself.'

With these words going round in his head, Jorge Lorenzo prepared for yet another of the hundreds of press conferences he has to sit through every year. This one was more important than most, though, because it was the presentation of 'his baby'. Milá began by saying: 'This biography is an exercise in transparency that has never been done before. It is virtually psychoanalysis. Stripping yourself bare in public is a rare thing for a World Champion who lives permanently in the firing line.' Jorge was ready to stand by the philosophy of his creation and he spoke as himself. 'I have always wanted to be different. I don't like people who are sheep, following the crowd. You have to be politically incorrect and question things.' When I heard him say that last phrase I knew that he had perfectly understood what it means to speak honestly: 'I have made a lot of mistakes in my life and I will continue to do so. But I want to be a World Champion and a good man.' This is the story of that journey.

24 October 2008, 20.30pm
Yamaha Hospitality, Valencia
EVERYTHING CHANGES

It is the eve of the Valencia Grand Prix, the final round of a successful but crash-strewn debut season in MotoGP for Jorge Lorenzo. I've just found out that the success of the Spanish edition of this book and the success of the rider in general have created enough interest to have the book translated for the English market. After the initial feeling of pride and excitement had passed, I quickly realised that this wasn't simply a case of translating but of rewriting. Because the whole backdrop, or the majority of it anyway, has changed.

By the end of his first season on the Yamaha M1 the stage on which Jorge's life was being played had undergone a makeover and, as the writing of the first book had demonstrated, it was all much more about 'Jorge' than it was about 'Lorenzo'. The way Jorge Lorenzo lives, thinks, feels and acts is usually a reflection of the events going on around him. That is why a change that may seem relatively superficial at first glance was bound to hide deeper, more interesting reasons that would require an update of his life story on both a sporting and a personal level. After all the intense hours I'd spent with Jorge between the end of 2007 and the start of 2008, I could sense that his new circumstances would tell us a lot about the events of the past year on every level.

As we sat at a table for dinner in Yamaha's hospitality unit at Valencia, where we planned to pick up from where we'd last left his biography, I realised that there was nobody left from the group of people with whom I had worked so closely last time around. There was no Dani Amatriaín, his manager for ten years; no Pere Gurt, his former director of communications; even his old friend, Dani Palau, wasn't there. They had all made way for a new inner circle, headed by Marcos Hirsch, his physical trainer and now his manager. Héctor Martín, who was signed up by Amatriaín as Jorge's press officer, was now in charge of all his press and PR activities while the renowned lawyer Ramón Sostres, who works for a host of top-level Spanish international footballers, had been hired as his new legal adviser.

At the age of just 21, Jorge Lorenzo has had to experience things that other people would not come across even if they were born again seven times over. In a little over two decades he has been through periods of great transition and change that have moulded him into the young man he is today. This latest development, however, is even more curious than any of the previous episodes. The decision to make drastic changes to his life, within his closest professional and personal circles, was entirely his own. The maturity and perspective he has developed over the last couple of years have allowed him, for the first time, to instigate such a change without the guidance and advice of others. This time it was he, and only he, who knew when, where and how to make the changes required to keep his career on the desired path. It is something that has come about after deep thought and through the responsible outlook of a young man who has enough independence to set the pace of his own life and decide who he wants around him and who he doesn't. However, no such change is straightforward or free of problems, setbacks, deliberation and suffering. If the break-up with his own father had been a heavy blow for him to take, splitting from the man who effectively took his place was always going to be painful too. However, Jorge does not want anybody to feel sorry for him. He hasn't been left completely defenceless; he is not a child playing grown-ups who needs a father figure to look up to. He races an 800cc motorcycle now, and both on the track and off it, in every respect, he has taken the step up to the big league.

As we sit at the table we scan through the first edition of the biography and discuss some of the things that need to be changed, which initially seem like quite a lot. I listen, surprised, to the avalanche of modifications he wants to make but I'm also interested in his reasoning. Jorge also listens to my opinion: 'We can explain that everything has changed but we shouldn't try to change the past.' I suggest that we simply turn a new page, figuratively and literally, detailing the present and the future with the optimism and strength that typify him. When I received the modified manuscript, agreed on by Jorge, Marcos and Héctor, the changes to the original version were minimal and I was reassured that Jorge had understood that he could not change where he has come from. All that has changed is where he is heading, and with whom.

But this is the difficult part. There is a great deal to tell. His first season in MotoGP has been about a lot more than nine months of racing and 18 Grands Prix. This is the biography of a double 250cc World Champion and the best rookie in the history of MotoGP. It is the story of his podiums, his poles, and his victory at Estoril. It is also the story of his crashes and his fears. It is the story of why some of the people who helped him to where he is now, people with whom he has shared many of his 21 years of life, are no longer around, and the reason for that is because Jorge has taken control of his life and he wants it that way. Ever since the day they met, Marcos Hirsch has repeatedly told him: 'Jorge, when you come of age you should sack us all. Take control of your life and only re-employ the people you want to work with.' And that is exactly what Lorenzo did in 2008. From here onwards, the present day will be mingled with the past and vice versa. It won't be easy, but then whoever said Jorge Lorenzo was?

Ernest Riveras Tobia

INTRODUCTION

Warm-up lap: entering 'Lorenzo's Land'

Whatever 'Lorenzo's Land' consists of, there is certainly no middle ground. Jorge Lorenzo is not an everyday guy. Everything about him is extreme and he is most comfortable dealing with, and surrounded by, the different and the extraordinary. The Lorenzo phenomenon is one of those things that you either embrace or repel. You're either a fan or you're not. Throughout his life he has left an indelible mark on the people and places he has come across, a trait that was once raw and unrefined but one that in recent years has allowed him to stand out above the rest as a champion both on and off the track. 'I am like a rough diamond', he says. 'I've not been polished yet and it's up to me to do that, I have to keep working on myself. I'm evolving. With the public, with my friends, with my fans. For example I don't think I've ever behaved badly with a fan but sometimes I've greeted them with a scowl. I shouldn't do that.'

Eugenio 'Cheni' Martínez worked as personal assistant to Jorge from 2006 to 2008 and he recalls an incident that changed Jorge's outlook on dealing with fans. 'In 2006 Samuel Eto'o, the Barcelona football player, came to Valencia and everybody within a 100m circle in the paddock was looking at him and asking him for an autograph or a photo. Samuel was obliging to everybody but he told them: "We can't stop, we have to keep walking!" Jorge has learned this little detail. Now he never says no to anybody but he doesn't stop walking.'

Fans either love him or hate him and if they're not trying to stop him for an autograph they're probably hurling insults. There is nothing in between. He leaves nobody indifferent – bipolarity, the experts call it – and that is something he enjoys; in fact he thrives on it. Jorge Lorenzo has just enough arrogance, enough insolence, to make him almost completely sure of himself. He is sincerity personified, and he doesn't hold back. Jorge is not the kind to hide – on the track or off it – although he has learnt that too much self-confidence can generate criticism and problems. 'He's a tough kid, cheeky,' was the diagnosis of 'The Doctor', Valentino Rossi, during post-season testing for Yamaha at Jerez in November 2007, the first time they had come face to face on a MotoGP track.

The material for this book was therefore a little unusual and the only possible objective was to get to the bottom of this combative, glory-hunting rebel, who sometimes looks at the world with defiance and arrogance and at other times with fear and a burning desire to learn and be liked. The devil in him has probably become more famous than the angel, because there have been plenty of controversial stories written about Jorge in the past. But his intimate side is interesting as well, and it's never too late for you to get to know him.

However, the only way to enter the world of a warrior like Lorenzo, by name (his maternal surname is 'Guerrero', meaning 'warrior' in Spanish) and by nature (his star sign is Taurus), is on the attack. The 'Lorenzo's Land' fortress has several doors and the only way to get in is by finding the key to one of them. Despite Jorge's youth it isn't easy to get a true idea of his character or understand it first time around. However, it is the small details, the little stories, that hold the truth and, when put together, they colour in the outline of a young man who feels he is now ready to start opening those doors.

11 June 2007
The day after the Catalunya GP, Montmeló circuit
Text written by Jorge Lorenzo entitled: **'IF ONLY I COULD...'**

Imagine that one day you were allowed to choose how you would like to be. What would you ask for? I'm clear in my mind. Actually, I'm not really but I'm going to write down the first thing that comes into my head. If only I could...

I'd like to have the speed and spring of Carl Lewis. I'd like to be richer than

Bill Gates and better looking than Brad Pitt. More attractive than George Clooney. I would love to have the political power of Bush and media influence of the Pope. To have the arrogance of Cantona and the character of McEnroe. The grace of Gandhi and the gentleness of Jesus Christ. The charisma of Nelson Mandela. The strength of Tyson and agility of Ali. The art of Picasso and the imagination of Gaudí. To be more intelligent than Einstein and as prolific as Casanova. To have the elegance of Zidane and the talent of Messi. To play football like Maradona and tennis like Nadal. To be as big and tall as Shaquille O'Neal. To sing like Sinatra. To dance like Elvis. To have the success of the Beatles. To drive like Alonso. To ride like Rossi…

Wait … just wait a second! What am I talking about? Is that what I really want? Surely I'm being naïve. The best thing about life is having defects and feeling comfortable with them. Trying to improve on your weaknesses and even turn them into a strength. To have a quality, to recognise what it is and then to squeeze everything out of it. Ay, if only I could! If only I could… As people we're never happy with who we are – especially when we're young.

Last night the whole team got together to have dinner and celebrate OUR victory. We only tend to do that at the Spanish races. We all know that at the end of the meal it is time for 'the boss', Dani, to speak, although yesterday it fell to me to open and close proceedings. Alex – who, by the way, I owe an entire column to, but I'm still thinking about it – also got his chance to express his thanks.

These are unique moments, those special shared evenings when you really realise who your 'people' are. The people who value your qualities and appreciate your defects. The people who make you realise that you don't have to share blood with somebody for them to be family. By the end of the meal you love yourself more and you value yourself more.

I've made my mind up. If I could choose, I'd continue to be Jorge Lorenzo.

After ending a five-year Montmeló victory drought with a dominant win that took him another step closer to his second 250cc World Championship, Jorge's article was a declaration of intent – the words of a man who had decided to be himself, to build his own personality over time, because his journey continues where others come to an end. For him, winning is not enough and he refuses to be just another person, just another sportsman.

What Jorge loves most is making other people happy. He believes that, as a rider, he is different from the rest and he wants that to be recognised. His former PR manager from 2006 to 2008, Pere Gurt, believes that Jorge Lorenzo's character may not yet have found a way to explain itself. 'That, or people don't want to understand it,' says Pere. Maybe that's why he sees this book as an opportunity to reveal himself – to come out from behind the fairing.

Jerez circuit, 1997
Final round of the 50cc Copa Aprilia
DISCOVERING A CHAMPION

Dani Amatriaín's routine at a circuit had not changed much over the previous ten years. As soon as a practice session gets under way Amatriaín takes a scooter and heads for one of the corners. A professional in his line of work knows that the best place to 'see things' is from trackside. Practice for the 50cc Caja Madrid Copa Aprilia in 1997 would be no different and there was nothing to suggest that this autumn day at Jerez was going to be special.

Practice for the youngsters in the Copa Aprilia was coming to a close. Lap by lap Dani began to realise he was watching one of them more than the others – a tiny kid who rode differently to everybody else. He didn't know it yet, but what Dani saw from trackside that day was a glimpse into the future. 'More than his speed, he caught my attention by the way he took the corners. It was as if he'd been doing it his whole life – like a professional.' It is now the end of 2007 and he closes his eyes to remember a moment that clearly holds a special place in his memory. You just know that he could describe every second of it.

'I was curious to see who this kid was, so I took the trouble to go to his box.' It was there that Dani would meet one of the key characters in this story – Jorge's father, Chicho Lorenzo. 'I asked him about his rider. I told him he'd caught my attention and I wanted to meet him. His father called him and he came out.' It was love at first sight, although they wouldn't realise that until much later. 'I remember it as if it was yesterday,' continues Dani. 'He was an unusual, curious character. His head was shaved, apart from a Mohican and two stars. His father said, "This is Dani Amatriaín." He [Jorge] looked at me with distrust. He had no idea who I was.' But their story together had begun because this little ten year old, with his skill and attitude, had made such a major impact on one of the leading talent-spotters in Spain.

A month after that first meeting Chicho Lorenzo travelled to Barcelona, where Dani was in charge of a school for mechanics called Monlau. While Jorge might not have known at Jerez how important this person was, his father certainly did, and he also knew how crucial his interest could turn out to be. Chicho wanted Jorge to go on competing in the Copa Aprilia but he was in dire financial straits. 'I've brought him this far,' Chicho told Dani. 'From here I don't have the means to take him further. Is there anything we can do?' Sincerity and candour, a Lorenzo trademark. At that time Amatriaín already had ten or eleven riders competing in the CEV, European Championships and Grands Prix. 'I couldn't give him the support he deserved,' recalls Dani. 'It was really difficult for me and I had no choice but to say no.'

Lorenzo's fledgling career was on the point of ending before it had begun, but Chicho was not, and is not, the kind of guy who accepts defeat. Dani's words would have been heartbreaking to anybody else, but Chicho refused to leave Barcelona without making one final attempt. As they said goodbye he handed Dani a videotape. 'Please, just watch this. So that you can see how we ride in Mallorca.' With that he left, confident in the knowledge that the sight of Jorge in action would be enough for Dani to take those crushing words back.

Jorge's father, who had seen the reaction his son's riding provoked among bystanders back home in Palma de Mallorca, was not wrong. The first thing Amatriaín did when he arrived home was load the tape into his VCR. His wife had his dinner ready on the table and was angry that he walked straight past it to the video recorder, but Dani's curiosity had got the better of his manners. 'I couldn't believe what I was seeing. The way he rode, how he slid the bike around. I was surprised by his audacity, his temperament, the way he controlled the bike and the way it was all so natural. He was so small that it was surprising to see him ride like that. And his stare ... he already had the stare of a champion.'

The video already forms part of Lorenzo legend and is something anybody close to him pinpoints as a key moment in his discovery. The first time I asked Pere Gurt when and how he'd come across Jorge he told me: 'I'll start by telling you about the first time I heard anybody talk about him. Dani told me he'd seen a video of this incredible kid. I remember he told me he'd discovered a bomb waiting to explode – a rough diamond.'

Dani Amatriaín lives for racing, and his experience and natural instinct for recognising talent drew him instantly to the screen, riveted by the image of a midget riding like a professional. From that day he made Jorge one of his pupils and always had him marked out as one of his favourites. Through Jorge, Dani envisioned the resurrection of an old dream and the quest to fulfil that dream became his life. His deepest professional desire had been to find a kid with raw talent and teach him from scratch – to train him as a rider and as a person, coaching him through every level of competition until that great promise was realised in the form of a great champion. 'I always thought that when I found a rider like that, who had all the natural attributes, everything else could be worked on.'

At Jerez Dani had already seen that this kid was different from the rest and now he could begin to witness it first hand. They would go to a circuit and Dani would take a 600, with Jorge following behind on a 50. 'I was virtually drooling because it was like having a professional behind me. Then I'd let him pass and I'd follow him from behind so that I could watch him and I realised that he'd picked up absolutely everything. He was like a sponge! I had to stop because he was getting faster and faster and I was worried he might hurt himself.'

Chicho Lorenzo had dug a diamond from the mine and delivered it – now it needed an expert jeweller to work on it. Despite his own obvious natural talent for riding and his vast experience, the first reality faced by Amatriaín was that this was going to be a difficult job – as difficult as the character of a World Champion. But Dani wanted to take it on and he committed himself to it with great conviction. Jorge came into his life as a challenge; he showed signs of being a thoroughbred racer and Dani backed him strongly, so convinced of his talent that he gave the youngster his own lucky number, 48. It was the number Amatriaín had always worn when he raced, during the late 1980s and early 1990s. It was a small detail but one designed to tell the world that Jorge was his great hope. Apart from 2007, when Lorenzo sported the number 1 plate as 250cc World Champion, Jorge stuck with 48 in tribute to his sporting father figure until the end of the 2008 season, when he'd brought their professional and personal relationship to an end. Indeed, as will become clear over the course of this book, the fact he discarded that number in favour of 99 for the 2009 season was just as significant a decision as it was to use the number 48 in the first place.

Exactly what the pair meant to each other – Dani to Jorge and vice versa – was best described by Jordi Pérez, team co-ordinator for Fortuna Aprilia, at the end of 2007. 'Other than his parents, the most important person in Jorge's life has been Dani. He put his life on one side so that Jorge would not want for anything. He gave up everything for him – not in a material sense but in terms of the affection he has shown him. Before giving Jorge bad advice he'd rather take it on himself.'

Winter 2002–Summer 2005
BACK TO HIS ROOTS

When he moved to Barcelona in 2000, aged just 14, Jorge cut his ties with Mallorca and with his past, leaving a lot of things behind, including his school friends. After the summer holidays following his second year at ESO (the name for Spanish secondary education from ages 12 to 16) he never returned to La Milagrosa, the state school in the centre of Palma where he had been studying. The change of scenery wasn't a particularly traumatic experience because, since he'd started competing in the Copa Aprilia, it had become normal for him to miss classes. For the same reason, his classmates weren't surprised when he suddenly disappeared. He was still virtually a child but he left to take up the life of a professional racer. His beloved island had become too small for the size of his aspirations.

Dani Palau was one of his friends from those days. They've known each other since the age of three. 'Whenever we played sport, if he lost or missed a goal or swung the bat and missed the ball he'd shout "Mierda!" ' he recalls. 'He still does it with the PlayStation. If he has a "virtual" crash he throws the controller on the floor!'

Palau lost touch with Jorge when he left for Barcelona in 2000. Two years later, out of the blue, Jorge called him. He answered, even though he didn't recognise the number. '¿Qué tal Palau?' It was Jorge, speaking as if they'd seen each other the previous day. 'It's a good job I was skiving school because otherwise I'd have had the phone switched off and maybe we'd never have spoken,' recalled Dani. 'In fact, I'm still not even sure how he got my number!' The pair swapped email addresses and hooked up online. Every time Jorge came back to Mallorca they met up for real.

Dani Palau became Jorge's only friend outside motorcycling. The rest of the time, anybody who had anything to do with Jorge was somehow involved in racing. He didn't even have friends his own age. Bikes came first – the most important and maybe even the only important thing in Lorenzo's life. But Jorge was starting to feel the urge to rebuild his links with Mallorca and Dani, his friend since the days when the only bikes they rode were plastic tricycles, was the best way to re-establish contact with the only life he knew away from the roar of engines and get close to somebody of the same age and with similar interests. In one of their many conversations Dani mentioned his studies and Jorge instantly saw it as a chance for them to get closer together. 'Graphic design? That's fantastic – you can do my website!'

In 2005, after turning 18, Dani Palau decided to follow in Jorge's footsteps and move to Barcelona to continue his studies in design. From the day he arrived, Dani and Jorge became inseparable – to the point that, until Jorge moved to London, they lived together in Alella, where they finally created the web page they'd talked of and dreamed about. They'd spend hours changing it, improving it, thinking up new ideas. It was always 'We can do this for the web' or 'We can do that for the web.' And since the Spanish for 'for the web' is 'para la Web', Dani's name changed from Palau to PalaWeb. 'At the start the website was a pig's ear, totally shit!' Jorge laughs. 'But we loved watching it get better every day. On an evening we'd put the things Dani had learnt in class that day into practice. It was cool!'

Following his final season with Derbi, in 2004, Jorge decided it was time to fly the nest and move out of the flat where he'd lived with Chicho until the age of 17. 'I went to live in Alella, near to Dani (Amatriaín). I didn't know anybody out there so sometimes I hung out with his daughter; we were friends. But it wasn't the same, I knew I was missing something.' The arrival of Palau was an important moment in his life.

They had a great time playing on the PlayStation, surfing the Internet and chatting online or playing online games – 'like GP500, which is really old' explains Jorge, as if to demonstrate his gaming pedigree. One afternoon things changed completely. Once again a telephone call would prove to be a key moment in the relationship between Dani and Jorge. 'I remember it well,' says Palau. 'I was in a park with some friends and the phone rang. It was Jorge.'

'PalaWeb, how would you like to be my Uccio?'

'What's an Uccio?' Palau didn't know anything about bikes. In fact, until that point, he hadn't even watched a race that Jorge wasn't competing in.

'Uccio is Valentino's buddy. He goes with him everywhere. It's just that Dani (Amatriaín) says he thinks you're a good guy and he wants you to come to all the races with us.'

'All of them? Even Japan?'

'Well, just the European ones for now.'

To the other Dani in Jorge's life, Dani Amatriaín, his manager and mentor, the positive influence that Palau had on his rider hadn't gone unnoticed. At the start, Amatriaín lent Palau a flat in Barcelona to help out with his studies and to make it easier for him and Jorge to stay in contact when Lorenzo was in town. Shortly afterwards, he signed him up to work for Motorsport48. 'I've been watching you for a month and I have to say that since I've known Jorge I've never seen him laugh the way he laughs with you.' For that reason, Dani

Amatriaín wanted them to be together the whole time. Amatriaín's project with Jorge covered both his professional and personal life: he knew that he had to take care of every facet of this young man's career if he wanted him to become a great champion. For a teenager, friendship is a basic and hugely beneficial part of growing up.

It was around 2005 when Dani Palau was offered the job of 'right-hand man' to Jorge. The first time the two friends found themselves together at a track was at Montmeló; the following weekend Palau was at Assen for the Dutch TT and he quickly became a team regular. In the end Dani never made it to Japan, but he didn't mind. The changes to his life were so plentiful and so important after Jorge picked up the phone – not once but twice – that the land of the rising sun could wait.

October 2006
Hotel Victoria, Palma de Mallorca
THE FASTEST RIDER, THE SLOWEST THINKER

When Jorge Lorenzo does something, he does it properly – and not just on the track, because his job doesn't finish the moment he crosses the line. If he has won, or finished on the podium, the follow-up to the Grand Prix is to speak to the press. Building a relationship with the media has always been an objective for Jorge and it is something he has worried about a lot. Right at the beginning, during those afternoons spent training with his father, one of the things they worked on was how to speak in public and answer journalists' questions. Those who remember his early days of racing in Mallorca recall the difference in the way Jorge used to speak to the local journalists compared with the other young riders. Little Lorenzo was confident and professional with his answers, copying the style of his heroes on television.

Spanish television reporter Marc Martín recalls the first time he went to interview Jorge at the Circuit de Catalunya, when he was still a child. Just when the camera was on the youngster and Marc was about to ask the question, Jorge held his hand up and said: 'I'm sorry, I've just remembered that before any interviews I have to consult my manager.'

Nowadays when Jorge arrives in a press conference room, tired and euphoric, he really has to make an effort to control his emotions and communicate his true feelings. It is extra difficult for him to then translate those feelings accurately into English for the international press. For this reason he always thinks through what he is going to say because he doesn't want to put his foot in it, even though the people who know him claim he knows more English than he lets on.

With the vast experience he has at explaining his thoughts after a race, doing it in English is now virtually his only worry. A press conference or group or face-to-face interview, in Spanish, doesn't faze him at all any more. Improvements can always be made, of course, and somebody might catch him out, but Jorge cares deeply about what people think of him and he doesn't want to be misunderstood. One clear example of his desire to learn and improve at anything he puts his hand to is the fact that, in November 2006, he decided to hire the services of a professional 'media coach'. Pere Gurt knew exactly where to turn, having recently attended a lecture by journalist and media consultant Miguel Ángel Violán at the Catalunya College for Journalists. Following a 30-hour course on public speaking, Jorge's stage presence and speech delivery are now virtually impeccable.

The first thing to catch Violán's attention on the autumnal Mallorcan afternoon when he met Jorge for the first time was that he seemed much younger than he'd expected. He didn't know much about racing and he didn't know what to expect from a World Champion, but he certainly didn't expect anybody this young. 'This little fellow is already a World Champion? And he wants to learn how to speak in public?' Miguel Ángel asked himself. The World Champion in front of him was just 19 years old.

Jorge wanted to create a good impression in front of the press and he'd finally realised that the way a message is transmitted is just as important as the message itself. He'd also experienced the problems that his impulsiveness could create once he was put in front of a microphone. Not knowing how to properly channel the overwhelming sincerity that had become his trademark over the years had got him into enough trouble to make him want to know how, when and how honestly he should speak at any given time. All of this surprised Miguel Ángel from the start. His experience had taught him that this was a common concern for politicians or businessmen, but with such a young man, who had quit his studies so early? 'He's either well advised or very intuitive,' he thought.

Even though he was well advised, this was pure intuition and while only Dani Amatriaín spoke during their first meeting in the Hotel Victoria de Palma de Mallorca it became clear that Jorge was not being forced into these classes; he was doing them because he wanted to. Jorge was silent during that first meeting, hidden behind his usual vice, his mobile phone. While Dani and Miguel Ángel drew up an outline for their sessions together, Jorge passed the time sending and receiving messages to and from his friends. 'Jorge wants to speak well in public because he knows that it will give him more appeal,' said Dani at the time.

And what about Jorge? 'Firstly, I want to do this because when I speak I want to give a good impression. Secondly, even though I like to read, I get the feeling that I don't retain the words very well or don't use them adequately.' Jorge had a passive knowledge of certain terms but was worried that he could have an idea in his mind and not be able to express it properly. He wanted to dominate language, both spoken and physical. He wanted to know how to handle himself in front of the press when they tested him with uncomfortable questions.

Even though Amatriaín hadn't instigated Jorge's media training there was something that had bothered him from the start of the youngster's career. He didn't want Jorge, through youthful impulsiveness, to say the wrong thing – even if it happened to be the truth. Miguel Ángel had to get it through to Lorenzo that with calm reflection would come more accurate explanation. In order that Jorge learned how to say what he was supposed to say he taught him a motto: 'I have to teach the fastest man in the world to be the slowest thinker.' That was the maxim of his work with Jorge, and anybody who knew Jorge before and after his classes with

Violán will tell you that it remains imprinted on his mind and is constantly applied.

'Miguel Ángel is somebody who always speaks slowly, calmly. He told me that he had once been shy like me but he had improved. He was different to the rest, you could tell that he'd studied how to communicate with others whereas I was still a bag of nerves. I'd sit down at the table, shift position a thousand times and play with my mobile phone when I got tense. He corrected all of that,' recognises Jorge. Violán, meanwhile, laughs when he recalls how 'he used to look at me like I was a freak, as if I was an alien!'

In just under a year they had ten sessions together. At first these took place in a business centre in Calle Vilamarí, Barcelona – a neutral venue without any distractions, where Jorge could take his first steps towards improving his communication skills. Later they moved to the head office of the insurance company RSM, one of Jorge's sponsors, on Calle Numancia, also in Barcelona. The exercises that made up the classes were varied but often consisted of reading out articles aloud in order for Jorge to gain more confidence when speaking. Violán would often interview him, at length, on any given subject so that he learned to improvise answers, sometimes backing him into a corner like a real journalist would. The idea, basically, was to prepare him for worst-case scenarios.

The success of the classes was easily measured by Jorge's willingness to continue with them, and on that level Miguel Ángel was achieving top marks. Jorge is a proactive person and, as such, he looks for a reaction to everything he does. He became hooked on the classes because he felt he was learning something. Jorge is hugely disciplined when it comes to things that bring improvements to his life, and his attitude towards it, so he turned up on time for every lesson. It seemed his capacity for learning had no limit, so the only option was to continue bombarding him with new things, moving on to exercises in mental co-ordination. Miguel Ángel gave him three balloons, which Jorge had to keep hitting into the air, answering a series of questions without letting them hit the ground. The reason for the exercise was because concentration is often his Achilles heel. Miguel Ángel continually repeated a phrase made famous by the

Spanish sports journalist José María García: 'At this level the difference between competitors is made by the one who has practised for an hour longer. So, let's continue.'

During one of their sessions, Miguel Ángel caught Jorge giving him an intense look. 'What's wrong, Jorge? Tell me anything.'

'Miguel Ángel, you like what you do, right?'

It was a question that didn't surprise his 'teacher'. 'Jorge is passionate about what he does and he can recognise that passion in other people,' he says. It is hardly surprising that Miguel Ángel didn't turn in an invoice for eight months. 'I was enjoying myself so much that I forgot I was supposed to be working and I didn't send them a bill!' When he did, he was paid within four days.

21 October 2007, 13.00pm
Sepang circuit, Malaysian GP
TEARS OF A DOUBLE WORLD CHAMPION

For some people, Jorge Lorenzo's attitude can at times come across as pure arrogance. For others, however, it is an example to be followed. Whatever anybody thinks, Jorge is the kind of rider who gets up on race morning with the conviction that nobody can beat him. He feels invincible. He has not been conditioned to lose and, as far as he is concerned, second place is for the first loser. In Lorenzo's mind there is no margin for error and he doesn't need anybody to put pressure on him because it comes as standard.

This is the Lorenzo we have come to know, but on the inside there is a completely different Jorge. Few people get to meet him because few people get close enough. One of the select group to have done so, and to have gained the authority to say whatever they like to his face, was Alex Debón. For two years he worked as Lorenzo's 'Sporting Director', gaining access to the man behind the visor thanks to the strength of his professional example and advice – and he told him things straight.

'You have tried to create an image, and it is not for me to tell you it's a bad one because when you're winning there's no such thing,'

Alex told him one day. 'But show people who you really are, take off the mask. This display of cool – what's it for? We've already had enough of that with Max Biaggi. A legend on the track, yes, but nobody really cared for him off it. You're different. Be yourself! If you were to show the world the person I know they'd realise what a great guy you really are. You are the way you were born. Don't try to invent a character! By the way, you've got a big nose. And you're not exactly good looking either.'

If only a few people are allowed access to Jorge's sensitive side, then fewer still have seen it in action. For a large part of his life he has always tried to block out any displays of sensitivity or fragility, emotion or sadness, considering them signs of weakness. But even though there have been few public occasions when we've seen Jorge with his guard down, there have been other times when his mind has said one thing and his body another, because circumstances have prevented him from controlling it.

In general, Jorge has a firm grip over his emotions, which is why those who know him well say that you have to hit him over the head with a flowerpot to make him cry. However, when he was crowned 250cc World Champion for the second time, in Malaysia in 2007, he could do nothing to stop the tears. He'd celebrated like a victorious boxer, having knocked his rivals out of the fight before the season's end, but when he returned to parc fermé at Sepang and saw Alex Debón, he collapsed onto his shoulder in a flood of tears.

Two months previously, at the British GP, when a crash in the race saw his championship advantage slashed, Jorge earned himself a telling-off from Miguel Ángel Violán for saying in an interview 'I can't cry over it like a little girl.'

'Jorge, crying is not something that is limited to one sex,' Violán told him. 'You shouldn't think that and least of all say it. Think about what you say, but don't always say what you think. Your words have a huge impact. You can't just shout your mouth off like that.'

Jorge had taken that lesson on board and parc fermé wasn't the only time on that emotional day that he cried. In the evening, on the set of the Spanish television programme 'MotoGP Club', Jorge burst into tears again while watching a video of his life. Thoughts of his parents, his friends in Mallorca and those closest to him at the time, like Dani Amatriaín, Alex Debón or Juan Llansá, broke down his defences once more. (Juan has been Jorge's most trusted mechanic since his days at Derbi. He's better known in the paddock as 'Juanito' although Jorge jokingly refers to him as 'Hollywood' or 'Holly', a dig at his Hitchcock-esque habit of appearing in the background on the television). As the video was broadcast, the director showed a close-up in the corner of the screen of Jorge crying in his pit box.

Jorge recalls: 'I cried because there are times you think you are not going to achieve something. There are difficult times, like when practice is going badly and you're trying your best but you can't get the job done, and you think you never will. Then you do it! If it were all easy nobody would ever cry. Interestingly, when I won in 2006 I didn't cry. Maybe I did in 2007 because I felt more 'alive' – I knew how to better appreciate my emotions. I valued what was happening to me more. The previous year I was probably more bothered about the image I was giving out, I wasn't myself. I was more worried by what other people might think of me. But in Malaysia I didn't care! Is that maturing? I think it's just doing things the right way. Being yourself gives you much more pleasure than trying to be something else and I think that I'm becoming myself more and more. That's why I cried. Because I truly felt it.'

In Spain Jorge had gained the respect of the general public thanks to his success on the racetrack, but the more this soft and sensitive side of his character came out, the more that respect turned to affection. The more he began to show who he really was, the more fans he gained. Behind every thoroughbred champion is a thoroughbred person.

Before becoming a World Champion Lorenzo had won himself few admirers. 'I am better than Pedrosa and time will judge if I am right or not.' 'Maybe my rivals are a little scared of me.' Comments like this, from February 2006, did his reputation a lot of damage. The impetuosity of his words and ways perhaps made him seem an unattractive personality, but the Lorenzo of today divides the masses. His nature is still to take things to the extreme, because he has been taught to win, but his sporting spirit and desire to constantly improve himself have also begun to turn him into the fine person, friend and colleague he is now showing he can become. The effects are beginning to be felt outside the confines of his pit box.

Jorge Lorenzo is a hero, and he's not ashamed about it. Spain is a country where heroes with character arouse passions of all kinds. 'If Jorge Lorenzo and Fernando Alonso say they'll win five world titles, they are seen as arrogant. If Raúl or Ronaldinho say the same thing they're seen as heroes,' Jorge once said, with the bitterness of a person who clearly felt misunderstood by both public and press.

I should mention here that the first time we went through this book together Jorge read this quote, which had appeared in a recent interview, and realised that his thoughts and feelings surrounding that particular subject had already changed. He felt that he had matured a lot in a short period of time and pointed out that he didn't stand by many of the things he'd said in the past. Another one of Miguel Ángel Violán's lessons came into play. This was something they had spoken about together.

Miguel Ángel, do I always have to tell the truth?

'That's a heavy question and not a normal one for somebody so young,' thought Miguel Ángel.

Jorge, you should never lie but you don't always have to tell the whole truth. You should only say things that you are sure you can stand by. The fact you're saying something you know isn't necessarily nice for other people to hear. Also, your thoughts evolve so it is better to play everything down, so that in the future you won't regret something you say now.

Comparing himself to Alonso, Raúl and Ronaldinho was an example of Jorge still not having the awareness to know when the time was right to speak out and when it was better to keep his mouth shut, a trait he is keen not to make excuses for. 'There are no excuses for it. If I said that and people didn't like it then there's a reason for that. Everything, or almost everything, that happens to you in life, good or bad, is deserved. In my case for thoughts that I have expressed or things I have done. I used to think that people didn't realise how good I was, how magnificent I was, etc. But now I think that if they didn't understand me at the time it is because I was doing something wrong. I deserved it, it was fair. Everything happens as a result of something you have done and sometimes I did or said things that weren't right.'

20 November 2007, 8.00am
Milan, Italy
TRENDSETTER

In Spain, Jorge Lorenzo is a sponsorship magnet. While other sportsmen are struggling to make ends meet, Jorge has run out of space on his leathers to fit the logos of companies who want to be associated with his image and on occasion his people have had to say 'no' to many of the offers that have come in. Towards the end of 2007 a new product found its way into the Lorenzo brand and a trip to Milan proved to be well worth making.

It was a flying visit like so many, if not most of them, are. And like most film shoots, it was a real pain. Even though it was for a 20-second television advert it felt more like a remake of *Ben-Hur*. Each take was repeated over and over. 'At the agency where we were, they're used to working with celebrities, actors and singers,' explains Jordi Pérez, who was the person designated to travel with Lorenzo. 'They treated him with extreme care, they didn't want to upset him. They kept asking him if he was tired!' After several hours of filming they finally sat down to watch the footage and check it was okay but it was Jorge who wasn't satisfied. 'Let's do another take, I'll do it better this time,' he said. 'They were so shocked they almost fell over! He's a champion in every sense of the word,' recalls Jordi.

The advertisement was for 'Prima', a brand of ketchup. In

September 2007 they carried out a survey to gauge Jorge's popularity amongst the general public. The response left them with no doubts. His notoriety level came back at 52 per cent, meaning at least one in every two people questioned had heard of him; 92 per cent of those people knew what he did and 60 per cent of them responded positively to the key question: 'Is Jorge Lorenzo a good example to follow?' Numbers aside, Jorge had also been a personal choice of the company's bosses. It wasn't that the directors of 'Prima' were huge motorcycle fans, but they had been captivated by that inimitable Lorenzo style on television and they were convinced that it typified ketchup; you either love it or hate it!

The filming schedule included only a half-hour break for a sandwich. The rest of the day was spent filming, watching Jorge squeeze sauce over French fries. With experts in such banal activities sitting watching, it suddenly dawned on them that he was distributing the ketchup in the opposite direction to most people – anti-clockwise. Apparently only one in a thousand do it clockwise, like Lorenzo. To normal human eyes it was a seemingly insignificant detail, but for the directors of the ketchup brand it was confirmation to them that they'd made the right decision.

At the end of the afternoon, and with time running out before they had to catch their plane, Jorge had to record a voiceover track. 'He had to say five or six phrases, each one about ten words long, and repeat them twenty times over,' recalled Jordi. 'When he'd finished, the sound engineer told him he could go. He said he'd be able to take a word from here, a word from there, stitch them together and sort out the levels and it would sound perfect. But Jorge shook his head. "The thing that needs to sound perfect is me, not the machine – I'll do it again," he said.'

The taxi driver out on the street was beeping his horn impatiently, and Jordi was looking anxiously at his watch. 'We're not going to make it,' he thought. But not only did Jorge stay behind to redo the voiceover, he insisted on saying goodbye to each individual member of the production team, the kids and even their families – more than sixty people. Jordi still laughs. 'I'm sure the first people to buy Prima ketchup were the production staff. You'll probably even see them at Mugello with a banner supporting Jorge!'

1998–2008
A DECADE IN THE MAKING

Once Jorge Lorenzo has left the circuit, he limits his racing to the PlayStation. He doesn't ride on the street – he doesn't even own a licence – so away from the track he has come to dominate, minus his racing leathers and on public roads, he wouldn't legally be allowed to ride a 250, much less an 800. 'I guess he thinks that riding a bike away from the circuit is dangerous, so he prefers to go by car,' says Cheni Martínez, his former assistant. 'If I rode a motorcycle on the street I'd end up hurting myself, I'm sure of it,' confirms Jorge.

Since we've mentioned Cheni again, what exactly does a rider's assistant do? 'Other than dress him, everything!' he told me. 'Jorge gradually changed, but believe me, it didn't come easy! Nowadays he's punctual but he always used to turn up late. He'd be in the shower or in bed, playing on the PlayStation, and I'd be saying to him, "We're gonna be late!" As far as I know riders in general are a bit of a disaster and I don't know how other assistants work, but with Jorge it was really difficult because he started out much worse than anybody else. We had a lot more ground to make up! For example, he's a poser, he's vain, but he's a disaster with his clothes. They are thrown all over the place, always inside out. He's the same at home or in a hotel. Like I say, he improved, but slowly.'

Jorge and Cheni spent hours and hours together in cars. When Jorge was in his third year of ESO, Martínez used to pick him up outside the Monlau school and take him to the gym. He'd sit in the front seat, rucksack on his lap, and not utter a word. 'One day I cracked and said to him "Hey, Jorge! Hello! Weren't you ever told to greet people when you met them?" And he answered, "What for?" '

At first glance this seems like the typical attitude of a bad-mannered child with little respect or consideration for his elders, but it is unfair not to consider the situation he found himself in at that time. Jorge was just 14 years old, a long way from home, out of his comfort zone, and separated from his family back in Palma de Mallorca. He was surrounded by strangers who supposedly worked for him. Packed in his little suitcase were eleven years' worth of dedication to motorcycles. Racing had moulded him body and soul, they were his life and his religion. The people who looked after Jorge when he arrived in Barcelona were in awe of his talent on a motorcycle, but they would have preferred that talent to be complemented by a little grace when he got off the bike. After a short time spent working with Jorge, everybody knew that teaching him and setting him a good example would be a crucial part of their job.

'Cheni is right,' recalls Jorge. 'I didn't say a word, but sometimes that was because it was worse when we did speak. We'd end up arguing, about football, for example. I was a Barca fan and he supported [their city rivals] Espanyol. We'd get fired up, get angry and then not speak to each other for hours. If it was a long journey, that was an uncomfortable situation to be in. The cure was worse than the illness!' They would laugh about it later, but Cheni eventually told Dani Amatriaín that if Jorge didn't change soon, he would quit. 'I think Jorge has certain things very clear in his mind. The good relationship we had was based on the fact I didn't automatically agree with him. I didn't ask him much and he didn't speak much. I suppose we met somewhere in the middle,' smiles Cheni.

Cheni once asked Jorge about his mechanics at Derbi and Lorenzo admitted that he didn't even know their names! It goes back to the same thing: he wasn't particularly bad mannered, it's just that nobody had ever told him that other people were just as important as he was. He'd spent his whole life being told that he was number one. He'd not been taught any social skills and he was also very shy. He needed working on constantly, 24 hours a day, even in the car. Team members from those early days tell countless anecdotes of Jorge being shy, of him not speaking, not even looking them in the face. You had to ask him everything twice to get an answer. One day it fell to the boss, Giampiero Sacchi [Sporting Director of the Piaggio Group] to set a few things straight. 'Hey, son. Here at Derbi we start the day with a "Good morning". Are you with me?'

During the Copa Aprilia seasons of 1998 and 1999 Cheni Martínez travelled all over Spain with Jorge, in a caravan. All the young riders who were competing travelled together and they would all be singing, laughing and messing around the whole time. All except Jorge, who would be silent, lost in his own world – and this was the kid who won almost every race. As time went on the others made it their mission to make Jorge laugh. The day they managed it, they cheered louder than they would have done if they'd won a race. If, at times like these, they'd know that Jorge once got sent home from school in Palma with a note from his teacher telling his parents that he had spent the whole day laughing with his friends, maybe his developing reputation for being serious and stern would never have stuck.

When Julián Simón joined up with the team for a private test at Almería, he walked past the telemetrist, Fabricio Manciucca, who was eating his lunch on the steps of the truck. 'Buen provecho!' ['Bon appetit'] said Julián. Manciucca's response is etched in the team's memory: 'I've spent two years with Jorge and he never cared if my food went down the right hole or the wrong one!'

'At the start of 2006 Dani told me that he wanted me to be permanently on Jorge's case but to gradually allow him to take care of himself,' recalls Cheni. 'The idea was to let the line out a little, then pull it back in. Slacken off if I thought he was improving, tighten up if he wasn't. Little by little he learned to fly solo.'

Several years later, on 6 November 2007, everything had changed – and radically. It was Jorge's first day as a MotoGP rider and he introduced himself individually to each and every member of his new Fiat Yamaha crew. From his new team manager, Daniele Romagnoli, to the telemetrist Carlo Luzzi, chief mechanic Ramón Forcada, his Spanish mechanic Javier Ullate and his beloved Juanito Llansá, he greeted and chatted with each of the men who would now be spending more time with him than with their own families. Men like Walter Crippa and Valentino Negri.

It may not seem such a rare thing for one human being to greet another, but for Dani Amatriaín one of the biggest battles he'd had with Jorge was convincing him that he needed more than a handful of throttle to be successful. You have to love, respect and look after your own. It is a long time since Jorge adopted and was adopted by his 'other' family in 250s. They may already be only a memory, but those three years together were long enough to ensure they left a permanent imprint on Lorenzo's soul. In fact, Jorge decided to commit that feeling to paper.

May 2007

A LETTER FROM JORGE LORENZO TO HIS TEAM

Home, sweet home … It feels so good to be back after almost a week in the land of rice! Anyway… today I'd like to talk about a group of people who make my dreams come true every fortnight.

Let's start with 'il capo', Giovanni Sandi, my Chief Mechanic and in my opinion the best technician in the [250] class. He's just turned 60 and he wears the scars of a thousand and one battles. With his experience, patience and optimism he always finds a solution to my problems.

Juan 'Holly' Llansá is my soulmate, my most trustworthy mechanic and a person who has shown nothing but loyalty towards me. We've been together for ten years and he has never let me down. There was a time when he used to change his hairstyle more often than David Beckham and when we go shopping in Chinatown in Malaysia or China he brings their whole economy crashing down with his haggling. Those poor Chinese guys…

Valeriano 'Vale' Rodríguez is the new and improved Gérard Depardieu (version 2.0) of the team. He's always been a sex symbol, although he recently got married and had a baby. Time to look after the family! The blonde fella who pushes down my back protector every time I throw my leg over the Aprilia – that's him. He's a top professional and never gets involved in any nonsense.

Ivanno Mancurti is a betting man. When my race is over, some of my mechanics have a bit of banter trying to predict the winner of the MotoGP race. He's the best, just as he is at tuning my Aprilia. He's also a softie and the team member who gets most emotional when we win, to the point of tears.

Carlos 'Carlitos' Suárez is the team 'rookie' because he's the only one who wasn't with me last year. He's the joker of the pack, he doesn't stop, and he talks more about girls than anybody in the team. His laugh is gravelly

from smoking so much and it still makes us all laugh.
Luciano Bonci and my telemetrist Loris Conte. Luciano is very quiet but
is probably the guy with the biggest heart. Loris always has a smile on
his face and is always there to help me improve those little set-up details
that can only be picked up by a computer.
They are all World Champions too, but like me they are doing everything
possible, and more, to add the word 'double' to my CV by the end of the
year. They are my mechanics. They are my friends.

He might have been unable to write a letter like that two years earlier, but a long time had passed since young Lorenzo had moved on to better things. If there was one thing Jorge had learned in his career so far, it was that you couldn't win races on your own – he was simply the first piece in a jigsaw puzzle. Each member of that team had brought something to Jorge that made his life easier, allowing him to focus on using his natural-born gift – racing to win.

September 2003
HITTING WHERE IT HURTS

There is no doubt that Jorge's father, Chicho, taught him to ride fast, but Jorge himself didn't know how he was doing it. He was certainly very brave, but he thought all he had to do was open the throttle. He only cared about winning – that came as standard – but he didn't know anything about setting a bike up. It annoyed him when things didn't go well, but he just didn't know how to solve his problems. When he joined Derbi as a 15 year old, in 2002, he didn't have a clue about mechanics. All he had was incredible hand-to-eye co-ordination.

'I have an ability, a special feeling that allows me to do things with my hand,' Jorge laughs, acknowledging the double entendre. 'I find it easy to be good on the PlayStation, driving go-karts too. My hand-to-eye co-ordination is very advanced.'

But because he didn't talk to anybody, his problems mounted up. He'd get off the bike and wouldn't know what to say. Even if he did know what was wrong he couldn't communicate his thoughts to his mechanics because all but one of them were Italian. He couldn't even speak with his chief mechanic! He'd just sit in his chair and leave them to prepare the bike. In his first ever 125cc World Championship season he broke his collarbone and finished up 21st.

'If you're giving it loads of gas but the bike isn't set up, that's pointless. If you get the bike set up you will always go faster,' Juan Llansá told him one day. It was 2003 and Dani Amatriaín had recently told Llansá: 'Juanito, Jorge wants you with him at Derbi.'

'He knew me because we'd worked together during the European Championship in 2001 and from his second season in Grand Prix until now I've always been his closest mechanic. Since then we've always been together,' recalls Juan Llansá, closing his eyes as he visualised those early days. 'Jorge is like a son to me. He has slept at my house, spent time with my two kids and my wife – I don't look on him as just a rider.'

Jorge and Juanito became inseparable, and over the past six years not a day has gone by when they haven't been there for one another. They searched for and found a common understanding and it has turned them into an ideal partnership. Nobody has ever had to teach Jorge how to work the throttle, so they turned their attention to learning to set up a bike. 'We worked on him concentrating on small details, memorising things. He learnt to isolate a problem, recognise a noise.'

Juanito Llansá has been, and still is, Jorge's maestro for everything they don't tell you in the manuals. Jorge has learnt about the spirit of a motorcycle – things that have nothing to do with metal, valves, electronics – and in the end they found the key to him becoming a champion. The words that Juanito vocalised that day back in 2003 did not fall on deaf ears: 'Learn!' Nowadays a rider has to be aware of how a motorcycle is being developed, if it is going in the right direction. Telemetry is a great source of information, but the most reliable data still come from the mind of the rider. Only he knows how the bike is truly behaving and it is crucial he is able to transmit his feelings.

'I've tried to make the kid learn how to communicate what a bike is doing, if the problem is coming from the front or the rear. I've fought with him on many occasions. I have always said that he needed to learn – more so now than ever in MotoGP. Now it is extremely important for him to get a good feeling from the tyres, the suspension, the chassis, the engine...' With the 250cc bike Jorge knew how and when he was going fast, but in MotoGP he had to start again from scratch. 'He has to get to the point where he can get off the bike and immediately tell the chief mechanic or engineer what's wrong with it. He needs to be able to distinguish if a problem is coming from the tyres or the suspension.'

The good thing for Jorge is that his beloved Juanito has stayed by his side. The story goes that it was one of their head-to-heads in Almería that gave rise to the winner in Lorenzo that we have come to know. It was 2003, his second season in the 125cc class, and Jorge was recovering from injury. 'Giorgio, you've spent all year waiting for new parts from Derbi,' said Juanito, looking him directly in the eyes. Jorge had rarely seen him look so serious. 'Look, son, before asking for more let's get 110 per cent out of this bike – let's squeeze everything out of it before feeling sorry for ourselves anymore. Because the bike isn't going to get any better than it is now. The most they'll give you is a couple of stickers and an aerial. Either you start getting the most out of this bike or you're finished! The longer you wait for new parts, the more time we're wasting. You have to understand that this is the Derbi and this is how you need to ride it. Either make it go fast or we're heading for the dole queue!'

One week later, on 7 September 2003, Jorge finished sixth in the Grand Prix of Portugal, equalling his career-best result in the 125cc World Championship. Two weeks after that he was celebrating his first win, at the Jacarepaguá circuit in Brazil. Juanito had pressed the right buttons. In a technical world such as motorsport it is not unusual to come across craftsmen capable of giving a machine that subtle touch that a computer can't. Juan Llansá proved that not only could he do that, he could do it to the human brain too. Jorge was quick to take on board his favourite saying: 'There are people who speak badly of you to do you wrong, and others who speak badly to you because they love you.'

'I've been in this business for 21 years,' says Juanito. 'I've worked with good 250cc riders like Luís D'Antín and Carlos Cardús but I still struggle to comprehend what Jorge has done. Yes, sometimes he learnt things grudgingly but it took him just three years to join motorcycling's elite. Sometimes I can't get my head around it but he has a special gift and he has been able to make the most of it. He continues to exploit that gift more and more and I still don't think he has peaked as a rider. He is starting to realise that he can go a long way in this sport but he needs to spend a couple of years maturing in MotoGP. When he finally hits the mark, I think Spain will have a second Valentino Rossi on its hands.'

'I'm going to have to be careful not to say things that I think may be true but perhaps aren't an accurate representation of the real truth,' said Lorenzo at the end of November 2007, explaining his first impressions of the Yamaha M1 to a journalist from the Spanish sports daily *AS*. 'If I'm not totally sure about my opinion it could be dangerous for me to voice it because here they make the bike just how you ask for it.' He knew that his feedback from riding the bike was going to be studied in depth by the team and he was conscious that he would have to choose exactly the right words if the machine was to be developed as he wanted it. But he also knew that he would be able to do that because Juanito was by his side. 'If Jorge told me tomorrow that all this was over … if he said "Juanito, that's it. This is as far as we go," the World Championship would be over for me because my job would be done.'

'Juanito is my guard dog,' said Jorge before his rookie MotoGP season in 2008. 'I know he doesn't like me saying that, but I feel calm because I know that everything is going to be okay in MotoGP, nobody is going to do me wrong. He's much more than that, though. He is the mechanic who suffers the most during my races, who has suffered the most throughout my career. There are mechanics who give their all during a Grand Prix but switch off when they get home. But if Juanito goes a week without touching a motorcycle he gets withdrawal symptoms! He can't wait to get back. When he writes to me on Messenger he doesn't start out with a typical greeting like 'Hola', he'll put something like "Let's win again this year." Other than his family, all he cares about is racing. He's not an engineer, he's not a suspension technician, but he changed everything for me at Derbi, put everything on the bike in its place so that I could rise to the top.'

The year 2008 was a time of happiness in the Llansá home. Juanito's daughter Zaida made him the youngest granddad in the paddock and his 'adopted son' Jorge, who has changed his friend's nickname from 'Holly' to 'Nonno' ('Grandpa' in Italian), produced great things on the track. Which is why Llansá laughs when he shows me two stones he picked up at Le Mans almost five years ago, which are now resting, he hopes for good, in the exhibition room he has at his house in Barberá del Vallés, near Barcelona.

The stones date back to 2004, their final season together at Derbi. 'Jorge had been losing it in a few races and when we got to Le Mans he was really on edge,' explains Juanito. 'So I picked two stones out of the gravel trap at the Bugatti circuit and told him a story. Well, it was more of a joke than a story.' Surrounded by Lorenzo memorabilia, including helmets, boots and pole-position certificates, there is a warmth about Juanito's face as he tells the story, but no longer nostalgia. He's pleased that Lorenzo learned a lesson from his joke. 'There was a guy riding a camel, lost in the desert for several days, and he suddenly sees an oasis. He kicks the camel to set off towards it but it doesn't move. So he gets off, picks up two stones and shows them to the camel. The camel just stands there. So he takes the two stones and cracks them together either side of the camel's genitals. The camel yelps and sets off running towards the oasis. After that, whenever the camel refused to move the man showed it the stones and it would quickly get going. So that's what I used to do with Jorge. Whenever he got pig-headed I showed him the stones from Le Mans and said, "We're going to get on together, right?" It eased the tension and he soon forgot whatever problems we were having.'

During his first season in MotoGP Jorge Lorenzo never once stepped out of line with his new team. In other words, the stones weren't necessary. Juanito had warned his new colleagues at Fiat Yamaha that Jorge had a strong character, but chief mechanic Ramón Forcada has been pleasantly surprised by his rider. 'He has got an incredible desire to work,' says Forcada. 'That's why he can sometimes get into a bad mood during practice, if things aren't working out. But that is the most normal thing in the world.'

Javi Ullate agrees. 'The relationship with Jorge has been fantastic. I think he has realised that throwing his helmet around or causing a scene doesn't get you anywhere, especially in a factory team. The things they say he used to do in the past, we haven't seen them at all.' So for the time being the Le Mans stones have not had to make a come-back, although Juanito warns, 'He'd better not change because I keep them in my suitcase. He'll be just like the camel!'

December 2007

Punta Cana, Dominican Republic

OPERATION HONDURAS

Before making the step up to MotoGP, Jorge Lorenzo took a well-earned holiday: 2008 was going to be a year of constant learning for him and he got the impression there was going to be little time to think about anything other than racing. He knew that, without a rest, it would be impossible to be fully focused and, as such, perform to his maximum. Even though this was something he'd learned a long time before, in the final race of 2007 at Valencia he convinced himself that it was impossible to win unless he was feeling 100 per cent fit. At Cheste he took it easy because he was already World Champion and he finished seventh. Knowing that his first season in the premier class would barely leave him time to draw breath, he decided to take a break by holidaying with a group of friends in the Dominican Republic, killing two birds with one stone – relaxation and recreation.

And why try to deny that at 20 years old 'recreation' is closely linked to one particular activity? Jorge is no different from any other guy his age when it comes to girls – and as with everything he does, of course, he goes into it all set to score top marks.

On 5 June 2007, at the presentation of the Catalunya GP in Barcelona's Port Olímpic, Jorge asked me what book I was currently reading. I can't remember what my answer was, but the interesting thing is not what I was reading but what he had read.

Ernest, when you finish your book you have to read 'The Game' by Neil Strauss. Read it and tell me what you think!

The Game is the story of a man who infiltrates an underground society known as the 'Pickup Artists', whose members take wagers over who can be the most successful Casanova. Within two years the author gets so involved that their techniques become second nature and he is given the accolade of the 'World's Number One Pickup Artist', renaming himself 'Style'.

On holiday in the Dominican Republic Jorge partied with Dani Palau, Ricky Cardús, a number of team members, including mechanics Carlos Suárez and David García, and a new friend the group had got to know during 2007, the tennis player Jonathan Susmozas. Their mission: to switch off, have fun and, since all of them except Palau were single, meet as many girls as possible.

The theory was pretty straightforward, but the reality is never that simple. For a start, hotels in the Caribbean aren't the best places to pull girls. They are full of families and newlyweds, and the same people appear at breakfast, in the pool and at the disco. However, invariably there will be a couple of girls around, on their own and looking for fun. Jorge and Jonathan began chatting up one such pair – a German and a Pole. As the guys gave the girls a gentle massage, in the hammocks by the pool, they felt confident they had them just where they wanted them. They seemed literally like putty in their hands. Just as they were making arrangements to meet up later, at the disco, a Honduran guy turned up – fit, bronzed, muscular. 'He was giving it the whole "boy next door" thing,' remembers Jorge. The Honduran was straight in there, his exotic accent working overtime. 'So shall I pick you ladies up from your room at nine?' The two girls went weak at the knees, Ricky Cardús fell over laughing and Jorge's face was a picture. Honduras 1 – Spain 0.

But the game wasn't over. A couple of nights later Jorge and Jonathan were in the disco, working their own brand of Spanish magic on two holidaymakers – dancing merengue and salsa – the two buddies winked at each other, it was looking good. The alarm bells sounded when the girls started to look at their mobile phones. Then came the bombshell. 'We have to leave in twenty minutes.' The lads followed them outside, only to find their Honduran nemesis sat on a wall. 'Hello ladies! Shall we go?' Jorge and Jonathan were indignant, Ricky Cardús and Palau were in stitches, although that only lasted the one night. 'The next day, Ricky got mugged by him too!' Honduras 3 – Spain 0. Game over.

'It's only because he speaks perfect English and he's already arranged to meet them,' claimed Jorge.

'And he's not as good-looking as you either, Jorge. It's just that he's tall, tanned, muscle-bound,' replied Palau.

'But Jorge's well built too!' interjected Jonathan.

'Yeah, but he's got no pecs,' said Palau.

'Who invited this guy to our hotel to screw our holiday up anyway? Pedrosa?' said Jonathan.

Jorge couldn't see the funny side and he went to take his aggression out in the gym. 'This is the start of Operation Honduras,' he said. 'In other words, I'm going to get more muscles to make sure this doesn't happen again!' He was deadly serious. 'When I was riding in 250cc I had to be careful not to bulk up and I was more bothered about stretching, about being flexible enough to fit behind such a small fairing. Now I'm in MotoGP, look out Honduras! It's war!' Other than losing a race, missing out on a girl is probably the thing that winds Jorge up most in life.

To add insult to injury, Jorge was again forced to taste defeat on the back of that holiday to Honduras. The six friends made a bet on their return home that the first one to remove their 'all expenses paid' coloured bracelet would have to pay for dinner for the other five. Jonathan underwent an operation and told the surgeon to leave the bracelet on, Palau took more care over his than he did of his own girlfriend, and even though they worked in a garage, Carlos and David managed to keep theirs intact – Ricky too. Feeling ill one day, Jorge ripped his bracelet off and had to pay up!

December 2002–December 2008
Hotel Barceló-Sants, Barcelona
AN UNCOMFORTABLE TRUTH

When Jorge Lorenzo crashed at the 2007 Italian Grand Prix in Mugello, some people just focused on his collision with Álvaro Bautista. Others, though, were more interested in the fact that Jorge got back in the race by picking up a 250cc bike that weighed more than 100kg as if it were only 100g.

It was an amazing change compared to the Jorge of 2002. That was the year he was introduced to his personal trainer, Marcos Hirsch. They'd arranged to meet in the Flash-Flash restaurant in Barcelona with Dani Amatriaín, who had also been trained by Marcos. Hirsch arrived to find Jorge sitting on a sofa, his feet hovering inches above the floor. 'One day this guy will be a great champion … if we can sort him out,' declared Dani, with his hand proudly gripping little Jorge's shoulder.

One month later, in December 2002, Dani came with Jorge and his father, Chicho, to the Hotel Barceló-Sants fitness centre in Barcelona, where Marcos worked. Dani told Chicho: 'This son of a bitch [meaning Marcos] is the only person who can sort your son's life out. If this son of a bitch [he was saying it affectionately] can't do it, you might as well throw in the towel.' Dani knew what he was talking about because Jorge was going through a difficult patch, and Marcos had been the only person capable of sorting his life out when he was a racer himself.

'Jorge was a sickly boy,' remembers Marcos. 'He wasn't eating well. He'd get a cold twice a month. He was tired, exhausted. Now, after six years of hard work, I can say with some satisfaction that we have had no injury problems in the gym itself. I have taught him to suffer, to deal with suffering and pain, and I have taught him the discipline necessary to be the best in whatever he decides to do.'

Marcos is strict and extremely demanding. He is not your everyday personal trainer – he took control of Jorge's health and his work involves in-depth analysis and genetic profiling. He is hi-tech, a trainer for the latest generation. 'The first thing was to sort out the kid's health. Then it was time to improve his physical performance. Muscle creates a mental state. When you are strong you feel secure, your self-esteem grows and you can tackle your job with more conviction.' Marcos's philosophy is clear: 'You don't play with your health. Certain people cannot train with me. For all the money they might want to pay me, I don't like wasting time.'

While others might be suffering, sweating blood, Jorge will most probably be enjoying himself. Even when Marcos signals the end of an exercise, Jorge wants to do more. 'Come on, let's keep going! Legs, pecs, whatever!' He loves lifting weights and when he starts to run out of steam he and Marcos come up with self-motivational sayings and phrases tailored to the occasion. 'Lightweight baby!' they'll shout, the phrase made famous by former Bodybuilding World Champion and multiple Mr Olympia Ronnie Coleman. 'This ain't heavy, son,' is the house favourite.

That's how things are now, but the early days were desperate. Jorge didn't speak for four months. Marcos would ask questions and get silence in reply. One day he finally exploded: 'That's it, kid. If you don't answer me tomorrow you can find another trainer.' But as Cheni had previously discovered, the cure proved to be worse than the illness. The more they got to know each other, the more Jorge went from doing whatever Marcos said to questioning absolutely everything. He contested every command and he thought he had all the answers. 'Is this exercise enough? Why don't we do this instead?'

'One day I just left him standing there,' recalls Marcos. 'I walked away.'

The next day Jorge called him. 'What's up? Aren't we training today?'

'What's the point if you already know everything? You don't need me at all.'

'Come on Marcos, don't get angry.'

'Jorge, this is your last chance. Next time I'm not coming back.'

The tension was premeditated, planned with a single objective: to get Jorge to react. Since then an intriguing, constantly evolving relationship has developed between the pair. A mutual respect was formed on the basis that Marcos always told Jorge what needed to be done and Jorge responded. 'Okay, I'll listen to you this time, but if it doesn't turn out like you said, and the result isn't what you promised, I'll never listen to you ever again.'

It is difficult to comprehend Marcos Hirsch's presence without actually meeting him in person. When people talk about the role of a personal trainer, they don't come close to what the Brazilian brings to Jorge Lorenzo. Between them they have always found strange and unusual ways of staying in touch and exchanging ideas, even when one of them was away at races while the other was in Barcelona. Marcos still keeps the mobile phone he used back in 2001, on which he has saved the hundreds of text messages that went back and forth between them at that time. One, for example, came when Jorge got tired of the way they raced in 125cc:

I'm fucking sick of 125cc. Let's see if we can move up to 250cc. These guys only know how to follow. All good for tomorrow.

In the gym Jorge and Marcos entertained themselves by coming up with names for themselves and for other people. Among Jorge's nicknames were 'Achilles' and 'Gladiator', and at that time he used to do a lot of stretching, which is how he came up with his first nickname for himself, 'lo gomat', which comes from the word goma, meaning rubber in Spanish and Catalan. 'Lo gomat' roughly translates as 'the rubber one'; it was also a reference to the famous Spanish soccer player, Ivan de la Peña, known as 'lo pelat' – 'the bald one'. Another text read:

I'm getting better every day. I'm like fucking rubber. 'Lo gomat.' Tomorrow I'll start cycling. Was I on the telly much? Was my interview on? See ya.

The text messages were a direct and immediate way to stay in touch. Jorge felt the need to communicate, but he also needed feedback and it was this necessity that led to their most curious invention. An old notebook would be their most original and reflective means of communication. Jorge carried it with him. He wrote down everything that had happened to him in a race, what worried him, the problems he'd had. And 2003 was a year of intense, explosive activity.

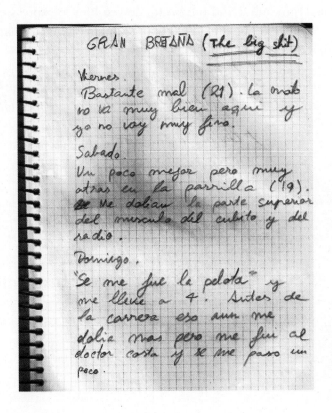

GREAT BRITAIN – (The Big Shit)

Friday: Pretty bad (21st). The bike isn't running well here and I'm not riding smoothly.

Saturday: A bit better but way down on the grid. I felt pain from the upper part of elbow and radius [forearm].

Sunday: I lost my head and I took four riders out. Before the race I was in even more pain but I went to see Doctor Costa and it eased a little.

On his return from a Grand Prix he would hand the book over to Marcos, who would read the entries and write his own reply. The book went back and forth. At 16 years of age there were a lot of things on Jorge's mind and the book allowed him to express exactly what he felt – like the time he got angry with his team-mate and former 125cc World Champion, Emilio Alzamora.

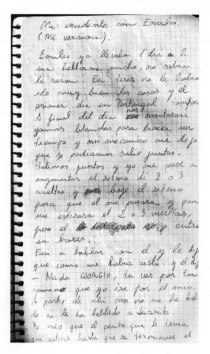 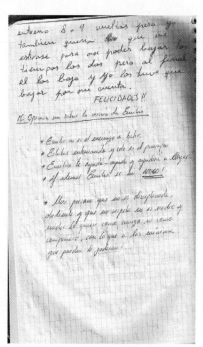

My incident with Emilio (my version)

Emilio hadn't spoken to me much for a day or two, I didn't know why. At Jerez things hadn't gone well and they didn't on the first day in Portugal either. At the end of the day we put some soft tyres on for a quick lap and a mechanic asked if we could both go out together. So we went out together and I picked up the pace for two or three laps. I slowed down so that he could pass me and give me a tow for two or three laps but he came in to pit. I went to speak to him and asked how he could have not seen me. And he said: forget it Giorgio. You do your thing and I'll do mine. Since that day he has barely spoken to me or Juanito. I think he thought I was supposed to tow him until the end of the session, eight or nine laps, but I also wanted a tow so that we could both improve our times. In the end he improved following me and I had to do it by myself.

Marcos's answer was:

CONGRATULATIONS. My opinion without hearing Emilio's version:
 – Emilio is not the enemy you need to defeat.
 – It was practice and this is only the start.
 – Emilio helped you, is helping you and will help you to make it.
 – Furthermore, Emilio is your friend.

A person who is not disciplined, obedient and respectful is nobody and nobody wants him as a friend or team-mate because as soon as they can, they will screw you over.

Jorge didn't always answer straight away or would sometimes forget to write down his thoughts at the end of a GP weekend. The book is plastered with requests from Marcos:

Monday 17 June 2003: The fucking Montmeló summary with every minute detail of the three days and your opinion on your conduct.

Thursday 17 July 2003: It was 2500BC when you last emailed me the notebook pages!!

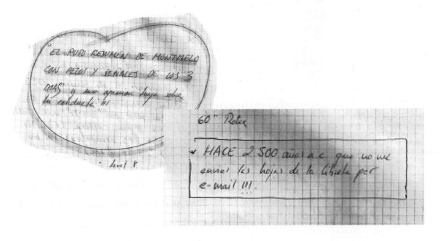

Marcos's threats usually had the desired effect – and especially one in particular. 'When Jorge looks in the mirror and says to himself: "I'm an Adonis, I look so fucking good," I tell him: "Watch it! I can take that little body I've given you away again in two months. You don't need it to ride a bike so do what I tell you!" In a professional sense, Marcos trained Jorge's body and in a personal sense he was his Al Gore – taking it upon himself to voice life's 'uncomfortable truths', the things other people couldn't say to a double World Champion. Like the time he wrote down the phrases Jorge was no longer allowed to repeat in public:

NEVER REPEAT
1 – I had an unfortunate childhood.
2 – My life is boring.
3 – I'm too busy.
4 – How can you expect me to be happy when I'm this depressed?
5 – I've got less than an unpaid child.
You should never waste time feeling sorry for yourself. Feeling sorry for yourself is for losers! And when you finally let yourself realise it, time has already passed. Your time is better spent fixing the things you don't like.
You're a man, not a machine. Especially when you get on a bike!

'Marcos has obviously changed me on the outside, but he has worked more on changing me on the inside. After my father, he's definitely the person who's had the most influence on my personality, on the way I am. He finds it so easy to communicate. He draws you into his world and makes you think like him – he is very persuasive. The only time I don't listen to him is when he talks about bikes. He doesn't have a clue about that!'

'Every sporting discipline puts different physical demands on the body,' says Marcos, 'so I work with Jorge to make sure he is prepared for any kind of physical effort. With that objective, in 2008 we added some new things to his usual weights regime. Now he plays indoor soccer once a week because it is a different kind of running and cardiovascular training. We've also incorporated Pilates and one session a week of self-defence.' Marcos is quick to add that the classes are not intended to prepare Jorge for a fight. 'I have always told him that if he has a problem in a nightclub or a bar he must walk away or tell security. He can't get involved because he has a lot more to lose than other people. But the fact is that after his classes this year Jorge could take out a guy with one blow.'

Marcos has a friend who is a black belt and has achieved a third dan in taekwondo. 'We worked with him to design a training programme specifically for us,' explains Marcos. 'He's not being taught how to hit people! The muscular and cardiovascular effort required in this discipline is huge, and we have made his programme even tougher than normal. In martial arts you spend your whole time with your tongue out and your heart pounding. That is why we do it – so that the physical effort required to ride the bike is as minimal as possible.'

In 2008, a wide range of medical staff took care of, and will continue to care for Jorge's health. 'A chiropractor takes care of his spine, while a specialist physiotherapist works on his forearms, ankles and any other area that needs working on to make sure he is fit and able to recover quickly and properly from any injuries,' says Marcos. 'When the weather is good we go to the beach to do specific physical exercises.' Strangely, Marcos is more proud of the mental work he has done with his pupil than the physical. 'Whenever he's had problems he has decided to lock himself in the gym, which is great. He has never let life get him down. He has been forced to grow up through a series of emotional batterings, but it has made him stronger and his skin thicker. If all the bad stuff means that from now on he can be happy, then it is more than welcome. Now Jorge looks at himself in the mirror and says: "At last, I am free, this is my life." And what more important thing can there be in life than being free?'

The relationship between Jorge and Marcos Hirsch is much stronger now than it has ever been. Each of them has put their heart and trust into the other's hands. 'I have always had the feeling that I am with Jorge for something more than just training him,' concludes Marcos. 'I've always thought, "Something is going to come out of this." '

Between 19 January and 5 September 2008
'FREE MAN TEAM'

'As a journalist I can recall some pretty weird interviews with Jorge,' says Héctor Martín, a young Spanish journalist who was made Lorenzo's official press officer in 2008. 'In fact, the weirdest interviews I've ever done in sport were with Jorge Lorenzo. In 2007 I went to Castellón to interview him. We did it while Jorge was walking around his hotel room getting ready for an awards ceremony. I was sitting on his bed and he was walking around, naked, talking away, sprucing himself up, putting his suit on...' What Héctor saw as 'weird' back then would prove, over time, to be something he now recognises as 'special', and key to Lorenzo's success.

Héctor Martín was one of the closest people to Jorge throughout his debut season in MotoGP, literally and metaphorically. The position of press officer turned out to include a few extra responsibilities that he was unlikely to have imagined when he took the job, which is why he laughs when he remembers how the pair first met back in 2003. 'The editor of [Spanish magazine] *MotoViva*, Gonzalo de Martorell, sent me to do an interview with Jorge when he was at Derbi. He told me to go and do it at the gym, and I refused. "You mean the Jorge Lorenzo from the telly?" I said. "That 15-year-old kid that talks like a grown-up? No thanks, I'd rather not!" But he was my editor and he insisted in the hope that they [Derbi] would buy some advertising space in the magazine. So I went with gritted teeth. I thought I'd have had enough after 15 minutes but they were three fantastic hours. By the time I left I really liked him. Then, when I was at the Catalunya Grand Prix, Jorge was riding through the paddock on his scooter and when he saw me he stopped to say hello and ask how things were going and how the interview had turned out. He'd only met me once before! Any journalist reading this will know how rare that is, because very few interviewees remember your face when you meet for a second time. I always remembered Jorge's greeting and it's something that rarely happened again with anybody else.'

Without realising it, Jorge had earned the respect of a person who destiny would reunite him with five years later – and there was no mistaking that this was the very same, irrepressible Jorge Lorenzo. 'The best part of that interview was when I asked him which was the better bike, his Derbi or the Honda,' laughs Héctor. 'And the kid just comes out with it and says the Honda! When the interview came out the poor lad got an ear-bashing from Dani Amatriaín. "Why the hell would you say that, Jorge?" he said. But I thought, "Hats off!" '

Over the course of 2008 Jorge has come up with a variety of different names for Héctor Martín: Noriega (a Puerto Rican Reggaeton star), Caniche (Poodle) and the latest, Mike – after Mike Di Meglio. 'Don't you think he looks just like the 125cc World Champion?' Jorge laughs and points. Héctor 'Mike' Martín and Jorge began their journey to becoming 'brothers-in-arms' in Rome on 19 January 2008. 'At the beginning, when I first started to work with him, I was really keen to see how he accepted me,' recalls Héctor. 'We had to go to Malaysia for the tests. I was travelling from Barcelona to meet him in Rome and he was coming from London. I arrived in plenty of time but I couldn't see him anywhere. The flight started to board and I started to worry, looking for him and asking the air stewards if he was already on the plane. Then he suddenly appeared out of nowhere … the last to arrive but totally laid back about it, like he is – like he continues to be.'

Jorge's trademark nonchalance showed itself on many other occasions during 2008, but Héctor still can't believe an incident with what is now known at Yamaha as the 'sofa of champions'. 'It was in Amsterdam, during a visit to Yamaha Motor Europe. We were at a lunch with Lin Jarvis and all the directors from Yamaha Europe. James Toseland was there too. It was like a welcome lunch for the factory's two new riders and in this really luxurious room there were two sofas in an L shape. Once he's done eating, Jorge goes and stretches out on one of the sofas for a kip! I was really anxious because there were all these top bosses from Yamaha there, but they calmed my nerves by telling me it must be the champions' sofa because Valentino Rossi had done exactly the same thing when he was there – he went to sleep too! I suppose geniuses must be like that.' That was the first of many occasions that Jorge would fall asleep on Héctor, most recently in December 2008 while they were waiting for his new passport to be processed. It was only a 15-minute nap but it was in a room full of people. 'He doesn't see himself as different from anybody else so he just goes to sleep. When he's not out on the track, he doesn't think about who he is, it doesn't worry him.'

It was a strange introduction to what would be a total career change for Héctor, who was used to life on the other side of the fence. As a journalist for *Diario de Mallorca* he had followed Lorenzo during 2006 and 2007, his 250cc title-winning seasons. 'When we arrived in Kuala Lumpur I realised that my work with him wasn't going to be limited to just being his press officer. Jorge is very independent when it comes to his professional life but he is quite dependent in terms of day-to-day things away from the track. Even though he'd been to Malaysia plenty of times, he had no idea where the car rental office was, the car park, or even the hotel! He didn't care! So as you can imagine, I had to take over, even driving an automatic for the first time in my life. Between that and being a little nervous anyway I stalled the car. Since then, if I ever stall Jorge says: "You've stalled it again. Just like in Malaysia, eh?" '

It was in a hire car that the pair shared one of their funniest moments of 2008, and one of the most dangerous. 'We were in Monterey on our way to Laguna Seca and I jumped a red light,' recalls Héctor. 'A police car followed me with his lights on but no siren, so I just kept going. He followed us for quite a while but never told me to stop. He must have been calling for reinforcements because when I did stop eight other patrol cars suddenly appeared! Dani Amatriaín opened the rear door and said: "I'll sort this out," but they shouted at him to shut the door and stay still! The cop came out with his hand on his gun. What a nightmare! This was at eight o'clock on the morning of the race, before the warm-up. In the end they didn't fine us or anything because we were close to the circuit with our passes on, but they gave us a real fright. I was really worried they'd take us in and I'd be to blame that Jorge couldn't race.'

While the professional parameters of his role as Jorge's press officer were clearly defined from the first day, the close personal relationship they now have developed organically. It was decided that, on his step up to MotoGP, Jorge would need an assistant and it was quickly agreed that the person should be Ricky Cardús, his friend and sidekick in a hundred and one adventures on and off the track. But Ricky was still busy chasing his own ambitions as a professional rider, focusing on the Spanish Championship, and could not work his own schedule around Jorge's travels. Ricky was at Jerez for the Spanish GP, but from Portugal onwards it was Héctor who had to become Jorge's right-hand man. 'The first night I stayed over in his motorhome was the night before his first win. We watched the movie *Rocky III*, Jorge mentally preparing himself for the next day, but the night had actually started with a game of Pro Evolution Soccer on the PlayStation. Jorge was staying on his own and at dinner in the Yamaha Hospitality he said, "Come back and I'll give you a beating at Pro Evo!" '

The pair were only separated in China because Lorenzo was in Yamaha's team hotel, but after Le Mans, where Jorge was still struggling from the injuries picked up in China, 'We were never apart,' recalls Héctor. 'He needed so much help that he couldn't even go to the hotel alone. He needed a hand getting in and out of the truck, putting his leathers on, his boots were a nightmare because he couldn't get them on … he even needed help to get to the bathroom. I suppose it was a series of circumstances. Between the injuries and the fact that Ricky couldn't travel, I gradually started to spend more and more time with him. Previously I'd been travelling with the guys from Motorsport48, with Pol and Aleix Espargaró, Joan Olivé, Pere Gurt … because Jorge would always go with Dani Amatriaín. But things changed the more I earned their trust.' From the basis of this trust grew a great friendship that now fills the limited free time they have together.

Text written by Jorge Lorenzo entitled:
'IN MY FREE TIME'

Tuesday, 26 August 2008. 7pm. We arrived in Bologna a few days before the race. On the following day I had an event for Chupa Chups, my longest sponsor, at a water-park in Riccione to celebrate their 50th anniversary.

We left our suitcases at the hotel and I got my Acer laptop out. Before going out for dinner I challenged my press officer Héctor 'Noriega' Martín to a game of 'Football Manager 08' (a football management game that has sold really well in England and has recently started to take off in Spain). We decided to start an English league season so I chose Manchester United and my rival went for Chelsea. The thing is that while the president of my club gave me just 14 million to spend on new signings, Chelsea had 60!

I had two choices: to make some good, cheap signings or sell one of my best players for a fortune – so that's when I decided to try and pull a fast one on the Poodle. I gave him my word that I'd sell him Cristiano Ronaldo for 50 million, but when he made his offer I upped the price to 55, and when he accepted that I nudged it up to 60. In the meantime I'd already nicked young Obi Mikel off him for 10 million and offered him 12 for Shevchenko. At the same time, Héctor was offering Barça 70 million for Messi but the player turned him down! With only a couple of days left of the transfer window, Chelsea made an offer of 52 million for Dani Alves! It's almost double what he is worth so Seville accepted. I suppose he had to follow in the spendthrifty tradition of the London club...

Whenever I get free time at the circuit, apart from being manager of Manchester United, I watch practice back on DVD or watch an episode of 'Lost'. I also had time this year to try my hand at my latest purchase: 'Cycling Manager 08'. At the moment I'm the manager of the Astana team and while I'm winning the odd stage here and there with my countryman Toni Colom, I'm busy getting Alberto Contador ready for the next Tour. At least I know they'll let me take part!

Finally, on a different topic, I'd just like to send my thanks to all those people who still believe in Jorge Lorenzo regardless of the results. We've shown once again that when everything is in place we're capable of absolutely anything. Big hugs from your rider, JL.

Héctor Martín has spent time on both sides of the fence with regard to Jorge Lorenzo's media commitments. When he was a journalist he followed him all over Spain, and he was in Malaysia to see him crowned 250cc World Champion. Now he is the one who organises the press conferences, television reports and interviews, and keeps a close eye on the ebb and flow of Lorenzo's relationship with the press. He is, therefore, the best-placed person to make an accurate assessment of its current state. 'He gets on well with the press and the journalists know they can ask him things they don't get away with, with other riders. Then they print whatever bollocks he comes out with! Jorge gives them plenty to play with and in any one interview they'll have a choice of headlines, although they always go for the ones that refer to Pedrosa or Rossi, even when sometimes there might be much more interesting things that's he's said.' Jorge likes to read everything that is written about him. 'But it's better that we don't give him the daily press clippings we receive because he'd go mad!'

Héctor has gone from being Jorge's 'employee' to being his friend, to the point that between the Australian and Malaysian GPs in 2008 they went on holiday together in Thailand. 'Jorge picked up a Buddha painting that was two metres high. He stopped to look in this art shop and then started picking up a load of paintings to buy. The first one was of Eric Cantona and to top it off he bought the Buddha one. It was so big that we couldn't get it back to Spain! We had to shove it in the Yamaha freight to Valencia from Malaysia. We killed ourselves laughing about that.'

The pair of them have found YouTube to be a good way of switching off and having fun together. 'Watching videos has become one of his favourite ways of relaxing,' explains Héctor. 'He likes watching videos of freaks. A lot of mornings in the motorhome, when he's struggling to get out of bed, I turn the laptop on and put a couple of videos on. He opens his eyes, starts laughing and gets up in a good mood.' Like a lot of people his age, 2008 was a year for another Internet-based discovery. 'Facebook!' laughs Héctor. 'All of his friends are girls! As far as he is concerned, Facebook isn't a way of keeping in touch with his buddies – it's a way to get laid! We all know he can be absent-minded and forgetful, but when it comes to racing motorcycles or pulling girls on Facebook he's got a special gift!'

'Jorge is very intelligent and he doesn't need any advice from me,' concludes Héctor. 'Although there have been times, like Valencia last year when the season was over and he said he'd be World Champion next year, I told him not to say that again – even though it is his objective. I said: "Don't put that pressure on yourself! What you have to say is that you're going to improve on what you did last year, which was fourth place. Then we'll see." It seems that the idea has got through because that's what he's been saying lately.'

Over the course of 2008, Héctor Martín was a first-hand witness to the changes in Jorge's professional and personal life, taking an active role in his development and growth. 'Since the split with Amatriaín he wants to know everything. He gets angry if we don't tell him. He doesn't oversee everything because the wheels are often already in motion, but he wants to know if there's anything going on.' Jorge has taken control of his life and the evidence was there initially in the small details, with his helmet in the final round at Valencia bearing a small inscription that read 'FMT', meaning 'Free Man Team'. For 2009 he changed his number from 48 to 99. The message was clear: Jorge Lorenzo was a free man. 'Now I make the decisions,' he says forcefully. 'I will ask the people around me for advice but I will be free to do what I feel like and what I want. In the past I had my hands tied a bit. A bit no, a lot! Perhaps I could have realised that earlier but life happens the way it happens and the important thing is to react decisively and not to regret the things you can't change.'

So Jorge Lorenzo is the captain of his own ship, but as his 'teacher' Miguel Ángel Violán reminded him on his Christmas card, in a message that almost felt like a farewell, extra freedom comes with extra responsibility:

Happy endings are as important in relationships as they are on the track because, as I constantly told you in the classroom, it is the final impression that is the most lasting.

So let this be our lasting impression: the pleasure of having had you as a pupil, watching you slide around keeping those balloons in the air and practising with you the healthiest of all exercises: questioning.

I wish you great success, as a free man, a responsible man.

'Responsible, sure,' says Jorge. 'I have changed but not much more than you normally change from one year to the next. I have grown, grown again and I will continue to grow. Things have happened to me again that don't happen to most athletes. I've had difficult times where I have had to make difficult decisions but my heart and my emotions have hardened so much that very few things affect me now.'

Jorge Lorenzo has started to worry about matters outside racing, for example, the direction of his career or financial concerns that were previously left in the hands of his former manager. 'I suppose that person has demonstrated to me that I can't take [money] for granted. I've had to change the people around me and start again from zero, putting my trust in others but with the experience and determination to stay on top of everything. Sometimes it can seem like you have a blindfold over your eyes with respect to certain things and you get so used to it that you're happy to have it. You don't want to take it off because you don't know what life will be like without it, you don't know that it could be better. My blindfold fell off unexpectedly and I suddenly saw everything through different eyes. I saw things I didn't like so I decided to change them. Marcos [Hirsch] gave me a hand. It is a tense situation but we'll keep going.'

It is already clear that Jorge is a person who tries to find the positive in every situation. He can find inspiration from virtually anything and he is always keen to learn from others. 'Jorge has read the autobiographies of Fernando Alonso, Rafa Nadal and Lance Armstrong, so that he can learn something from each of them,' reveals Ricky Cardús. 'What I'd like to know is whether sportsmen like them will sit down and read Jorge's.'

No Excuses is one of the books Jorge Lorenzo has read recently. It is the autobiography of Kyle Maynard, who suffers with a rare disorder called congenital amputation, meaning he has no elbows or knees. Despite his disability, Maynard became a wrestling champion and is now a renowned motivational speaker. For Lorenzo, the book provided a source of inspiration at the start of his MotoGP career and is the reason why he consciously refuses to make excuses as he fights for his ultimate goal – as impossible and unreachable as it may sometimes seem.

November 2007
Text written by Jorge Lorenzo entitled:
'DOES PRACTICE MAKE PERFECT?'

We are all born with a quality, a talent to do something with our life. I believe that we all have the opportunity to become good at at least one thing, if we are able to discover what our talent is, of course. It is not easy and the majority of people never realise what their gift is – maybe because destiny has never opened their eyes to it, or because other people saw it but didn't say anything, or even because they know it but are too lazy to do anything about it. Other people don't realise until it's too late – when they don't have time to practise and catch up with people younger than them.

For example, they say Albert Einstein had Asperger's syndrome (autism). They say he was an eccentric, with few social skills (he hardly ever spoke and was so involved in his work that he would forget to eat and he had a strong character, even with his friends). He found it really difficult to maintain casual conversation. On the other hand, he was a genius at what he did, literally. I've got friends who are riders, sportsmen like me, who have a huge talent to ride a motorcycle but can't kick a football to save their life...

Maybe I'm wrong, but I have always believed that I was born to ride motorcycles. Yes, I know, you're wondering how I know I was born to do this if I haven't tried anything else. I think it too sometimes. Sometimes I stop and wonder if I could have been a great painter, sculptor, writer, lawyer or footballer ... What if my natural talent for any of those things was greater than my ability to ride a motorcycle? I'll never know the answer to that but what I can tell you is that there are more things that I'd be bad at than good...

I'm not complaining. At the end of the day I've just become a double World Champion at the age of twenty. It's a good thing we never listened to the people we overheard in the past saying: 'They'll never win anything.'

Practice. They say practice makes perfect and there could be nothing closer to the truth. I've never seen anybody practise something on a daily basis and fail to become at least slightly good at it. Obviously, to be the best you need to have the talent, otherwise there would be millions of heroes in this sport. But for me there is no doubt that practice, channelled in the right way, can allow somebody to be good at whatever they choose.

That initial feeling of panic and clumsiness will always be there at the start because your subject knowledge is non-existent, you don't know how anything works. After a few hours you start to become familiar with what you're doing and you start to improve, even though you must think before you act. After a few months you start to do it well, even though you still make rookie errors. After a few years you become a natural and you don't even have to think about it. Your subconscious is working for you. It's always the same: you practise, practise, practise. I've spent a huge part of my life sitting on a motorcycle and I can tell you that it is a place where I have felt every emotion this life has to offer. For the second time in my life I have achieved my dream. To do so a third time is a question of lots of practice … and luck.

Talent, practice and luck. If anybody wanted to describe the key to the success of Jorge Lorenzo, or of any other sports star for that matter, they need few other words. The first part comes as standard for Jorge, who was blessed with an incredible natural talent to ride. The opportunity to practise came as soon as he was old enough to reach the handlebars and he hasn't stopped since. And luck? Luck will come into it on the day he truly needs it.

1

X-DENTRO: ON THE INSIDE

Jorge Lorenzo, up close and personal

*T*ime to relax … with a book! It would be better for me to leave my games
console on the bedside table and choose something with a bit more culture
instead. Along with music, reading is one of my great passions. The last book I
bought was because the protagonist is like me. He doesn't mince his words:
Joaquín Sabina.

Extract from a text by Jorge Lorenzo, published in Marca on
24 April 2007.

13 December 2007, 12.00pm
Mau Mau bar, 265 Portobello Road, London
THE RED LIGHTS GO OUT, THE SPOTLIGHT COMES ON

From the moment I started to visualise in my mind how I would
write Jorge Lorenzo's biography, I gave a lot of thought to how it
could start. Even breaking the ice with him would be different to
doing so with somebody else of his generation because, even though
he left school early, he is still much better read than most people of
his age, which is a nice irony.

It was the text that opens this chapter, written by him and
published after the 2007 Turkish Grand Prix, that gave me the answer.
Lorenzo had just read the latest biography of the Spanish singer-
songwriter Joaquín Sabina and had been moved by his confessions to
the Madrid-based journalist and writer Javier Menéndez Flores.

One of the many anecdotes of Sabina's life served as the inspiration
for my starting point. During his years of exile in London, Sabina
wrote his first songs and began to make a living from them by

busking on the Underground and performing in restaurants and cafés. It was in one such establishment on Portobello Road, the 'Mexicano-Taberna', where he played in front of George Harrison on his birthday. The ex-Beatle, impressed by Sabina's talent, gave him a five-pound tip.

Visiting Jorge in London, aware of his admiration for Sabina and his knowledge of this story, I thought the same restaurant could be the perfect starting point for our journey. But despite putting good old Google to task, I couldn't find an address for the 'Mexicano-Taberna'. Even so, I wanted to tap into Jorge's sentimental side by taking him to the most similar place I could find to the venue made famous in Spain by a rebel with an identical penchant for shooting from the hip.

Ernest Riveras: So here we are. London, Portobello Road. Joaquín Sabina must have spent a lot of time in places like this!

Jorge Lorenzo: I've read Sabina's biography. It's a really honest book, without limits. It really had an impact on me, the way he spoke so sincerely, telling the whole story without holding anything back. I haven't seen that in many books. In that respect it's probably the most powerful book I've read. It shocked me, and I like that idea.

ER: So what did you think? That if you ever told your own life story you'd want it to be that way too?

JL: Well, it's a bit different. Sabina has had more of a life than me, he's older. He's got a much more … how can I say it? A more chequered past. I can't start dishing the dirt like that because I'm a professional sportsman and I have sponsors to take care of. I don't just depend on my talent and my voice.

ER: In other words, we're not going to talk about hookers and drugs, or drink whisky until six in the morning?

JL: We can if you like but I don't have many stories like that to bring to the table! [Laughs]

In the end, the Mau Mau bar was chosen as the place where Jorge Lorenzo would begin to tell his story. Once we'd sat down his mother María, who had accompanied us to our own particular starting point, left us alone. 'I have to go and buy fish otherwise I won't be able to produce the menu Marcos has given us for the next few days.' The Lorenzo menu, created by his own personal chef and trainer, Marcos Hirsch, has become famous in Spain and Jorge doesn't miss a single day – not even at Christmas, apparently!

JL: I decided I wanted to do the book if I won the title. I thought about it at the start of 2007. I saw that I was quite a good writer and I even started a diary. I wrote it for three days and then packed it in! But a book has always been a dream of mine. Marcos always said I was too young to write my life story and that he'd never buy a book written by Nadal, by me or by any young sportsman. He reckons we don't have anything to say, but I don't think that a 60 year old is going to write a better book just because he's older. You can be a 20-year-old genius, even though that's not my case. I just hope that after reading it people find it interesting, that they discover things about me that they didn't know and see me as I really am.

We ordered two cafe lattes and I decided to go back to Sabina. After spending a few days with Jorge, I had begun to notice that his face changed according to the surroundings, the topic of discussion or his mood. If we spoke about bikes he put on his serious face, the focused look of a professional discussing his job. If we talked about winning, his face would light up. And at the exact moment that the waitress came over with the coffees, Jorge had a different look altogether. He was staring, unblinking into the distance. It was a look I'd seen before – the one that tells you his heart is open, ready to share his most intimate thoughts. It was simply a matter of kicking things off in the same way Javier Menéndez Flores had done with the maestro Sabina.

ER: Jorge, are you prepared to tell all? How far do you want to go? Do you want to open all of the doors and windows to your life? Do you want to be completely honest?

JL: People have to enjoy reading this book. It has to draw them in, be interesting and they should find out new things about me. I want them to see that even though I am a sportsman, even though I am a double World Champion, I am still a normal person. But going back to your question, I don't think you can ever tell the whole truth. You'd end up being a very lonely person if you always said exactly what you thought! Also, if I tell everything now then people would lose interest, don't you think? Then we'd never be able to write another book again!

Jorge laughs. In close company he feels comfortable and safe. We're up and running! Now it's all or nothing time. I want to know everything he's learnt, what he hopes to learn in the future, his life, the way he sees it, his hopes and ambitions. For now we'll open just one of the doors into the private, personal world of Jorge Lorenzo – the one the media have never been allowed through and perhaps the one he has never previously opened himself.

THE BURNING QUESTION: WHAT IS CHARISMA?

I'm so glad that I know more than I knew then
Gonna keep on tryin' till I reach the highest ground

Red Hot Chili Peppers
'Higher Ground', Mother's Milk, 1989

Catching Jorge off guard is always difficult. He's always on his toes, always alert to what is going on around him, to what people are saying about him. It is a characteristic that has probably always formed a part of Jorge's personality, but it is one he has worked on and refined as he has grown up and matured.

He always has his hand on the throttle, ready to react, and while it is an approach that has produced results on the track, it is not one that is likely to guarantee success in day-to-day life. He really cares about what people say about him and never misses an opportunity to answer back if he hears something he doesn't like, often without considering the consequences of his words. In the past his spontaneity has made him a headline writer's dream, and on several occasions he's been forced to pay dearly for it. In more than one encounter with the media, or the general public, 'Lorenzo' has been taken over by 'Jorge' and this led him to question himself. Why do I come across badly to people when I meet them for the first time? Why can't I find the right words to express my true thoughts? How should I approach the media? How can I be myself without offending anybody?

Jorge wants to find a formula that allows him to be himself in public: a rebellious and direct young man who isn't ashamed of his success and who wants to share it, while at the same time expressing his own ideas and way of being without provoking unnecessary criticism or being rejected. It is only relatively recently that Jorge began to question the value of always saying what he thought. He had grown up without any kind of filter on his thoughts and words and it had proved a costly chink in his armour. He was used to speaking without prior consideration, letting everything on his mind break loose without regard for the consequences of what he was saying.

'In this game people say one thing and think another. That bores me, it's not my style. I am direct and sincere.'

That phrase could well be credited to Jorge Lorenzo, but in fact it came from another 'Giorgio' – a world champion of the fashion circuit, Giorgio Armani. If Armani can get away with saying something like that it is because his career, his experience, his success, his professionalism and even his age have put him on the kind of pedestal that gives people licence to say pretty much whatever they want. They don't offend anybody because the aura around them is so golden and the respect they have gained is unquestioned.

Jorge Lorenzo craves that kind of licence but despite his success, experience, professionalism and dedication, he is still in the early stages of his career and the wrong kind of honesty has worked against him on a number of occasions in the past. Maybe one day Jorge will reach the top of his game in the same way as Giorgio Armani has. He's certainly showing signs of having that potential, but there is still a long way to go.

Jorge's will to constantly challenge himself has helped him overcome a lot of the criticism that has been levelled at him because of his occasionally arrogant approach, and if he didn't have that attitude he wouldn't be here today. He refuses to conform to what is generally expected and he constantly tries to improve himself. He wants to know things and in a way he is trying to make up for lost time, even though he may not always be conscious of it. And while he has become accustomed to providing answers, he is also a mine of questions. 'What is charisma? How can I have charisma?' he asked Miguel Ángel Violán, a specialist in the tricky field of public speaking. 'The way you look at people, the way you laugh, walk, smile, your body language, hand gestures, the content and tone of your voice … throw all this into a blender and you'll have a cocktail of charisma!' he answered.

This intriguing part of Jorge's personality, the part that divides so much opinion about him, seemed like a good place to start.

ER: Jorge, have you always been interested in charisma, in being different to everybody else, standing out?

JL: I think so, even if I didn't know it. I didn't used to be sure how I wanted to be – what was best for me, which way to go in life. I suppose being arrogant has stuck with me. I don't like people who are submissive, people who have no personality. I think it is a major defect – definitely not the worst, but I don't like it. I don't like half-measures either. I wouldn't like to be one of those people who spend their whole time pretending to be humble, saying: 'We'll have to wait and see what happens in the race, fifth place would be okay…' and then go out there and win. But I also realised that if I continued like that then the only people who would like me would be the ones who've liked me since I was young – the people who thought I was a good person anyway. It had a limit, a ceiling. If I wanted to break through that, show people who I really am and have them like me for it, I had to make sure I wasn't too arrogant.

ER: Is that when you asked yourself what it took to be seen as charismatic?

JL: Of course, I wanted to learn the character traits that generate 'charisma'. I like watching other people. Ronaldinho, for example, is very charismatic. He's got a good face, he's always smiling and he looks like a nice guy. Then you've got someone like Eric Cantona. He was arrogant, the enfant terrible. But in 1997 he was chosen by Nike to be their big star ahead of other great players. Nobody really knows what is the best way to be but personally I'd prefer to be Cantona or John McEnroe than Ronaldinho. Since I was little I was always captivated by arrogance and since my dad was like that too, a bit cocky, I followed his example.

ER: So, unlike most people, you're a fan of the anti-hero…

JL: I know. I realise that and I've changed my opinion over the years, especially through reading. The more I read, the more I realise that it is possible to change – especially since I read *How to Win Friends and Influence People*. That had a big effect on me. It talks about the attributes you must have for people to like you. How to be a friend to your friends. We know that it's good to be generous, to look after people, be polite … but a lot of the time we don't apply that logic to our lives because we're stressed out, not concentrating, whatever. There are other interesting concepts that we skip over too. I must admit I find some of them difficult to put into practice because I have to read things a few times before they stick. I probably forget half of it or more. And then it's the typical thing – you follow the rules to the letter for the first few days but then you forget.

ER: Why were you so convinced you needed to change?

JL: I noticed that when I went out with my friends, people I didn't know seemed afraid to talk to me. Until they got to know me a little, they didn't talk to me. It was because I was so withdrawn and egotistical, in a way, so people didn't appreciate me. I found that strange! So I started to watch how my friends behaved, to see if I could work out what was wrong with me. Above all I was getting it wrong when I first met people and I've improved on that a lot, although I still have some way to go. I've even improved with my own friends – now I think I'm a good friend to them. They tell me how much I've changed. The person who says it most is Ricky [Cardús]. He used to say I was rude. When I arrived at his family's restaurant I didn't even bother to say hello. He says my head was so big it hardly fitted through the door!

The book helped me but I'm still learning, without pushing it. At the end of the day I think that, without becoming obsessed by it, the most important things will naturally stay with me. My philosophy is that you have to get used to acting like the person you want to be ... until eventually you are that person.

Throughout my conversations with Jorge, I began to realise that he was constantly reflecting on what he'd just said. On many occasions he'd pause and I'd be asking him about the next thing, but he'd want to go back and clarify exactly what he meant by his last comment.

JL: I think I have a weakness in 'cold' situations. During a race, for example, a few laps have to go by before I feel comfortable. It can take me a while to get confident and up to speed. It's the same thing with people. If I haven't seen somebody for a while I feel uncomfortable for the first ten minutes. Maybe I've got a handicap in that respect.

ER: A lot of people around you will probably say that you can act how you like as long as you keep winning...

JL: I think it was Carl Lewis who said that humility is only false modesty on behalf of the mediocre.

ER: Do you believe that?

JL: Well, things aren't always that black and white for me. But I think that people who criticise people for being cocky do so because they are not in a position to be cocky themselves, or don't know how to be. Obviously, there will be some people who don't want to be and that's a good option if you really believe in it. But those who demonstrate complete confidence and self-belief are sometimes criticised for it by the people who don't have it, and can't have it.

TALENT ISN'T EVERYTHING

We like to think we make a sad man happy

Red Hot Chili Peppers
'Good Time Boys', Mother's Milk, 1989

23 October 2007
Text written by Jorge Lorenzo entitled:
'25 KEYS TO BEING A NUMBER ONE'

A number one must have talent. It is possible to be a champion without talent, but you can't be a number one.

A number one must be brave, because without courage it is impossible to see the opportunities that tough competition sometimes offers.

A number one must be persistent because there are always difficulties to overcome. Every year, in every race.

A number one is only satisfied with being number one. Second place is not enough.

A number one must not be arrogant. He is the owner of his silence and a slave to his word.

A number one must be humble. We are equal and we can all learn from each other.

A number one must have the eye of the tiger, because when a sportsman loses the hunger that has taken him to the top, he is finished.

A number one knows how to accept defeat and how to learn from it. There is more to be learnt from defeat than from victory.

A number one learns from his mistakes; we are humans, not machines. Imperfect beings, who can improve day by day.

A number one never throws in the towel.

A number one must have charisma; even though he may be the best on the track, he still has to be accepted by the public.

A number one must have belief in his ability. If you don't have it, who will?

A number one needs the luck of a champion.

A number one must shave his head halfway through the season (ha!).

A number one must have personality; a weak character can be brought down by the silliest thing.

A number one never wins alone; behind him there must be a group of people who are just as competitive as him.

A number one must be positive because a positive attitude leads to a better job and better results.

A number one must enjoy what he does. Be happy.

A number one is patient. After the storm comes the calm.

A number one must always go to the toilet just before a race … in case of emergencies!

A number one is calculating, when the situation requires.

A number one must be a gentleman and recognise when his rival has been superior.

A number one must be intelligent. Motorcycle racing is about strategy.

A number one must be thankful, because it is only with the support of his sponsors, team, family and friends that he has been able to become the best.

Finally, a number one must be a person.

The '25 keys to being a number one' was clearly written by a person who recognised the need to add hard work and effort to the blessings of talent and luck. Jorge has started to place the same demands on himself off the track as he does on it. Of course, he is still not perfect and he can't be a 'Number One' every day, but at least his attempts at being so are being recognised by the people closest to him.

Writing down what he considers to be the keys to it was an important step. Applying them to daily life would be as big an achievement as winning another title, if not bigger. Jorge has the skill and also the desire to do that. In Spanish they call somebody like that a 'crack', derived from the English adjective 'a crack rider' or 'a crack team', but Jorge has always rejected the term. Cheni Martínez used to call him that when he was a kid and Jorge didn't like it. He once said to Cheni:

Why do you call me 'crack'?
Because you're so good on a bike.
Yes, but I work hard too!
I know, Jorge, but as much as you practise, if you don't have the talent you'd never make it. Lots of people work hard and don't make it.
That's because they don't work as hard as me.

ER: Why don't you like being called a 'crack'?
JL: Well, I accept it because everybody likes a compliment. It

would be nice to think that I win things because of my talent, because talent is not something you can buy, but I have been lucky to be good at something, I've trained hard to be good at something and really I'm only good at the one thing! I'm a specialist, so that term is too big for me.

At the heart of the matter is Jorge's belief that talent alone is not enough. He truly believes that hard work and sacrifice are even more important and are the factors that really make the difference. He doesn't like to be called a 'crack' because he thinks it's referring to his natural ability and doesn't reflect the hard work and perfectionism he always brings to his job. He has trained hard and made sacrifices for as long as he can remember, and his tireless commitment and professionalism are often commented on by anybody who has the pleasure of working with him. It is easy to understand how Jorge often connects better with people in the same place as him, people whose feet have spent more time on the footpegs than they have on the ground in their own quest to be the best.

JL: There are so few sportsmen prepared to work hard that even somebody who doesn't have the talent can reach the very top just by working hard. I was able to make the difference in the titles I won by being the person prepared to sacrifice the most, by being the most focused on that objective. I was the one who put the most energy into it. It's not just about working hard in the gym or on the bike – you have to live your whole life with that goal in mind. The mere fact you think it and have absolute faith that you will achieve it makes the entire universe conspire so that your wish comes true.

ER: So basically it annoys you that people talk about your talent because it takes credit away from the number of hours you put in?

JL: Since you ask, I'll give you an example. Right now I'm not as flexible as I used to be. Two years ago I really was, but not any more – I don't need to be. But if I decide to stretch, if I do the splits and hold it for two hours every day, within two months I could be as flexible as a professional gymnast. Or if I pick up a football … if I don't know how to kick it then I won't suddenly be able to play like

Ronaldinho – it's unlikely I'll ever be able to reach the same level as him – but if I spend months practising I'll at least end up being able to juggle a ball. If somebody really wants something and they go after it, usually they will get it. At the same time, if you don't believe you are going to get it then it's impossible that you will. There are a lot of riders who want it but they don't know how and they're not prepared to sacrifice themselves for it. They think they are, they think they're sacrificing enough, but they're not! They say to themselves 'Yeah, this is great, I'm a rider, this is cool. I'm famous, I can pull whichever girl I want...' but racing is not the main thing in their life. It may be only 50 per cent of it because there are things that are equally as important to them. Already that means there are too many things going on in their head. At this level, if racing is not the most important thing in your life then you can't do it, you can't compete with your rivals – least of all beat them! You cannot become World Champion, because you have other objectives in life. Objectives that may be more satisfying in the short term but only serve to distract you from your ultimate goal.

ER: Don't you think that Dovizioso wanted to be World Champion too in 2006 and 2007? Don't you think he gave everything to achieve it?

JL: He will think he gave his maximum but he will be lying to himself because nobody does that. Nobody gets close to their maximum, not even me. He will think that he didn't win because he was riding a Honda. There are very few sportsmen who will say, 'I deserve what happened to me and there are no excuses. I didn't know how to do any better and I've done things wrong.' That is the only way to be the best, the only way. People who make excuses don't get to the top. I know riders who haven't made it for just that reason.

ER: Don't you ever make excuses?

JL: Yes, yes, of course. Everybody makes excuses! It is difficult to admit your mistakes. Swallowing your pride is one of the most difficult things you can do. It's your ego. We all make excuses every day. You moan about something that's happened to you, what bad luck you're having, that the bike wasn't running well or the tyres weren't the right ones – most riders use these excuses – even Valentino sometimes! We all do it but it's not the right way. In an ideal world we wouldn't make excuses at all. We'd be honest and admit that something is our fault. I do that sometimes but it's not easy. It's implanted in our brain, since birth. Making an excuse makes you feel better about yourself. Even when you reflect on a problem and start off by saying, 'I don't want to make excuses but…' – you've already done it!

May 2006

CUTTING THE UMBILICAL CORD

Say what I want
Do what I can

Red Hot Chili Peppers
From 'The Power of Equality', Blood Sugar Sex Magik, 1991

JL: My father is very obsessive and on top of that he has screwed things up in a big way on several occasions, but to me my father is still like a God. He taught me everything I know and without him I wouldn't even be writing this book, even though he has certain opinions that are wrong. My father did the best he could for me, but he wasn't the best father. I mean in terms of showing me affection and bringing me up. As far as teaching me to ride a motorcycle is concerned, I don't think many fathers could have done a better job.

They say that during the first five years of life our brain has an unlimited capacity for learning and the development of all aspects of intelligence, so the input from our parents is decisive. It is clear that the first few years of Jorge's life, spent surrounded by motorcycles and his father Chicho's passion for and dedication to them, were critical in forming the champion he is today and shaping his achievements up to now. The natural talent for riding that he was born with has been encouraged, nurtured and moulded by Chicho, who had a vision of Jorge as a future champion.

The relationship that developed between Chicho and Jorge Lorenzo was certainly special. Father and son were virtually inseparable for the first 18 years of Jorge's life – the first ten of which were dedicated body and soul to 'playing' at bikes and 'being champions'. The next eight years saw them doing it for real, with Chicho programming Jorge to win, fulfilling his own dreams through his son. Few people really know Jorge like his father does – partly because, in many ways, he is a reflection of himself – and it's for this reason that sometimes only Chicho could understand Jorge's reactions, the way he acted, his lack of manners and even his disregard for others.

Jorge had (and perhaps still has) certain ways that were only appropriate in the enclosed world inhabited by his father and him during those formative years. Generally, though, things are different now. There are other, more important things in his life – and his father is no longer his shadow and mentor. Now his team are his 'family' at a racetrack and many of them have got to know him well. They understand the young man who, over the years, left many people scratching their heads or saying that Jorge was careless, absent-minded, disorganised and spared little thought for things that didn't interest him. Chicho once told Cheni Martínez, 'Jorge is smarter than all of us put together! He's happy to let people do things for him as long as they're prepared to do it.'

During June 2006, as Jorge desperately tried to recover his form on the track, away from it an entirely different battle was taking place between his father and manager, on the pages of the national and international press...

The following is an extract from an article published in *Diario de Mallorca*. Jorge Lorenzo's father, Chicho, says, 'I've been left without my son, but I hope he values what I have done for him'

The father of Mallorcan motorcycle racer Jorge Lorenzo has declared war on his manager, Dani Amatriaín. Chicho Lorenzo has claimed in an interview with 'Diario de Mallorca' that 'it is not normal' that the parents of 'a 19-year-old boy don't know where his money is', before claiming that it has been invested in property.

'I've been left without a job and without a son, because at the moment he is no son of mine. I am hopeful the same thing happens to

him that happens to all sons. That he values everything I have done for him,' says Chicho Lorenzo, who says he hasn't spoken to Jorge for eleven days. He also points the finger at Amatriaín: 'He's his manager and the boss of the team, which are two conflicting jobs. As a director he's already taking 20 per cent, plus the percentage he takes as an agent, but it's not about what he earns. I don't know where my son's money is and it is not normal that the parents of a 19-year-old boy don't know that. We don't know what kind of contract he has with Aprilia ... I wish I'd have looked after the money myself. That way I'd know now that it is all for him. The number of cases where an agent has fleeced a sportsman is incalculable.'

The following is an extract from an article published in *Diario de Mallorca*: 'Lorenzo defends his manager against criticism from his father'

The 19-year-old rider from Mallorca has released a statement requesting the closure of 'a catalogue of false claims that, regrettably, have been made public' and respect for his 'private life, with the attention turned to my career as a professional and a sportsman. Anything that happens in my private life will never be allowed to interfere with my career.' The Mallorcan added: 'My life as a sportsman is completely separate and it is, and always will be, directed by a group of professionals who have my complete trust.'

The following is an extract from an article published in *Diario de Mallorca*: 'Daniel Amatriaín brings charges against the father of Jorge Lorenzo'

'...the kind of personal comments he has made need to be dealt with in court, where I have already appeared in defence of my honour as a person and a professional.' The press release goes on to thank 'certain sections of the media for the invitation to contest some of the humiliating accusations about my person and my professional attitude, which have been published recently'.

In the same statement, Amatriaín indicates 'I am aware of the source and intentions of these statements', adding 'even so, I must decline this invitation for a variety of reasons:

(a) Firstly, in the name of professionalism, since I view it as inappropriate to publicly discuss matters concerning the personal life of one of my team members. My responsibility and respect for them has always been of vital importance to me, as a person and a team manager, and the prestige I have gained among my fellow professionals relies on it.

(b) I do not believe that these matters are open to debate in the media, however serious and severe they may be.

(c) The most important reason is that the kind of comments that have been made must be brought before the Courts for Justice, where I have already appeared in defence of my personal and professional honour, as much as a matter of respect and professionalism as one of gravity and seriousness,' reads the press release.

Comments made by Chicho Lorenzo on Dailymotos.com

I am being crucified by a lot of people for everything that is happening, some of them intentionally and some without knowing the true cause. The only thing I can say is that I am fighting for the safety of my son my way, the only way available to people with few financial resources like me. Going to court is fine for people who can afford to pay for it … At the end of the day this is yet another example of the fight between the powerful and the weak and you know how the saying goes: the law is powerful on the weak and weak on the powerful…

As for the people who say I'm only in it for the money, I can tell you that is not true because if it was I'd have kept everything my son earned before he came of age. The fact is I never had control of it because I had so much trust in the person who was looking after him. Fair enough, call me stupid or naïve if you like…

The thing that has moved me to start this crusade was seeing how often my son was crashing, due to a decision that was completely wrong, and seeing that despite the evidence on show nobody was doing anything to get to the root of the problem, which was no different to any other young sportsman under so much pressure. Among the group of professionals surrounding him, he needed a sports psychologist or a professional adviser, somebody who was legitimate and honest. With respect to these comments I have supposedly made, which have been published with the clear intention of bringing me harm, certain things I said have been manipulated and others taken out of context. It is very easy to do and there are journalists who specialise in it. I would like to express my thanks to the press who have been objective and impartial and dedicated themselves to what the media should be about, which is providing information without taking sides. The readers can make their own decisions on where the pieces fit together.

Whatever your views on where 'the pieces fit together' it was clear that the professional approach Chicho had taken to his relationship with his son since those early days on the wastelands of Palma was now becoming clouded by emotion, a protective instict and, without doubt, his trademark stubbornness.

ER: The roles that you and your father took on were very well defined from the very beginning, weren't they?

JL: I've always seen my father as a figure of authority. It's not that I saw him as superior to me, but he has always been in control of my life. And now he isn't.

ER: There was a turning point in your relationship with him – a 'before and after' moment. Tell me about the time between the races in Turkey and Mugello, in May 2006.

JL: My father has his ideas and he thinks that only his ideas work, that you can only achieve things by taking them on board. After the Italian Grand Prix at Mugello, when I found out what he had said, I couldn't believe it! It was really heavy! I remember one thing in particular that he said: 'If my son wins tomorrow, it will be like giving a hit to a drug addict.' Incredible! At that time I thought, 'Is this guy really my dad? Either he's desperate or he's gone mad. What the hell is up with him?' But in the end I was able to understand him too. Firstly, because a father never wants to see anything bad happen to his child and very few do so intentionally. Secondly, I put myself in his shoes and realised that from the age of three to eighteen he has always been by my side, taking care of everything ... Sure, it's not right that he should think that the objective is to be recompensed with money, that for the seeds we planted together you should give me a basket of fruit ... But to have worked so hard for so long and then to one day fall out with your son, and for him to not want to know you anymore – I can understand it.

ER: But it's not like you cut your ties completely with your father. You just told him it was time to move on, that he wouldn't form a part of your new workforce.

JL: Yes, but I also told him not to bother coming to the races. I sent him away, so I can understand his reaction. Coming to the World Championship was his life. He loved watching his son race. 'Don't come to the races, don't speak to me, I don't want to know you...' I can understand that it must have been tough to hear those words. That's why he did what he did, but at the same time I have always said that I would have supported my father. I would have given him more than he could have possibly asked for. But what he said was so harsh, so strong, I still don't feel like helping him right now. Obviously if he was in a bad way I would, but not just now...

ER: In other words, the problem was money.

JL: My dad asked Marcos [Hirsch] to act as an intermediary and tell me that I owed him a percentage of the money I earned. He said that he deserved to recoup his investment, reap the fruit of the seeds he had sown. Marcos told him no, he said he didn't agree and he wouldn't do it. That's where the conflict started. My dad got mad, instead of being smarter with Marcos, who had always been a help to him.

ER: Have you forgiven him?

JL: Everything in life can be forgiven.

ER: What about him? Has he forgiven you?

JL: Well... He still has his own ideas, the same ones he had back then. But at least he lets me get on with my life in peace. If I can help him out now and again I do. I went to Mallorca for the opening of his school. We don't exactly call each other every day but we get on.

ER: Did he celebrate when you were crowned World Champion?

JL: In 2007 he did, but I'm not sure about the year before. I'm sure he wasn't completely happy when I won at Mugello in 2006. It sounds crazy but my father is a very logical person – he does everything logically. Ask Marcos, he'll tell you the same, that my father is a genius, a craftsman, with some incredible ideas. But sometimes he can go a bit crazy and he doesn't know where to draw the line. Personally I don't think anybody in this life has the whole truth, nobody is 100 per cent right. At the same time I'm sure my father wasn't 100 per cent wrong about certain subjects ... not many anyway, but definitely some. At the start I didn't want to break up with him, just change things around. I understand that is hard to take. To be separated from your son after 18 years together, training him ... But he brought it on himself because he didn't want me to continue with Dani [Amatriaín]. If he'd have got on better with Dani, he'd still be here now, but that's the way he is. It's all or nothing with him and when he gets really angry you can't calm him down. He used to say: 'Since I've got nothing to lose, I don't care.' That didn't make sense to me and it hurt me the way he went about it because it wasn't right. I know that he didn't want anything bad to happen to his own son. There are people that anger you because you know they want to hurt you, or make life difficult for you, but that wasn't my father. He wanted the best for me and he thought his way was the best, but it was obvious to me that he was wrong. Only he and maybe four other people thought his was the right way. Even the press and some of his own friends turned against him!

ER: But now the relationship has recovered a little. When you were with us in America [working as a guest commentator for TVE at the USGP in 2007] I asked you who you were calling to see how well you were doing as a commentator and you said your father.

JL: Yes, because my father tells me things straight. He'd never tell me I'd done something well if I hadn't. If I want the truth, I ask my father.

One year on from these initial conversations, which took place either in the Mau Mau bar or at Jorge's house in Chelsea, in December 2007, it was time for an update. We needed to find some free time again, between charity events and award ceremonies, to revisit some of his thoughts and opinions. The best way to hold Jorge's attention was to meet up with him near to the place where he feels most comfortable – the gym. Whether it was over lunch, after training at the Hotel Barceló-Sants in Barcelona, or beforehand in one of the small offices made available to us at the complex, Jorge was just as receptive and eloquent as he'd been twelve months earlier.

The relationship with his father had been much better during 2008 and I'd been told that Chicho Lorenzo had been watching Jorge's rookie season in MotoGP with keen interest from their home in Mallorca. In fact, I'd had a chance to catch up with Chicho at a round of the Spanish Championship at Jerez in June. He was looking after a young rider, Joan Perelló, and in between practice sessions I took the opportunity to find out his thoughts about his son, who had been badly injured two weeks previously at the Catalunya GP. 'The same thing has happened to Jorge ever since he was small,' said Chicho. 'When things are going well he gets confident and relaxes a little. The crash in China after three poles, three podiums and a win was an example of that.'

Chicho's opinions on this matter were already well known and have been mentioned in this book by Jorge himself, who shares his father's opinion, but he saved his most surprising thoughts for later in the year. After the split between Jorge and his manager, Dani Amatriaín, the one thing nobody expected was that Chicho would take Dani's side, having already made it clear that their relationship was really bad.

JL: My father will always be my father but just because we have the same blood or because he brought me into this world does not mean I'm always going to agree with everything he does or let him get away with everything. He is different and he does things that can catch you by surprise. I'm a little bit immune to it because I know he does very strange things sometimes but, honestly, what he has been doing lately and in particular that interview … it left me pretty stunned, yes.

The interview Jorge was referring to was given by his father to Toni Silva from the newspaper *La Voz de Galicia* on 22 September 2008. It had the headline 'I would like Dani Amatriaín to continue as Jorge's manager' and it read as follows:

The MotoGP World Championship title has already been decided in favour of Valentino Rossi, so with the excitement of the title chase over before the end of the season, other news has captured the interest of the paddock, such as the separation of Jorge Lorenzo from his manager Dani Amatriaín, a partnership that has lasted a decade. Off-track matters have led Lorenzo to make the break from a man who, for a long time, has had a tense relationship with Chicho Lorenzo, the rider's father. However, the Galician now insists that 'as a manager' Amatriaín is one of the best in the business.

'What do you think about the separation?'

'I'm more worried now than I was with the previous situation. As far as finding sponsors and guiding a young rider through his sporting career is concerned, in my opinion Dani is one of the best.'

'More worried? Why? We have all seen that Amatriaín and yourself have not exactly been the best of friends in recent years.'

'Yes, but I recognise that Dani has done his job as manager well and now there is a void to be filled. I don't think Jorge will find a professional who is able to do the job as well as Amatriaín can.'

'Does Lorenzo need a manager or is the infrastructure at Yamaha enough?'

'A rider has a lot of contracts to sign, with the team and with personal sponsors, and all of that needs to be taken care of by a manager.'

'Were you surprised when you heard about the split?'

'I'm not surprised by anything anymore – this is an elitist world and there are a lot of interests and money moving around. There are surprises every day.'

'So you'd like Amatriaín to continue managing Jorge?'

'The father of any sportsperson wants them to be looked after by the best. My differences with Dani were never about how he managed my son's career or his role as his manager. The differences were for other reasons altogether and so yes, I would like Dani to continue as his manager. You have to give him credit for the job he has done – the results are there to be seen.'

Chicho's statement was remarkable, not only because it seemed to go back on his previous comments about Dani's management of Jorge but even more so because Jorge was in the process of ending his professional relationship with Dani – a situation that would seem like the ideal opportunity for him to settle his differences with his son.

ER: Don't you think that after what had happened with Dani, this could have been the moment to patch things up with your father and recover your relationship?

JL: The truth is that it seems that whenever there is an opportunity to let things go back to the way they were, to fix his relationship with me, my father prefers to go the opposite way.

VALENTINO ROSSI: A LEGEND IN THE FLESH

You were always my favourite
Always my man

Red Hot Chili Peppers
From 'Savior', Californication, 1999

'I am not different. Or, what I mean is, I'm like everybody else and truly everybody is different. If you compare yourself with others you see similarities but everybody has their own paranoia, their virtues and their defects. There is a whole world inside every person!' More than anything, this comment – one of many – was a statement of intent from Jorge Lorenzo. One of his biggest motivations in life is to differentiate himself from everybody else. He doesn't mean to be pretentious, he simply has a healthy desire to create a style that sets him apart. 'I just think he wants everybody to look up to him,' observes Cheni Martínez.

Sometimes it is easier to create a persona by observing and being inspired by someone whom one already admires – and even though Jorge might not admit it out loud, the person he looks up to (as, of course, do many others) is Valentino Rossi. Interestingly, some of Jorge's first fall-outs with his father were about Valentino. Chicho isn't exactly Rossi's biggest fan, but he'd always insisted that 'The Doctor' was a better rider than Biaggi. So Jorge, partly because he liked to ride like him and partly because Max was Rossi's biggest enemy, rebelled against his father and became a Biaggi fan. 'The truth is that I started siding with Biaggi to wind my dad up in the Harada era. In 1997, when Biaggi signed for Honda after Aprilia decided they didn't want to continue with him, nobody thought he could win the title because, at that time, the Honda wasn't a winning bike. So when my dad used to go on about it, I'd say, "We'll see." And Biaggi won the first race at Shah Alam by 13 seconds! But then it developed into a difficult season, with a couple of crashes, and they arrived in Barcelona with Waldmann holding the advantage. I was at my mother's house watching the television. Biaggi led the whole race until two corners from the end, when Waldmann passed him and won! I was so upset that Biaggi had lost, I cried.'

Rossi himself admits in his autobiography (written in 2006 with Enrico Borghi) that he was a Biaggi fan as a youngster. In 1993, aged 14, Valentino had a Biaggi poster on his wall. Jorge didn't quite go that far, and he had probably already realised that Rossi was the more complete rider, although he couldn't say so. If you were a Biaggi fan, you were a Biaggi fan. Nowadays he has no trouble at all admitting that Rossi is the greatest there has ever been, although he hasn't come to that decision totally on his own: there has been the occasional push in that direction over the years from people like Juanito Llansá. 'I said to him, "Jorge, if you have to look up to somebody, focus on the best … and that's not Biaggi. You can have your own heroes, but the best of the lot is Rossi." Now he needs no convincing – especially since riding alongside him in MotoGP, on the same bike. He realises that to win so many titles on one of these things, you have to be seriously good!'

Even so, Jorge can't resist his rebellious side, claiming the best race he ever saw was won by Biaggi. 'I can remember perfectly Max's first victory at Suzuka in 1998 – his first on a 500! Nobody expected him to win there, people wouldn't have bet a single dollar on Biaggi. It's a bit like in football, when you're a fan of one of the smaller teams and they play against Barça or Madrid, you don't expect them to win. But not only do they win, they win 5–1! Doohan crashed but Max was already five seconds clear. It was incredible. I liked Biaggi's character – his wheelies, his designs, his numbers.'

Valentino, though, is a person who interests Jorge both on and off the track. He has always been aware of Rossi's incredible personality and also fascinated by his charisma. There's that word again: 'charisma'. Jorge took the opportunity to discuss Rossi's special personality with somebody who could give a professional opinion and explain clearly and authoritatively how and why Valentino finds it so easy to communicate effectively with so many people. Miguel Ángel Violán recalls: 'We used to speak about Rossi, and analyse his public appearances. There is a technique in psychology called psychomorphology, which refers to the way a person can transmit their character through their facial expressions and posture. In Rossi you can see a person who is naturally happy, congenial, creative, artistic, good fun but with a competitive edge too. Jorge's expression, on the other hand, made him seem like a serious person who can't even muster a smile.'

'Try to smile,' Miguel Ángel Violán would say.

'But what if I'm not happy?' Jorge would reply.

'Just try to be. People want smiles! You'll win more fans. It might not feel natural at first, but it will come.'

It is ironic that destiny has taken Jorge as close to Rossi as any rider could possibly be, sharing team colours, a garage (albeit with a wall down the middle) and maybe even the posters on the walls of young fans all over the world. Who would have thought it? When he joined Yamaha at the start of 2008, Jorge was keen to get to know Valentino personally. As well as learning from him on the track, he was eager to discover some of the secrets that make the World Champion such a media phenomenon. The first time they addressed the press together was actually at the Catalunya GP, on 9 June 2007. By then the secret was out that they would be team-mates in 2008, although Jorge had become disconcerted by rumours that their pit box would be divided in two, with Rossi switching to Bridgestone tyres while Lorenzo stayed with Michelin. It was a topic Jorge wished to avoid when talking about Rossi in one of his articles published in 2007.

July 2007, German GP
Text written by Jorge Lorenzo entitled:
'THE ALIENS HAVE NOT YET LANDED'

Yes, you read it right: they're still not here, they haven't landed yet. And don't worry, there are no signs that they're about to – at least for now… 'There is too much imperfection in this land,' they may be thinking. Maybe their technology and intelligence are light years ahead of ours so to conquer us wouldn't be a big enough challenge for them. I don't know, maybe they don't even exist.

What I do know is that here on earth, where we humans live (usually), we don't get visits from aliens (I know … some people look like them, that is true) and even less likely is a visit from a god from another galaxy. And just when we do find somebody we think has paranormal powers, he goes and crashes one Sunday afternoon.

When Valentino Rossi crashes, it is not like seeing any other rider crash. When people here in the paddock see that number 46 machine spinning across the track, they can barely believe their eyes. My race had finished and I was tucking into a lovely plate of spaghetti carbonara, watching the MotoGP race, when I saw Valentino trying to pick his bike up out of the gravel. I had to blink several times to make sure I wasn't dreaming.

It's always funny to listen to the comments from everybody in the garage when we're watching the MotoGP race, passionately 'discussing' the more controversial incidents. It is one of the nicest and funniest moments of the weekend so it's always a shame that on lap ten we have to rush off to the car and get out of the circuit before the post-race traffic jams start.

Anyway, I digress. When a rider crashes the standard comment would be: 'Look! So-and-so has crashed!' If it's a rider who tends to spend more time on the floor than he does on his bike it will be: 'So-and-so again, what a surprise!' But when Valentino crashes there's a unanimous cry of 'Nooooooooooooo … it can't be!' And everybody looks at each other in disbelief.

That's what you get when you're a seven-times World Champion. That's what you get when you're considered by most people (this writer included) as the greatest rider of all time. And that's what you get when you hardly ever make mistakes.

Having said that, my friends, if you still believe in aliens you can stop looking. You won't find any around here.

DECEMBER 2007

ER: Let's talk about Valentino. Inspiration, icon, example, rival?

JL: I think he's the model for any rider. When people talk about Rossi, it's not like talking about Doohan or Rainey. They are talking about somebody even more special. Rossi has been an extremely important person for motorcycling. He has been an inspiration for a lot of riders, for a lot of youngsters. He has had more impact than any other rider in history, he's done more than anybody to help the sport grow and he has given motorcycling a whole new dimension.

ER: But, for example, is Valentino the model for your celebrations?

JL: If Rossi hadn't started celebrating like he does then maybe it would never have occurred to me. Who knows? Obviously he was an inspiration to me in the beginning. The thing is they were so good, and there were so many ... they were so funny and so smart. I had a few ideas and I thought it could be good fun but I never did anything thinking that I could become Valentino Rossi II.

ER: You were a Biaggi fan. At what point did you change and start watching Rossi?

JL: It was always obvious that Rossi was extremely good but I wanted to believe that he won because he was lucky, or because he had a better bike. Once I started out in the World Championship myself I stopped watching out for Biaggi because I started to be more concerned with myself and less about other people. That's when I started to realise that Rossi had something – that it was no coincidence that he kept winning every weekend.

ER: And there came a point where you publicly stated that Rossi was the greatest of all time. When he was told about that he said: 'Wow, at last he's admitted it, but it's taken a while!'

JL: I don't like that. Even though he thought it, I don't think he should have said it. I never thought he'd say that! I didn't imagine he would. Even though he's the best, and he's won eight titles, he could have said, for example, 'I appreciate the comment and Jorge is also a great rider.' I would have expected that from any other rider, but not him.

ER: I remember at Jerez, when you were doing a report for TVE with [former 500cc World Champion and current TVE commentator] Alex Crivillé, we asked you if you'd like to have a corner named after you. And you answered: 'I wouldn't want a corner named after me even if I win the World Championship. I'll only accept it if I pull off an 'X-fuera' [overtaking on the outside] in that corner.' Can you seriously imagine yourself with that kind of legendary status?

JL: To be a legend is something huge. It depends how well I do in the future – on my results, on how I evolve. Right now I'm a long way behind Rossi, in terms of personality. We are two completely different characters, even if our celebrations may be similar. To create a better character than Valentino has managed over the years is very difficult. I've just got to find my own way and try to make my own character be as attractive as possible, to create a character that is different, very different. Maybe that way it can become legend.

ER: From what you say it sounds like you'll only be happy when you've established your true character…

JL: Yes, but when you're younger it is more difficult because your personality changes so regularly. Bit by bit you become more secure in yourself and you change it less. The more sure you are of yourself the less you self-analyse. But you always want to improve those aspects of yourself that you don't like and if you stop self-analysing altogether then you can't improve. It's a tricky one, isn't it? It is a vicious circle and it's difficult to break.

ER: They say that the first challenge is to beat your team-mate, that he is your main rival. And now you've got Valentino next door!

JL: So far, and I say so far because right now it's not just anybody

I've got alongside me, it's Valentino Rossi, but so far, unfortunately for my team-mates, I've been lucky enough that things have gone well enough for me to go badly for them. With Rossi it is a bit different because we're not technically in the same team. The mere fact there is a wall between us means we're in different teams, we're on different tyres, and for either of us at any time that could be an easy excuse as to why one of us hasn't beaten the other, or why we haven't got the result we wanted. I think it would be difficult for either of us to sink our team-mate...

ER: There was a lot of talk that Valentino wanted to veto your signing, like he did in 2006 with Casey Stoner.

JL: In my opinion, I think it is true that Valentino vetoed the Stoner deal because Colin Edwards was in the team at that time and Valentino also wanted to cover his back by not having a hungry young rider in the same garage. But after Melandri left, Yamaha didn't have a youngster. They had the best, in Rossi, but they also had to look to the future, to his eventual replacement. They were the factory that expressed the most interest in me. To get an offer from a factory that, alongside HRC, is the best in the world – as well as the fact that Yamaha have had better riders than Honda over the course of their history – I can tell you that to get that call and be told that you are their future ... that was nice, make no mistake! What Valentino thought about it didn't worry us too much.

ER: Don't you think you should have a man-to-man chat with Valentino?

JL: I'd like to. But I guess we've both got more important things to do than sit down and talk. It's hard to imagine the day when we say, 'Okay, let's sit down and talk.' I'd like to but it's not going to happen. I'd like to be able to learn things from him because he's an interesting person both on and off the track. But it's not to be and that's normal – I'd do the same in his situation. You don't give your food rations to your enemy! If you can avoid it, then you avoid it. If you can stop the other guy from moving forward, do it. But that's as far as it should go. If you can prevent another rider from coming then fine, but you shouldn't wish bad things on anybody. I'd like that to be the philosophy between us.

ER: You were being very cagey about whether you were going to stay in 250cc, but you'd already made the decision at the start of 2007, hadn't you?

JL: I wanted to move up to MotoGP as World Champion but if I didn't win it I wanted to move up anyway because I thought I was physically up to it and my riding was too. I never once thought about continuing in 250cc but I owed it to Aprilia to keep it under my hat. In 2006, two races before Japan, we made the decision and we signed the contract at Motegi. My preference was to move straight up to MotoGP in 2007 but Dani thought it was better for me to consolidate myself in the 250 class. Also, at that time Yamaha thought it wasn't a good idea to suddenly break their contract with Colin Edwards. They could have done, but they weren't convinced by the idea.

ER: We have spoken a lot about Rossi but you haven't described him to me as a rider yet. What's he like?

JL: What can I say about him? He's got everything. He has worked on everything to the point where he is good at everything. Maybe the only part he could still improve is his starts. He brakes well, really hard. He has good corner speed, he accelerates well. He is a great strategist and he wins a lot of races with his head. He's just extremely fast. He's also a racer – he's not necessarily one for practice, even though he has like 50 pole positions ... he's won over 100 races. He is very strong when it comes to a mental battle and he has talent. And I'm sure the level of his talent means he doesn't have to be as physically well prepared as other riders.

The Fiat Yamaha Team was officially presented to the press on 19 January 2008 in Milan – the 'Dream Team', as some people called it, referring to the nine world titles that Valentino Rossi and Jorge Lorenzo had won between them at that point. 'For any rider your team-mate is your main rival and I'm happy it's him because he is a very quick rider and I hope that he helps to improve the M1, so from that point of view he is a good team-mate', said a smiling Lorenzo. 'Valentino ... what can I say about him? Valentino is the most complete athlete that this sport has the honour to possess. He has everything and he puts on a show both on and off the track. It will be difficult to get to his level, although I'll obviously be doing everything to try and get there.'

After a year of sharing the same garage, or should I say sharing the same team, Jorge has a much more detailed opinion of Valentino, although their famous 'conversation' has yet to happen...

DECEMBER 2008

JL: We have never had an in-depth conversation. The relationship is cordial, but I've noticed that he puts a kind of barrier up. He doesn't want any kind of friendship with me and as far as I'm concerned it is not exactly essential to have one either. So we are polite with each other, we say 'hi' and that's it. Whenever we have to spend time together, like for example at the races when they send us out together in a convertible to wave to the public, we try and exchange a few words so that the situation isn't too tense, but you can tell that neither of us completely opens up.

ER: And do you think that's a good thing?

JL: I'm not the kind of person that thinks that just because you're risking your life racing against another person on the track, just because your livelihood depends on it, you can't look each other in the eye. Personally I would like to get on well with all the riders but because of the time constraints and the reality of a Grand Prix weekend it is just not possible. But I'm not one of those who think that just because you are my rival, you can't be my friend.

ER: But you don't seem to look for that middle ground either. Do you think that any attempt to make friends is a sign of weakness?

JL: It shouldn't be that way but ... maybe if somebody has a lot of interest in getting on well with somebody, that person could possibly interpret it as a sign of submission. Of conceding ground. And Valentino, with good reason, will think that he is above his rivals. He is made to believe it by his fans and by the media and I'm sure he thinks that he is better than everybody else. The reality is that it's true, because right now he is the fastest rider and he won the World Championship.

Héctor Martín has also been a first-hand witness to this intriguing relationship, or lack of it, with Valentino and he sums it up really well: 'Neither of them wants anything from the other. I have been with the pair of them on the way to an autograph-signing session in Australia and they didn't say a word. They sat opposite each other in silence. It was lucky that on the way back Colin Edwards jumped in and he is so easy-going and such a good laugh that it broke the ice and the atmosphere was completely different. They even started talking! Valentino is really chatty but not with Jorge. And of course Jorge is his usual self – shy and very proud.'

The famous partition that separates Lorenzo and Rossi and their crews within the Yamaha garage provided plenty of column inches for newspapers and magazines in 2008. And even though they would both be using the same tyres in 2009, Valentino was quick to insist that the divider would remain. 'At Yamaha there are two top riders fighting for the championship,' reasoned Rossi. 'The wall improves harmony and if it worked so well this year, why change it? If Lorenzo wants to, he can pull his side of the wall down, but I'll be keeping mine.'

Jorge no longer cares about the wall, although he still can't quite understand why it is there. 'It was Valentino's decision, not mine,' the Spaniard explained to the Italian press. 'But now that we are both on the same tyres the wall is not necessary, we don't have anything to hide. We are a proper team now and I think the wall is a sign of weakness from Rossi. Even when you think about our achievements, he has eight world titles and six of them were in the premier class, whereas I don't have any [in MotoGP]. I don't understand it.'

Either way, according to those people closest to Lorenzo – new and old – far from being detrimental to Jorge, which is what Valentino might have hoped, it has actually been beneficial. 'The wall takes the pressure off a rider,' reckons Javi Ullate. 'Without the wall, the riders watch each other, keep an eye open. I think it has been a good thing and it would be a mistake to remove it now. This way, Jorge is more focused on himself and less concerned about what is going on "over there". Valentino is not stupid and he knew that Jorge was fast, that he'd be fast straight away. He thought that if he handed over information, as soon as things got difficult, there would have been problems. Rossi is strong both on and off the track and he wanted to mark his territory. Whether they had the same tyres or not there'd have been a wall there, but even though Rossi didn't realise it, Jorge has actually been much more relaxed with it there. If Valentino allows you to be his friend it is because you are not a threat to him. And since that isn't the case, the relationship is the minimum, nothing more.'

'The wall has been more of a good thing than bad, much more positive than everybody thought,' adds Juanito Llansá. As a long-term observer of the way Jorge thinks and feels, he has a different viewpoint. 'Jorge doesn't like to share a garage. He is a winner and he likes to work alone. We all remember what it was like when he shared with Héctor Barberá.' The final word goes to Marcos Hirsch: 'Our mental preparation includes the depersonalisation of rivals. We are not competing against Rossi or anybody else. Jorge is racing against unnamed obstacles. The Lorenzo I know is an impossible nut to crack. He couldn't give a toss about the wall! In fact, not only would I keep it, I'd make it out of stone. I'd go and find some nice rocks, make it look pretty and build it a metre and a half thick. If there has to be a wall there at least it ought to be a nice one, like an old Catalan country house, with a touch of rustic style. That way when Jorge wins nobody can claim he was given a hand.' On 30 October 2008 Jorge Lorenzo was quoted in the Spanish daily newspaper *AS* as saying: 'I get more excited by beating Rossi than Pedrosa.'

A RIVALRY THAT DIVIDED A NATION

I am playing for a better day

Red Hot Chili Peppers
From 'The Righteous and the Wicked', Blood Sugar Sex Magik, 1991

The 250cc Italian Grand Prix at Mugello, in 2007, saw Jorge fighting for the lead and then crashing after a collision with Álvaro Bautista. He got back to his pit garage and virtually threw his bike to the ground. He punched one of the wall panels and left. He would return later with tears in his eyes, apologising to everybody for his attitude. Juanito Llansá knows better than anybody that it is better to leave him for a while and let him calm down before trying to say anything. He also knew when 'the bull was under control', at which point he told him: 'Regardless of whether Bautista's move was right or not, I have told you before, Jorge, that you are going to come up against riders who are just like you were three years ago – riders who are hungry and don't have the equipment. When they're hungry, they bite!' Juanito had hit the nail on the head and Jorge knew it. How many times had he been told in the past that he was too aggressive and too reckless?

JL: I picked up my bad reputation in 2004. It was at Assen, in the Dutch TT, when I ran onto the grass and came back to go from fourth to first in half a lap. I made some pretty risky moves to get past Locatelli, Dovizioso and Stoner. But it was the Czech Republic Grand Prix at Brno when they really dismissed me as a good-for-nothing. I didn't have any pace at all in that race and Barberá was on it. The guy was in good shape back then! I had gone fourth fastest during practice but that was in the wet, I was much worse in the dry. As soon as the race started they got away from me. I was in a group fighting for eighth and ninth position, five seconds behind the lead group! Barberá was quicker than anybody in the race but not by enough to escape, so he started mucking around, letting people pass him, looking around, slowing the group down … I was getting faster and faster and I caught them with two laps to go. I got into the group and passed five or six riders in one lap. I was up to third! Then, in the first corner of the final lap, I moved up to second behind Barberá and on the next straight I passed him. I was leading! The pair of us were fighting for the win when we got to the slowest corner on the track, which you take in second gear. I was in front and Barberá passed me on the inside, but he was in too hot and he ran wide. I passed him back and we brushed together but I was back in front. Two or three corners later I closed the turn-off really tight, and I was braking so hard that he almost ran into the back of me. It was a bit risky. I made it look as though I was going to take the corner really slowly but then

I suddenly let off the brakes. It could have been dangerous for the guys behind me, yes. Braking like that, Barberá panicked and because of that he got passed by five or six riders. Dovizioso was then my main rival over the final few corners and he was right behind me on the drag up the hill. His Honda had better acceleration [than my Derbi] and when he got so close that I could hear the noise from his engine and see his shadow on the ground, I decided to close the corner off again and brake when I was already leaned over. If I'd have braked in a straight line he'd have been able to steal my line into the corner and there would have been nothing I could have done about it. So it was an unusual move on my part and that was when I started to get a reputation, not for being a dirty rider but for being risky, a bit crazy. After the race Dovizioso was saying: 'Hey! You shouldn't do that! You shouldn't do that!'

ER: But you really earned your reputation as a risky rider, a killer … call it what you will, in 2005 didn't you?

JL: 2005 … yeah. That time I was out of order!

It is an honest response, said with a smile. He looks at the ceiling and then moves quickly to explain.

JL: Well, maybe I wasn't out of order but I did have the wrong idea of what a good overtake was supposed to be. Since I'd got into a run of them all working out for me, I was trying anything, anyhow. I would see a gap and even if it wasn't the right corner I'd dive in there. Sometimes I didn't even think about it, it was like a passive decision. 'Should I go for it or not?' I occasionally wondered. It was in a couple of these races where I ended up touching wheels with my rivals and going 'arse over tit'.

He describes the action with vivid hand movements.

JL: At Montmeló, and in Germany … I wasn't decisive enough with my manoeuvres. I went in there too relaxed, thinking I was through and didn't have to push any harder. Big mistake!

ER: You mentioned Montmeló, where you ran into Alex de Angelis, and Germany – the famous collision with Dani Pedrosa. Is that when the rivalry first started? This animosity that looks set to divide the country's MotoGP fans?

JL: Germany was my fault, completely my fault, but what wasn't right about it was Dani's attitude afterwards – the indifference he showed towards me. That was where he first tried to show the public that he was ignoring me.

Jorge stops in his tracks. He knows this is an important subject, so he thinks his words through carefully before continuing.

JL: Pedrosa knew perfectly well that it was me who had knocked into him and that it was me that crashed, but after the race he said something like: 'Well I don't know what happened. I just heard a noise behind me, somebody hit me, my exhaust broke and I almost crashed.' It was a complete lack of respect and I didn't like it. That was the only thing I criticised him for! Fair enough, at the time I didn't acknowledge that I was to blame. I did that later, after I'd seen the video, but everybody is guilty of being proud, especially when you're young. I was 17 years old and the way Pedrosa treated me wasn't right – neither was the role of the victim that he played at the time.

ER: So the follow-up to that came two races later in Japan...

JL: Yeah! That's a long story, though.

I suppose he could tell by my face that I had time for a long story. I guess he knew when we agreed to put pen to paper and write his biography that the time would come when he had to discuss 'uncomfortable' issues, and his confrontations with Dani Pedrosa had filled thousands of column inches in Spanish newspapers and magazines in that summer of 2005. In fact, the constant comparisons with Pedrosa had occasionally got to him. 'Why does Dani Pedrosa, with his boy next door image, get such good press yet I don't?' he'd asked Miguel Ángel Violán. 'He used to hate that,' remembers Violán.

Juanito Llansá has his own views on the matter. 'Jorge and Dani Pedrosa are completely different. They are poles apart. Dani is cold, impassive, while Jorge is vivacious, sometimes too extroverted. The thing is that Pedrosa started winning before Jorge did and we [Spain] had been going through something of a drought in terms of titles, so people had started watching motorcycle racing again because of Pedrosa. Naturally, the fans had taken to Dani more. When Jorge emerged on the scene, and started winning too, people had got used to Dani's character and thought that Jorge was too cocky. But that's just the way he is! The fans already had their hero, but then somebody totally different came along. Now the fans had to be shared out between the two.'

ER: Come on, Jorge, talk to me about Japan.

He sighs and takes a mental run-up. Suddenly, his mind is back in Japan, in 2005.

JL: I qualified second fastest at Motegi and as usual at the start of the race I was struggling to get on the pace. Hiroshi Aoyama escaped and behind him a second group of two riders had formed – de Angelis and Pedrosa. In the third group there was Stoner, myself and … I think it was [Sebastián] Porto. I didn't get going until the halfway point and then I closed on the leaders. I even closed the gap to Pedrosa and de Angelis, which had been over four seconds. I kept making up more and more ground until two laps from the end I was within a second of them both. On the last lap, I was right with them. I remember trying to pass Pedrosa in a first-gear hairpin four corners from the end but I couldn't. On the exit from that corner I made a mistake, opened the gas too early and touched his rear wheel. I briefly lost control of the bike and as I fought to get it back they pulled a few metres out on me. In the next corner I was about twenty metres back. I don't know what was going through my head but I told myself I had to try it there.

His eyes are twinkling again with the intensity of the moment.

JL: It had to be there because next up was the long back straight at Motegi where we get up to sixth gear and my bike was slow. It would have been impossible on the straight. They looked miles away but I was so keyed up, so excited about what I thought was going to be remembered as a legendary ride, I just had to try it. I braked so hard … I don't think I've ever braked like that before! I had the front brakes on the limit, I gave the rear brake a little nudge too, and the bike just got totally out of shape, it crossed over and started fishtailing. Having said that, it was slowing down! In just a few metres I'd dropped my speed from 200km/h to 60. I went past Pedrosa like a streak of lightning and thought to myself: 'This could still work!' Then I saw de Angelis leaned over, virtually facing the opposite direction to me…

His hands are working overtime now, he can remember every detail.

JL: But I'm still thinking: 'This could still come off!' I was praying that we didn't crash, even though we were obviously going to collide. I wanted us both to come out of it. I managed to save the first impact but within a couple of tenths of a second I'd crashed … de Angelis too. I was exhausted – my heart rate at 190bpm and my tongue hanging out after working so hard to catch them. De Angelis got back up and rejoined the race but I was so tired that when I picked the bike up I couldn't hold it and it fell over the opposite way! I made a dismissive gesture with my hand and walked away.

ER: Which is when the real show started!

JL: Yeah, the real show started after the race. And what a show! I was just relaxing a couple of hours after the race, having something to eat in one of those cabins at Motegi and Dani [Amatriaín] came in.

'Jorge, we've got a meeting with Race Direction in an hour.'

'What about?'

'About the incident in the race.'

'But why, if it wasn't my fault? I haven't done anything!'

I got annoyed. I got really annoyed! All the journalists came, like a pack, asking me about it. They were all in my favour: 'They can't do this to you,' 'It's an injustice,' etc. That was before they'd even heard the result of the hearing! De Angelis and Pedrosa had both lodged complaints and all three of us were called in. I remember there were a few journalists waiting outside the door of the room because they weren't allowed in. I was inside, sitting down, and I could see Mela [Chercoles, MotoGP reporter for the Spanish daily *AS*] standing on something, taking photos through the little window above the door! In the meeting were Paul Butler, Claude Danis and Javier Alonso. Obviously Pedrosa was there with Alberto Puig, de Angelis was with the Sporting Director of Aprilia MS and Dani was with me. They took my statement first. I said fair enough, I'd gone in too deep but I was still on the right line because de Angelis had gone deep too and ran really wide. When he returned to the racing line he ran into my bike. Then de Angelis opened his mouth and it all came flooding out. He said it was incredible, that I was crazy and that he didn't know why I'd gone in like that, that he couldn't have done anything to avoid the crash. At that point we asked them to take a look at the video because de Angelis had got a bad start – he did a wheelie at the start of the race and blocked off another rider. We wanted them to see that there were other dangerous riders, not just me! There were other illegal things going on! Then it was Pedrosa's turn and he gave me a total slagging off. Instead of defending me, or not saying anything at all since it didn't actually have anything to do with him – the incident hadn't affected him and he'd actually finished second as a result – he said he'd seen me come flying past and smash into de Angelis from behind. It was two against one and they suspended me.

Jorge pauses before concluding his tale. He breathes calmly and you can tell that he is speaking honestly.

JL: The truth is that at that point they both went down in my estimation as sportsmen and as people. I wasn't too bothered by Alex de Angelis because he's Italian and the fans aren't so keen on him but I didn't expect it from Dani Pedrosa because he was a World Champion. Having gained everybody's respect, including mine, for him to operate in that way left me feeling cold and I thought it was mean. I still don't understand his actions that day in Race Direction. My understanding is that sportsmen should help each other and never try to do each other wrong. We compete on the track and settle our differences like gentlemen, face to face. In my situation, totally defenceless against Race Direction, I would have appreciated the gesture of defending me or at least trying to defuse the tension. If I were them I'd have been more conciliatory. At the most I would have condemned their actions and asked for it not to happen again. We have both read Lance Armstrong's autobiography, something we have both said in public, and one of the things you learn from it is the value of sportsmanship. Well, in this case he didn't learn from the story and he took the opportunity to hit me while I was down.

ER: So it's fair to say that while you weren't exactly the best of mates before that, the animosity between you and Pedrosa multiplied as a result…

JL: It goes way back, since forever … well, not forever.

Once again he takes a moment to think about what he's going to say, before saying exactly what he thinks.

JL: The bad relationship between our managers, Alberto Puig and Dani Amatriaín, has definitely influenced our own [relationship]. I don't think it should ever have been that way because at the end of the day we are the ones getting on the bikes to race and the only things we should be worried about are opening the throttle and giving the thousands of fans watching the race something to enjoy. The fact is that Pedrosa doesn't see it like I do and he has taken sides to the point that it has made any kind of relationship impossible.

ER: Are you saying that you have paid the price for the fight between Amatriaín and Puig?

JL: I don't think I should have to pay for anything. I think people should show themselves for who they really are and my virtues are that I am honest, I speak the truth, and I accept the consequences of my actions and words. That and the fact I'm not influenced every five minutes by what one person or another says to me. It's like Joan Olivé. Before he was with Puig we knew each other quite well and we used to chat. We're friends again now but when he was with Puig he didn't even look at me! Julito Simón's the same. We used to be friends at the track –

I followed his races and he followed mine, and I'd be happy for him when he did well. Since he signed with Alberto Puig he barely says 'Hi'. It's the same with his mechanics, they daren't even chat with other teams. That's the way it is! The same thing happens with Dani Pedrosa. The only time there's been any good feeling between us was at their happiest moment – when they won the 125cc title for the first time. Alberto Puig congratulated me for finishing third in Malaysia and asked how the race had been. They almost seemed like nice people! So in front of all the press I lifted Pedrosa's arm as the champion. It was the only time they have ever seemed prepared to open up to other people.

ER: And when did it go bad again?

JL: The next time we saw each other. In the next race!

Jorge Lorenzo is aware that everything he says about Dani Pedrosa is going to be put under the microscope, so he takes care to make sure there are no misunderstandings.

JL: Listen, I want to make it clear that I don't know Dani Pedrosa. I don't know if he's a good person, if he's a nice person … but as a professional he is a fine example.

It is an opinion commonly held in Spain that the ongoing rivalry between Jorge Lorenzo and Dani Pedrosa is likely to attract the millions of television viewers necessary to reinstate MotoGP as one of the top national sports. Even before Jorge Lorenzo's crash in China, the Spanish and Portuguese Grands Prix had been watched by more than four and a half million viewers, a 42 per cent market share. Motorcycle racing hadn't been so popular in Spain since Alex Crivillé won the 500cc World Championship in 1999. Pedrosa winning at Jerez and Jorge in Estoril – and with both of them having led the World Championship – had clearly aroused a lot of interest, but what seemed to capture the public's imagination most was the question of a simple handshake between the two rivals.

Shortly after the opening race of the season in Qatar, when Lorenzo claimed second place on his MotoGP debut, he was invited on to the set of the TVE programme 'MotoGP Club', which is shown throughout

Spain on the evening after each Grand Prix. I was presenting the show and I asked him:

ER: Jorge, you were on the podium with Dani Pedrosa. Did you say anything to each other? Did you shake hands?

JL: In Qatar everybody who saw me on the track – mechanics, riders and race officials – congratulated me on my performance. But Dani Pedrosa didn't. He didn't say a word to me, didn't look my way, didn't congratulate me. He didn't even wave or hold his hand out at the end of the race.

ER: And do you think he was supposed to be congratulating you and not the other way round?

JL: When somebody finishes their first MotoGP race on the podium, the least he can expect is a wave. I'm not talking about friendship, just a simple raised hand. It's a question of good manners. Everybody is responsible for what they say and do. If I was him I'd have been congratulating a rookie who finished second. Dani Pedrosa disappointed me.

Such an unexpected and honest response hit the headlines in Spain, even though a general election was going on at the same time. And at every public appearance Lorenzo made in the following weeks, he was asked about Pedrosa, his manager or the handshake.

ER: That was quite a palaver wasn't it? Looking back on it now, with hindsight, would you still say the same thing?

JL: Yeah I'd do it again because I believe that it gives off a bad image when two riders from the same country, representing millions of people, can't get on. Trying to shake hands with Pedrosa isn't a bad thing. It is a good thing, for the sport and for the country. At the time I thought it was pretty unpleasant that he didn't want to shake my hand but it's not the biggest worry in my life. I would like our relationship to be cordial because we're both putting our lives at risk on the track, we're battling fairing to fairing and yes, it is good that there's a rivalry on the track, but off it we should be presenting a picture of the good sportsmen that we are.

A mere handshake had become a matter of national debate. Everybody had an opinion on the subject – and since Lorenzo was the only one prepared to speak publicly about it, with Pedrosa opting to state his case silently, Jorge bore the brunt of the pressure. Even members of his own team were telling him to take the sting out of the situation as soon as possible. 'It always seemed that it had to be him who took the first step,' says Javi Ullate. 'I also made the mistake of thinking that it was down to him to sort it out. It was another unnecessary problem. It was a ridiculous situation, that wasn't getting anybody anywhere. I asked myself, if rivals can't greet each other, then how is it that Pedrosa can greet other riders? He is civil with Rossi and Stoner, but not with Lorenzo. What has been proved is that not talking to somebody doesn't make you any faster. Your rivalry is on the track, when the race starts, not walking through the paddock.'

ER: Then came Jerez. Something happened there that you haven't wanted to speak about. Do you want to break your silence now?

JL: Well at Jerez I set pole, again, and it was my turn to be interviewed on television. As soon as I'd finished it was Pedrosa's turn. So I was stepping off the platform and he was stepping up. I offered him my hand and he said he didn't want to accept it. 'I'm not shaking,' he said. So I just walked past him, but I waited until the end of his interview and said, 'Have you got a second for a chat?' We went into a corner and I told him that I didn't understand why he wouldn't shake hands. He said, 'I'm not shaking hands because of everything you have said about me in the past. Because of all the bullshit you've said about me, I'm not shaking hands.' I told him that I thought we should at least put a good face on it because it was good for the sport and for Spain. He repeated that he would not shake hands. I left and as I walked away from him he shouted after me: 'No, because in the end I'll come out as the bad guy.' I looked at [Colin] Edwards and he asked: 'What's up with him?'

ER: And then of course the next day was the race – 130,000 people packed in for the Grand Prix of Spain…

JL: I was quickest in almost every session at Jerez and I think even my race pace was better than Qatar, but for some reason Sunday was different. I don't know if it was warmer, or windier, but the track was different and I couldn't go at the same pace I had in practice. I was more uptight and riding slower. At the same time Dani went completely the other way. He got a really good start and went much faster than he had in practice. He escaped at the front and then Valentino passed me. I tried to chase him and even though he made a mistake at the end of the penultimate lap, thinking the race was over, he was too far ahead of me. I finished third and I was even more disappointed than in Qatar. I got stressed out because of my lack of experience in MotoGP and I was also struggling a lot with my forearms.

ER: So then you got back to parc fermé, with everybody watching. Do you know that there were 4.2 million television viewers waiting to see if you shook hands? It looked as if you were waiting for an opportunity. Were you thinking about offering him your hand at that point?

JL: No. I waited out of courtesy because I felt that the riders who had finished in front of me should go up the stairs to the podium first. Plus, I'd already offered him my hand on Saturday and he'd rejected it, so there was no point trying again. In fact, I've heard a story from that day – and I don't know if this is true – but some people who were in parc fermé overheard Alberto Puig, when he was hugging Dani and congratulating him, saying: 'Don't shake hands, don't shake hands.'

ER: And to top it all you did shake in the end because HRH King Juan Carlos forced your hands together!

JL: The King came to the race and whether through his own initiative or because he'd been told about the situation by his advisers, he pulled us together and said: 'You must get on with each other. From now on you have to get on.' He took our hands and clasped them together. Dani tried to come over as cordially as possible because the cameras were on him but I'm sure he didn't find it very amusing. I'm sure that if instead of trying to talk privately with him on the Saturday I'd have held out my hand to him in public it would have come across terribly if he rejected it. But it wasn't my intention to turn him into the bad guy because there are no good or bad guys around here. There are simply things that are done right and things that aren't and in my opinion Dani was not behaving in the correct manner. But I've behaved badly on plenty of occasions during my life and I'm sure I'll do so again. I just think that the right thing to do at that time was to shake hands and at least look like sportsmen, like gentlemen. It was a question of manners, of principles...

'I told Jorge that the next time they were together on the podium he should offer to shake hands – especially if Dani finished ahead of him,' said Héctor Martín. 'I told him he'd look like a real gentleman! But unfortunately there wasn't another opportunity.' When Lorenzo won at Estoril, two weeks later, Pedrosa wasn't on the podium. Likewise at Misano and Indianapolis. The next time they came face to face was for another rumble in Japan although this time, unlike 2005, it took place on the track instead of in Race Direction.

ER: In Japan you almost took the pair of you out on the last lap. Was there something personal in the attempt to try and overtake him at that point on the track? Because we all thought you could have passed him on the back straight.

JL: As if! I'd set pole again in Japan and I had a good pace on race tyres but I got a bad start, again. The three of them passed me – Stoner and Valentino escaped but Pedrosa was still in range. Over the last few laps I could see him but I couldn't catch him. Why? Because even though he has never been good on the brakes he could brake much later than usual with the Bridgestones, about the same as I could with the Michelins. We Michelin riders were handicapped all season against the Bridgestone guys on the brakes, it was tricky. He could brake late, stop the bike and then use the Honda's acceleration and the good grip from his tyres to get away from me. The only way for me to make up ground was by taking the corners faster or by taking more risks under braking. I was right behind him, following him, but I couldn't make a pass anywhere so on the last lap I thought, 'I'm going to have to risk it.' I got closer than I had been over the previous laps, there was about a metre between us. I had no choice but to try it there because he'd have pulled away from me on the long back straight – he was accelerating away from me there and I'd be 50 metres behind him by the time we hit the brakes. With the tyres I had there was no way for me to make that up so when I saw him go slightly wide I tried to go up the inside in the middle of the corner, unexpectedly.

It annoys the hell out of you when you've spent ten laps playing cat and mouse in the knowledge that it's impossible to pass. So you try it. You see a little gap and you go for it, knowing that it is risky because you don't want to crash and you don't want to knock the other guy off either. But there is a big difference between fourth place and third…

He stops talking and takes a few moments to think. He knows that my real question is whether or not he is aware of what would have happened if he'd knocked Pedrosa off. But he is still visualising the race.

JL: It just winds me up! Dammit! [He's virtually shouting now.] It winds me up that I have to compete at a disadvantage for the whole race and I can't get past. So as soon as the other guy makes the tiniest mistake, I'm going to go for it.

ER: But if you'd have crashed, you'd have been to blame. There was no doubt about that.

JL: But, man … I was at a disadvantage. Big time! The next Michelin rider was 25 seconds behind. I was well over the limit and when you can see that a rival is one or two seconds clear there's nothing you can do, but whenever you get even a small opportunity you have to try and take it. Maybe if you're third and it's for second you might think twice about it but from fourth to third it's another story – it's the difference between standing on the podium or not. Some people might say it's not very ethical because there is the risk that the other rider might end up on the floor too, but…

MAKING UP FOR LOST TIME

Sometimes I feel like I don't have a partner
Sometimes I feel like my only friend

Red Hot Chili Peppers
'Under the Bridge', Blood Sugar Sex Magik, 1991
Jorge is an independent, intelligent and observant person … when he is interested in something. He knows how to be with people and

at the same time enjoy those moments of solitude he saves for himself. And even though it may seem strange, he doesn't like to talk about racing when he's not at the track. Travelling around the world is the part of the job he struggles with most. 'Right now I am very happy. A man can get used to the good things in life very quickly, which is why it is important to reflect every day on how lucky you are and on the good things that life is offering you. Sometimes I stop and ask myself: what would I have given five years ago to be a World Champion?'

'Jorge is person who wants to improve – he's never satisfied because he knows he could have done something better,' says Jordi Perez. 'Jorge Lorenzo needs support in certain personal aspects because he is a World Champion and he knows how to ride a bike but in life he sometimes needs a little guidance. He's not a diva, he is very normal. As long as he has a bed to sleep in, he's happy!'

'Even without a bed, he sleeps well,' adds his mother. 'He can sleep anywhere!'

I have every reason to believe María, having seen the evidence with my own eyes. When I went to interview Jorge in London he slept at the airport while we were waiting for our luggage and then again in the taxi on the way into town. However, the day he really surprised me was at Laguna Seca, during the 2007 USGP, when he was working with us as a guest commentator. We were preparing to do a live link from pit lane and with moments to go before the director cued us in, I turned to Alex Crivillé. 'Crivi. Where's Jorge?'

'Look at him, he's over there!' And sure enough, seconds before we went live, and amid all the tension that goes with it, there he was on the pit wall, fast asleep, having stretched out to catch some sunshine. The most amazing thing about it is when he wakes up, because it's like he just switches himself back on.

His mother always tells him it's bad manners to sleep in public but Jorge is unconvinced: 'Personally I gain more from sleeping than the bad effect it could have.'

'Chicho, his father, was like that too,' concludes María with resignation.

'When I was little,' adds Jorge, 'I used to ride on my father's motorcycle with him and on the journey between work and home I'd fall asleep in his arms. It was only 15 kilometres but I'd be flat out.' It is an unusually nostalgic anecdote from Jorge, who embarked on his professional life before his personal life took shape. He has had an intense and complicated upbringing and it has led to certain shortfalls in his character that he has now begun to address and improve. He was a difficult teenager, but nobody can deny that he is finding his path in life and it is a path he's happy with. It's also a path many young people never end up finding.

ER: Everybody says that you didn't used to recognise other people's hard work. You weren't grateful and you didn't even address them properly, but you don't come across as bad mannered to me. Was it just a case of nobody telling you how important it was?

JL: I was like that mainly because I had a father who was like that too. Let me explain. He was a shy person, distant, like me. He liked people to think he was full of confidence, the hard man ... he tried to give the impression that he was like Clint Eastwood. He was a fantastic trainer, so creative, with so many ideas, but from a social perspective he wasn't. In my opinion he didn't have a personality that was well suited to being sociable, because he hadn't worked on it, he didn't realise it was important or maybe he just liked being the way he was. That's my dad! Surly, affectionate on occasion, but he found it tough to let it show. When you're little you tend to lean more towards either your father or your mother. I'm sure there could be cases where it's an equal split, but not many. More often than not kids lean towards one or the other – especially if they split up and you go to live with one of them. Living with my father, I picked up his good points and his bad ones. One of the bad ones was being distant with people.

ER: Did you tend to hide yourself away in your own little world?

JL: Yes. In a way it was a good thing because it allowed me to concentrate on races, on practice sessions, and not be distracted. But at the same time I lost something very important in life – friendships. Did I have friends? Yes, but I didn't treat them like friends. I didn't know how to treat them! I had no idea how to get along with others. That side of me had been neglected, I hadn't been brought up well in that way.

ER: So you never had a 'social education'.

JL: Exactly. I'd spent most of my life on a motorcycle, trying to go faster, only listening to my father because he was very demanding and we used to train a lot. It was all very methodical, my father with the stopwatch in his hand. My social life was on standby and there came a point when I realised that had to change.

ER: When was it exactly that you realised the importance of others? When did you decide personal relationships were so crucial?

JL: Definitely when I went to live on my own. I was very untrusting of people and I didn't even realise what I was missing out on until I started to enjoy being with people. I must admit I'm still a long way off where I want to be and there are still a few creases I'm trying to iron out but people say I have improved. If I compare myself, say, with Ricky Cardús, I'm still a long way off the kind of class he has around people. But he grew up in a family where that was instilled from an early age. On the other hand, he hasn't quite made it as a motorcycle racer … and I think that's probably why. But he is one of the nicest people I know and an example to follow in that sense. I'm delighted to be able to call him a friend and I feel lucky that he calls me his.

ER: Are you saying that if you're too well-mannered you can't make it as a racer? You can't win?

JL: Dani [Amatriaín] used to say you could. He used to say that you could be like that and still become a good rider. I wasn't sure but now I think he's right because I have won. I've already uncovered the secret, if you like, and now I can concentrate on being a better person. Now I think you can get on well with people and still be fast but if you're as well mannered as Ricky, if you have so much respect for your family and you are so grateful to them for the help they've given you, then you can put yourself under too much pressure.

While the family is always a crucial aspect of preparing a child for life, school is undoubtedly another major factor. Jorge wasn't really there long enough to find out.

ER: When you were at the Monlau school you were able to

combine work and study, but there came a point where the studies got left behind. How did you take that decision?

JL: I remember being at Dani Amatriaín's house in Alella. The three of us sat down – Dani, my dad and myself – to discuss it. My father was insisting that I left school because I wasn't enjoying it! He said I used to come back upset because I had to do my homework and I was neither happy nor focused as a result. Dani said I should continue for a year and finish my ESO, because there was only a year left and I should do it. Me? Well I'd never enjoyed studying and when you're a kid, if you get the chance to quit school then you take it! All I cared about was racing.

ER: Do you regret leaving school now? Now that you're so keen to learn and improve yourself?

JL: I don't regret it because it turned out well. If it hadn't, I'm sure I'd be regretting it. Now I make sure I learn things, keep up to date on what's going on in the world. Now when I like something I try to learn about it. I'm not the kind of person who's obsessed by knowledge but I'm learning. Whether it's through intuition, watching others or a lesson. It was also difficult travelling back from a race in Australia and having a maths exam as soon as I stepped off the plane on the Tuesday. At the end of the day it worked out. We took the decision and the following season, in 2003, I did really well in my racing and I was focused on it. If you have a set target like that then school can be a distraction. I wasn't happy because going to school was an inconvenience. Also, when you miss half of the classes through absence you end up behind with your schoolwork and behind with your racing. If you're going to do an exam you have to study for it and I had enough on my plate with racing. It was my first season, my bike wasn't working properly and I was worrying about school … so I think from that point of view it wouldn't be right to say my dad did the correct thing but it didn't turn out badly either. Nobody knows what might have happened if I'd continued. Maybe if I'd stayed in school things would have turned out the same, but in leaving they definitely turned out well.

THE GLOBAL ART OF SEDUCTION

I'm part of you and you're part of me
Why did you go away
Too late to tell you how I feel

Red Hot Chili Peppers
'Knock Me Down', Mother's Milk, 1989

After spending so much time talking to Jorge's family, friends and colleagues, I was left in no doubt that the thing he likes most after motorcycles (or as much as, depending on the time of year) is girls. In that respect he is typical of a kid his age and his eyes twinkle with a mixture of angel and devil when I bring the topic up.

ER: Jorge, let's talk girls. What you know about them, how you win them over...

JL: Until I was 15 I wasn't interested in girls at all. I had my first girlfriend in Santo Domingo [Dominican Republic] – she was born on exactly the same day as me. She was gorgeous and we spent a week together. Later I met another girl in Mallorca but it didn't go any further than a bit of kissing in the cinema. Then there was Eva. I was with her for almost two years and she's still the only girl I've been in love with. The problem is that we started to fight. Also, I used to look into the future and I saw myself aged 25, still with the same woman, without having had the chance to experiment. That wasn't what I wanted! I honestly thought that we'd split up and I'd find someone else that I'd like just as much. Or a few! I've met plenty but so far none of them have been like her. I don't know if it's because I compare them all with Eva or if there really hasn't been anyone the same. I'll find her one day. I'm not in a rush but it is definitely something I want, because it brings me stability. In the meantime I'll just enjoy experimenting! I can see myself getting married in the future but before that I need to make some mistakes, find out what I like about girls and what I don't by meeting a lot of them! Why? Because when I finally make a decision I don't want to get it wrong.

Being in love is the best feeling you can have. But if you can enjoy yourself beforehand, even better! [Laughs]

ER: You mentioned Eva. Was breaking up with her so you could focus on racing during that rough period in 2006 one of the biggest sacrifices you've made?

JL: Definitely. I had to make a choice and Eva, as well as my father, lost out. At the end of the season I saw her again but it wasn't to be. In fact, it was me that lost out with Eva. I thought I was the 'king of the jungle' and I wanted to experiment before settling down. I thought, in fact I still think, that I'm too young to have a serious relationship. Since then I've realised that it's not easy to find a woman you're comfortable with, who you can laugh with, who understands you, who loves you … I don't regret anything because we were going through a rough patch but I'm convinced it wasn't serious enough for us to end it altogether.

We have spoken a few times about his interest in self-help books and when he reads one, Jorge has it very clear in his mind that he is doing so in order to learn some direct lessons. To help him in the art of seduction, he went for *The Game* by Neil Strauss. His objective wasn't to become the world's 'Number One Pickup Artist', as Strauss would put it, just to 'pick up' a few tips. As macho as the Lorenzo we've come to know in the paddock seems, he turns shy when it comes to talking about women and the lessons he learnt from this hugely popular book.

ER: You seem to be a little reluctant to talk about what you learnt. But if you're happy to talk about what you've learnt in other subjects, what's wrong with talking about women?

JL: Telling you would be like a magician giving away his tricks! Honestly, I'm interested in how seduction works – what it is that attracts people to each other, why it is that sometimes you can have a really good run of form with women but other times, even though you are exactly the same person, you go hungry. It's something that interests me and I'm trying to find the answers. I'm going to stop there because I'm already giving too much away! Ha, ha!

ER: Fair enough, I don't want to scupper any future conquests. But what do you look for in a girl?

JL: Intelligence is very important to me – probably more so than other guys my age. I've been with some really good-looking girls who just didn't excite me as people. I didn't even last a week with them. I couldn't connect with them, they didn't fulfil me. I like girls who are smart and have character, a strong personality. I like them to be mature and to know how to act. And, of course, I have to be physically attracted to them.

Palau once said: 'Jorge is strange. He is very honest but at the same time introverted. He is in his own world – he's not very communicative. I'd say something like, "Shall we go to the cinema?" and he'd be like, "No, I'm going to Italy for a presentation, didn't I tell you?" "No, you didn't tell me!" But when it comes to talking about women, he doesn't shut up!'

ER: Does it help being Jorge Lorenzo, World Champion?

JL: There are phases. At the end of 2007, the high point of my career so far, I went through a dry spell with women, totally different to the summers of 2006 and 2007, which were better. Maybe I got too demanding, too selective, and I was turning too many of them down. Maybe I was also enjoying spending time with my friends so much that I took that over being with girls. On the other hand, a few months earlier I'd been hooking up with one a day, or four a week anyway! To be successful you have to have self-confidence, a strong and solid personality. More than being good-looking, you need to believe that you are. Believe in yourself, make sure your self-esteem is high. You also have to be polite but a bit cheeky too – make them laugh, communicate with them.

'He wanted to get on well with girls,' recalls Miguel Ángel Violán. 'He wanted to know how he could be better at talking to them. It all comes down to a matter of communication.' If even his teacher knew of his love for the subject, it was pretty obvious that anybody else who knew Jorge did too.

ER: What about at the track? Is it easy to pull women?

JL: Yes, but I haven't because I am too focused on racing. Although now that I've got the new motorhome … No, I'm only kidding. You go to the circuit to work. A race weekend is no time to be pulling women. That is for outside, when you have to be a bit of a rascal, without getting carried away. If you're too nice there's no attraction. If they come on to me too strongly I don't trust them. I don't like brazen women.

ER: Have you ever had any complaints?

JL: None so far!

He laughs wickedly. Despite the time we've spent together, in London and at the races, the age gap between us makes it difficult for me to witness that Lorenzo style in action. It's not like we can really go on a night out together, although I almost managed it in Monterey, California, back in 2007. TVE had invited Jorge as a guest commentator for the MotoGP, as there were no 250cc or 125cc events at Laguna Seca. After dinner he fancied going out, but the production team were exhausted. 'Go on then, I'll go with you,' I said. But the party lasted just five minutes – the exact time it took us to get to the door of the first bar.

> *'How old are you, kid?' the doorman asked Jorge.*
> *'I'm 20.'*
> *'I'm sorry. You can't come in.'*

They wouldn't let Jorge into the bar. He'd only just turned 20 and it doesn't matter how many world titles you have to your name, in America the law is the law. You have to be 21 even to go inside an establishment that serves alcohol, even though Jorge doesn't drink. The experiment was over before it had begun and we went back to the hotel.

In July 2008 Jorge crashed out of a wet race at the Sachsenring, but there was an even bigger shock waiting for him when he returned to Spain. A girl he had been on a couple of dates with was making television appearances claiming to be Jorge Lorenzo's 'special friend'.

But what really annoyed him was that she appeared topless on the front cover of a magazine while claiming to be his girlfriend!

ER: Have you noticed a change in 2008 in the way you get treated by women?

JL: Not just women. In general I've realised this year more than ever how some people try to get close to famous people for their own interests. Some people, not everybody luckily. This year I've had experiences of that kind.

ER: You're referring to your 'girlfriend', who appeared naked in a magazine.

JL: Yes, the girl who appeared on the front cover of *Interviú* claiming to be my girlfriend. I didn't see that one coming! I'd never thought that could happen to me. It's like a slap around the face that suddenly makes you see things as they really are – that there really are people with bad intentions out there. People with their interests but no scruples! There was no way she was my girlfriend. We'd been out together a couple of times but that was it. I couldn't believe it.

ER: Has it made you approach relationships differently? More cautiously?

JL: No, even though I know it could happen again. Although now I have had that experience and I suppose I am more cautious. You have to watch people closely.

COMPETITIVE MODESTY

Calling calling for something in the air
Calling calling I know you must be there

Red Hot Chili Peppers
'Easily', Californication, 1999

Jorge Lorenzo likes a challenge. He is motivated by the challenge of bettering himself, of raising the bar, every day. His life is as fast paced off the track as it is on it and it's perhaps because of this that he's not had a chance to really enjoy his achievements or assess his failures. For every mountain he has climbed, he has then found himself at the foot of another. 'You always want what you can't have, and when you have something – even if it is what you have always dreamed of and even though you have spent your whole life working for it, when you get it, you put it on one side and start looking for the next thing. I find it difficult to truly appreciate the good times, but at the same time it is important for everybody to have objectives in their life.'

Jorge knows he's a lucky man. He knows that his is a privileged existence, but he also knows that the world of a popular, rich, good-looking 21-year-old racer is not real. It has a best-before date and after that it'll all be over. After he won his second title I was curious to know how it had affected him, so I talked to two of the people who were spending most time with him at that point. I asked the men who had been witness to both the highs and the lows what they would be like if they were Jorge Lorenzo:

If I was 20 years old, like him, and I had the things he has, would I behave like an idiot? Maybe. Jorge is a much better person than a lot of the circumstances around him allow him to appear. (Jordi Pérez)

If any of us were 20 years old and a double World Champion, maybe we'd lose our heads a bit. But I've never seen a situation where Jorge has shown signs of losing his. (Cheni Martínez)

Jorge is certainly independent in his opinions and in his way of thinking. He relishes being different but, at the same time, he wants everybody to like him and, when he opens his heart, to love him. It sounds like a contradiction in terms, but it isn't. The thing is that for him, as for everybody, the first step to opening your heart is to open your mouth. In other words, the message is the key. In September 2006 Jorge found this out with the help of his 'communication guru', Miguel Ángel Violán.

'When I was speaking to him, I could read the responses on his face,' remembers Miguel Ángel. 'It was like a computer – I could hear his brain going bip, bip, bip! Jorge is a very intelligent guy and he has an intelligent gaze. He is extremely talented and he has a huge capacity for analysis, observation; a cool head when making decisions. I'm sure it is a by-product of his job because, as a rider, he has to be very calculating on the track. Now it is a case of applying that to other areas of his life. He will achieve whatever goals he sets of himself.' It was also very important to instil in him that success could not be allowed to go to his head. Miguel Ángel Violán was qualified to answer any question on the matter but even he wasn't prepared for Jorge, who caught him out in his trademark unpredictable, impulsive style:

If I am humble, can I continue being just as competitive?

Violán was stuck for words. 'I told him I'd answer that in the next session and asked a friend for help. That's quite funny isn't it? A "coach" asking another "coach" for help.' The friend in question was Alex Rovira, a best-selling author and professor.

' "If I am humble, can I continue being just as competitive?" Who asked you that? Jorge Lorenzo? Goodness! Hmm... I'll answer it with an article.' This is a story that has been untold up to now. In response to Jorge's concerns, Alex Rovira published an article written specifically for him in the weekly magazine edition of Spain's biggest daily newspaper, *El País*. There was no need to tell Jorge it was for him, because he would realise that straight away. He read it, he was moved and he took note.

Article written by Alex Rovira Celma, *El País*
PROSPEROUS HUMILITY

Humility, when genuine and sincere, moves people through its modesty. Its very etymology refers us to the essential, to the earth. The word humility comes from the Latin humilis, which in turn comes from humus: that which nature discards and is then enriched by, fertilising the soil and creating growth.

Humility tells us to eliminate the excess so that we can focus on the essential. It also invites us to learn about the limitations that make us human and allow us to become aware of what remains for us to work on and how we can grow. For this reason, a sincere expression of humility is not a sign of naivety or weakness. On the contrary, it is a sign of clarity and inner strength.

Far from fragility, humility shows us the greatness of the person who demonstrates it, precisely because it is born of a feeling of self-insufficiency: there is always something to learn or somebody to learn from; it is always possible to do things better. A person can always question the worth and sense of what they are doing in their personal or professional life and from there find new challenges, develop new skills, learn new lessons or build new bridges. That is why humility goes hand in hand with consciousness and has such huge power for change because from it the perspectives of thought and actions are infinite, since they are born from common sense, reasonable doubt and the frankness that recognises there is still a lot of work to do before the embodiment of quality in every aspect: in oneself, in relation to others, in our actions or creations, in life.

Fortunately, the richness generated by humility is not fuelled by the drug of success, a drug that creates a bottomless pit of addiction, or the carrot hanging in front of the donkey's nose until it collapses through the exhaustion created by its own wishful thinking. Maybe for this reason humility has much more to do with accomplishment than success; with fulfilling an agreement or promise; with doing a job well; with completing what needs to be completed. That way the humble person does not cover himself in glory or become distracted by his or her success but continues to work and take enjoyment from the task, as they should, in the knowledge that success is not the end product but a sign that cannot be afforded too much attention because not only does it distract, it also misleads and can even generate the severe and acute levels of stupidity and self-importance that emerge as a consequence of collective adulation.

Neither should humility be confused with false modesty, which is still an extremely hypocritical form of vanity. Indeed, humility is precisely the opposite of vanity and while the latter makes us blind, distances us from reality and separates us from others, humility reveals and brings us into contact with what is real, with the essential, with the truth that we find around us and within us.

It manifests itself in the small things, in the details, in codes of communication that are anything but flamboyant. They are simple, basic, but of huge value to the recipient. In this way, the humble details become the kind of gifts to which we perhaps attribute the most worth, because they are genuine. These are the gifts we remember with the perspective life gives us over time and we know that it is these gifts, and only these, that last because we hold them in our memory, more than material possessions, and nothing and nobody can take them away.

Nowadays, when almost anything is within our reach – whether we pay in cash or in easy-to-manage instalments – we forget the value of the essential things in life, the things that cannot be paid for with money and that are humble in their essence but that have unquantifiable, sometimes even infinite, value. There are several examples:

•Knowing how to listen, affording somebody our silent attention, resisting our own need to speak and opening ourselves to the necessity of the other person to feel attention, company and respect, is without doubt a gesture of humility that nourishes a relationship and enriches the values of friendship.

•A simple, genuine smile can bring us together, improve initial acquaintance and even change the course of a bitter conversation or relationship.

•Gratitude is also a wonderful gift that is born through humility and recognition for another person. Through it, the two sides of a friendship become stronger. How little it takes to be grateful and how gratifying it is to be appreciated.

•And what can we say about the tenderness of touch? Humility in its very essence, born as it is through the unity of skin, of nudity, of bringing us back to the pure essentials. Through touch, we can express feelings that words cannot.

•Knowing when to be quiet, when not to bother or disturb, is a valuable gesture of humility. To leave somebody alone when that is what

they want. To shield them from advice they don't want to hear, help they haven't asked for or the company that only serves to disturb them – that lack of company that we sometimes find hard to understand because it requires us to swallow the same pill and deal with the silence or solitude that we so fear ourselves. To respect another person's need for solitude can represent a huge gesture of humility at a time when silence and tranquillity are such precious commodities.

The list of 'humble gifts' is in itself infinite. They are all around us, they are cheap and they nourish the roots of any relationship. In other words, they prosper because they are self-sufficient. They are gifts that can be given and at the same time received. No material items need to change hands, they rely merely on our disposition towards another person, even to ourselves. This is why it is worth putting them into practice, because they create healthy growth: they stimulate imagination, confidence, respect, commitment and joy, among a whole host of other intangible assets. It is maybe here that quality of life and relationships, in the main part, resides.

This was truly a 'gift' for Jorge. According to Violán, 'It was one of the best self-help articles that I have ever read. Basically, he is saying that if you are humble you will never let your guard drop. You will value the strengths of your rivals instead of underestimating them, so you will never relax, you will always be at 100 per cent. If they beat you on a motorcycle you will be forced to take your hat off to them because you will appreciate their effort. But if you refuse to let them beat you then you will be more competitive. So not only does being humble not reduce your competitiveness, it can increase it!' The processes of cause and effect are never definitive, but the motorcycling world certainly saw a much more competitive Jorge Lorenzo in 2007, and a much humbler one too.

For Jorge being humble is also a matter of knowing how to enjoy what he has, including all the money he earns, which is plenty. Jorge is thrifty, 'pretty tight-fisted, actually' he admits, and while most of his character traits are typical of his Galician ancestry, his approach to money has much more in common with his native roots in Mallorca. 'He has a shrewd, almost simplistic view of life,' says Violán. 'Money merely serves its purpose.'

ER: How important is money to you? Do you know how much you earn?

JL: Anybody who says it's not important is lying. Nowadays I have an idea of how much I earn but I don't get a definite figure until the end of the year. For me there are things that are more important than money. Money is good if you know how to appreciate it. People who are born into it and are used to having it can get bored with it. Because I've never had it from the start, I appreciate it more. But I have to keep looking at it from the same viewpoint, because if I keep earning money I could end up getting used to it. Then you're back to square one. I've always been quite thrifty, I've never thrown it away. I've got friends who'd spend 500 euros on a mobile phone. I'd never do that – I don't understand it.

ER: Do you think some people try to get close to you because of 'who you are'? Because you're Jorge Lorenzo, a World Champion?

JL: At the end of the day we're all with people because we have certain 'interests' at heart. There's always a reason why you're with somebody, even if those reasons might not be honourable. But since I have never had an interest in a person for economic or social reasons, I don't suspect others of being with me for those reasons either. I think if it does happen you have to be blind not to see it, to not see that somebody wants to be your friend for a particular reason. I don't have any enemies … at least I don't think I have. At least that is what I try to believe. Although I'm sure I'd be a bastard of an enemy to have!

ER: What do you say to people who say you're arrogant, that sometimes you're a little full of yourself. How would you sell yourself to them?

JL: I can't sell them anything. They've made a decision about what they like, I'm not it, and that's that! It's like if you don't fancy a girl. As much as she tells you she's going to love you or she's going to take care of you, if you don't fancy her you'll move on. Everybody likes to be liked but I can't convince people with anything I say – only by the things I do. I also have to say that I've always enjoyed having an enemy to motivate me. It sounds absurd, I know! Sometimes I like to get angry with a friend and wind him up. Sometimes I just feel like it! It's a mixture of pleasure and discontentment because I've upset a friend, but I like doing it.

Jorge Lorenzo settles into his chair. He looks at me and bursts out laughing. He realises that he's opening up and vocalising feelings he's not used to sharing, so he decides to shatter this momentary intimacy and go back to a language in which he is much more fluent.

JL: It pisses me off that people criticise me, but I also like it because I wouldn't be happy if everybody liked me, I'd lose a lot of spark. Also, if I was more normal, I don't think my fans would be as passionate. I wouldn't be as popular with them. My fans might feel betrayed if I were to change so that everybody liked me. At the same time, I can assure you that all those people that don't like me, if they were to spend a day with me they'd change their mind. But since that is impossible I have to try and win them over during the few minutes they see me on the television. To make it real I have to change my whole life, so that those ten minutes are a reflection of the truth, because otherwise it doesn't wash. But like I said before, if I could take those fans out for lunch or dinner, they'd change their opinion. Most of them anyway!

ER: What would you say to them?

JL: That the Lorenzo they see on the television is different – different from the Lorenzo among friends. It is a role I have played since I was little and I can't change it. It is really difficult for me. I have a role to play with all the different people I know – I behave around them in the same way I always have. With my mother, my father, everybody ... I have a different personality with all of them. The personality I have with the general public is one I have to work on – for my own good and for my own needs, especially so that the public Lorenzo is closer to the real Lorenzo. Right now they are light years away from each other.

The real Jorge Lorenzo is easy to like. He knows that the key is to get the friendly, sensitive and even vulnerable Jorge closer to the 'wild child' you see jumping around on the podium. He feels proud of the way he has changed in recent years and feels sure that he has found his true self. While he is still only at the beginning of his journey, the path has been marked out. It will be many years yet before 'Jorge' and 'Lorenzo' meet in the middle, with the medium of motorcycle racing there for him to express himself, convince himself and, above all, convince others.

ER: Jorge, have you thought about how long you want to race for?

It is a purposely loaded question, because I'd heard that Jorge had recently been toying with the idea of keeping his career quite short.

JL: I can't see myself racing at the age of 30. I'm saying that now, although next year I might think differently. Maybe I'll retire, get hungry for racing again and come back. What I don't want is to end my racing through injury. The longer you race, the bigger the risk of that happening, and I don't even crash that much!

He would crash eight times in his debut MotoGP season, the most recent low points of a rollercoaster life. Two intense decades of hard work and huge achievement have left him precious little time to reflect on his past or plan his future – and he is still at an age where most people's lives have hardly begun.

2

X-FUERA: AROUND THE OUTSIDE

The family, plus one

Text written by Jorge Lorenzo entitled:
'THE KID WITH THE STARS'

A Juan Bautista Borja replica helmet hovered inches above the ground. Inside it a head – completely shaved other than for a Mohican down the middle and stars either side – belonging to a 10-year-old child called Jorge. That was me. Actually, at that time most people called me 'Giorgio' – George in English. Those who couldn't remember my Italian nickname just called me 'the kid with the stars'.

I've always liked to be different, that much is obvious. It's fair to say I've always been drawn to bizarre, out of the ordinary things. Since I was small, really small, I have tried to go against the grain. While my classmates supported Barça or Madrid, I was a fan of Ajax Amsterdam ... well, I was young. I grew up at a go-kart track. It was a small tarmac circuit next to a waterpark, where German tourists would come to have fun between swimming sessions. Every moment, however small, that the track was free I'd take the opportunity to practise riding on an XR70 four-stroke.

I was the main attraction, the focus of attention, the king of the jungle! And I loved it. Everybody needs to have their ego massaged, not just kids. The people who went by there and heard the noise of my bike would be curious to see what was happening so they'd come and look. They'd stop in their tracks when they saw some little pipsqueak going sideways into every corner – each one looking as though it would be his last ... but no, everything was under control. After thousands of hours of practice I'd mastered a level of control that defied the laws of physics. I hardly ever crashed.

But, my friends, roll up because the show is not over! When my father forced me to come back in because there were some go-karts waiting to go out, the moment arrived when I'd remove my helmet. To the delight and surprise of the 'audience' the aforementioned pipsqueak would reveal his freaky hairdo! It was great fun at the time, but you'd have to pay me a lot of money to cut it like that again!

As time goes on, as people we change the way we think, act and dress. I remember shaving my head to a grade two the following year. To be honest I didn't care what kind of image I gave off to people. I just wanted to be comfortable and ride my bike. Obviously a few years later you start to get interested in girls and things change. You start to care more about your image and you change your haircut, your wardrobe, the vanity kicks in…

One thing I can say about life, which is so full of surprises, is that whatever your thoughts are today, they may not necessarily be the same tomorrow. But that's not a bad thing – it just shows that day by day, year by year, we improve. Enjoy the journey. Be yourself.

There have been many twists and turns in the short life of Jorge Lorenzo, the kid who started out with stars in his hair and ended up with the world at his fingertips.

FROM NAPPIES TO KNEESLIDERS

In the world of motorcycle racing family relationships are controlled by unwritten rules which state that, at a certain point, and at an increasingly early age, young racers need to be looked after by professional people if they are to reach the top. Without a team behind them it is highly unlikely that a rider will become a champion, and while it may be true that a team is like a family to a rider, their actual family is rarely seen inside a pit garage.

It is a world that demands professionalism from the earliest stage, with kids who show racing potential learning that the concepts of 'family' and 'home' are different for them. They are surrounded by professionals from within the sport who begin to make decisions that define and shape their destiny – and, given their young age, it is inevitable that many of those decisions have an effect on their personal life. It requires extreme generosity on the part of the families concerned to allow the natural barriers they've built to protect their child to be broken down by outsiders.

Starting a career in motorcycle racing when one is so young is tough, requiring significant sacrifices and intensely hard work, particularly when the necessary education and training are carried out by people other than the child's parents. However, this unwritten law varies with every rider: the 'family factor' is often what sets riders apart and each family is a whole different story.

With the general consensus being that it is essential to have top-level human and technical support to succeed in this sport, the ways and means of obtaining them do vary from one individual rider to the next. Also, the vital importance of the lubricant that oils the wheels of this machine – money – can never be forgotten. Money is just as important as talent. Only the most professional set-ups have the budget to see such a project through, which is why families often turn to a manager as the person who can help their child scale the ladder of success.

There are managers who discover talent by chance, arriving on a family's doorstep all ready to convince them of their child's bright future, with tales of titles and championships. However, the more normal scenario is that when a kid shows some talent for riding, and then starts to stand out, the desire for him to reach the top comes from within the family, and they seek out a professional who can help to open the door to the world of top-level motorcycle racing. This was the case for Jorge Lorenzo.

Being the parent of any top-level athlete brings with it special demands and sacrifices, notably allowing others to take on a role that is more naturally their own, and that is especially the case in motorcycle racing. One of the biggest things a family must do is take a step back – not only from the sporting interests of their child, but also from their daily concerns. Families have to understand that the undertaking of a career in racing represents a point of no return in the relationship with their offspring. The only constant in their relationship is that it will continue to be a source of great happiness and, occasionally, desperate despair. In Jorge's case the family were unable to recognise that their point of no return was on the horizon and, when it arrived, that severance was cataclysmic.

From 4 May 1987 until 1990 and his first motorcycle
'BOSS OF THE BALEARICS'

'Jorge was born on 4 May 1987 in the Son Dureta Hospital in Palma de Mallorca. You could tell pretty much straight away that he was a fighter,' said María Guerrero, Jorge's mother, when asked in an interview with TVE to recall his earliest days. The destiny of Jorge Lorenzo Guerrero was marked out before he was even born by a father who carried an unusual passion for motorcycles in his genes.

Chicho Lorenzo, from Porto do Son, Galicia, Spain, was born in Caracas in 1957. He moved to Palma de Mallorca determined to succeed as a motorcycle mechanic, armed with two important credentials – his natural passion and the experience he had gained at a workshop in Galicia. He was also a seasoned motocross racer. Chicho met María Guerrero in Palma. She was a dynamic woman, a hard worker and a dreamer. Before long, their lives would become inextricably intertwined.

Chicho was working in a motorcycle repair shop and was heavily involved in the amateur racing scene on the Balearics, while María was a motorcycle courier (she rode a Vespa) when they received the news of Jorge's impending arrival. 'As soon as I found out I was pregnant I stopped riding the bike,' she stresses. The Lorenzo-Guerrero lifestyle was the perfect blueprint for nurturing a champion. While he was still in his pram Jorge was surrounded by a passion for racing, the sounds and smells of motorcycles, and the rush of speed.

Jorge's mother is warm, friendly, sincere and affectionate, oozing with pride and constantly talking about her son – and she cannot remember a single day when motorcycles did not form part of their routine. 'Bikes, bikes, bikes,' she says, recalling the mantra and mood of her home. Jorge was part of it from the day he was born.

Chicho Lorenzo, an experienced riding coach with a reputation for training promising youngsters, quickly recognised that Jorge was championship material. 'He always wanted to win, always,' he repeats over and over in the aforementioned TVE documentary. María doesn't question it: 'His father always knew that Jorge could go far, he never doubted it.' Before he could even walk he was making engine noises and grabbing the handlebars of any motorcycle within reach. He probably cried like a two-stroke when he was born. The little kid seemed destined for success.

It was a winning formula – a rider with real potential and a father with the passion, the will and the means to prepare him for life as a racer. Jorge's mother respected her husband's wish to train the toddler as soon as he was able, patiently going along with Chicho's obsession. María's attitude, in fact, has always been ideally suited to the role she was destined – and willing – to play. She played it grudgingly on occasions, too, because she didn't want Jorge to miss out entirely on his childhood and that wasn't always the easiest position to defend.

1990–1997
FROM PALMA DE MALLORCA
TO THE COPA APRILIA

Jorge had barely stopped teething by the time his parents watched him ride his first motorcycle. It was a mish-mash of a bike, built by Chicho for his son to try out his first few laps, and probably unrideable by any youngster who'd not grown up familiar with the smell of gasoline, like Jorge. That first motorcycle, the first crash and the first moment of panic for his mother were enough for his father to realise that he had a rough diamond on his hands. Those first sessions took place on wasteland near their house.

'I have good technique thanks to my father because he trained me so well,' remembers Jorge. 'I have always been very competitive. I've always wanted to win, win and win. At Aquacity we did staggered races. We'd start out with a handicap, from the slowest to the fastest, separated by the time difference between us in practice. And because I was always the fastest, of course I would always start from the back. The idea was that we'd all head into the final corner with a chance of winning. I don't know how I did it but I would make passes and make more passes and I always won. Each time my dad would make me start from further back. That is what enables me to make those kind of passes now, those kind of late charges.'

That first bike was only the start. Chicho Lorenzo had meticulously worked out every step Jorge would have to take to make sure not a minute was wasted in his preparation for the great future he had planned for his son. It was a training programme that he hoped fitted perfectly with a fun-filled and happy childhood – a formula of guaranteed success. Jorge wasn't even four years old when he competed, without a licence, in his first official race – a round of the Balearic Motocross Championship. The photos from that time show the face of a smiling young boy, who was far happier to have his hand gripping the throttle of a motorcycle than the controller of a Scalextric.

Jorge remembers his father's methods well. 'We were always riding short sections, doing exercises – in particular a figure of eight. There were two tyres, separated by between ten and fifty metres. Or sometimes only five! When we did the five metre version at the start I was really clumsy but on the second day I'd improved and after a year I was like a machine. I became incredibly precise in slow corners.'

Chicho dedicates a whole chapter of his book to the benefits of the figure of eight, which he describes as 'the miracle exercise'. According to the book, 'The figure of eight covers a huge part of motorcycle racing because it covers braking, corner entry, picking the right line, throttle control and concentration.'

'Then we practised making the bike slide without using the brakes,' continues Jorge. 'My dad took the brakes off the bike and I had to learn how to slide it to a stop – on tarmac! To stop the bike I just had to fold it – lean over and fold the front outwards. I'd have to do it through a series of corners. While the other young riders in Mallorca were clocking up laps at the circuit, we would be working to a set objective. And we'd always do it with a light covering of oil in the corners.'

This father and son partnership was unbreakable during the first ten years of Jorge's apprenticeship as a champion. Other than classes at La Milagrosa school and holidays in Galicia with his grandparents, every waking moment was spent training, practising – Chicho and his little 'Giorgio', as he liked to call him. 'Giorgio' or 'Jorge' Lorenzo? Is it only the name that has changed? 'I've always been called Giorgio, my dad started to call me that when I was really small. It stuck until I joined Derbi in 2002. In Italy they'd get confused – they thought I was Italian and I'd have to tell them I was Spanish! So I went back to Jorge. My mum calls me "Giorgi", but I prefer "Jorge".'

Chicho's work initially took place in a small workshop beneath his house before he moved on to the Aquacity Waterpark in Mallorca and then to minibike circuits. It allowed him to organise his days around Jorge so that all their free time could be dedicated to what they both loved the most – riding motorcycles. In the couple of hours between leaving school in the morning and returning in the afternoon, Chicho would take Jorge to some wasteland or other near their house so that he could ride for a couple of hours. When Jorge turned five his family opened a minibike circuit of their own at Aquacity and it was there that he discovered the thrill of dragging his knee on the ground, enjoying the feel of the tarmac and inventing different ways of riding. That year he contested his first minibike races – this time with a proper licence. 'Lorenzo' was about to take off.

'We set ourselves up at Aquacity,' remembers Jorge. 'That's where I remember starting to watch the races on the television. A group of us used to get together to watch them. I remember in 1998 we were all waiting to watch the Dutch TT at Assen. It was the 125cc race that Melandri won, when he set the record [as the youngest ever Grand Prix winner]. The Dutch TT always takes place on a Saturday and I seem to remember it was at a different time to usual. My dad told me and my friend Rubén to let him know when it started. He had to go and hand out flyers at the entrance of the waterpark. They were actually discount tickets for the go-kart and minibike track. Anyway, it was a really exciting race and we completely forgot to tell him! When the race finished we went to find him. "It's finished and you didn't tell me?" he fumed. He punished us by saying we couldn't watch the 250cc race but we saw it through a crack. And Luís D'Antín was fourth!'

Jorge had a happy and healthy childhood, with his father by his side, taking care of his training and probably planning to live out his own dreams of being a racer through his son. However, as his father insists, there were still plenty of occasions when they took time out to enjoy things away from the circuit: trips to the mountains to collect mushrooms or asparagus, fishing, off-road riding, and the hours upon hours that Jorge spent at Aquacity playing with his friend Rubén, diving for the 'treasure' left by tourists at the bottom of the pools – rings, bracelets and coins. Of course, one of his favourite pastimes was to shock passers by with his incredible skill on a motorcycle.

'Rubén and I used to prepare a really small, twisty track for the minibikes. I'd take the slowest bike and I'd always beat him on the final lap, in the final corner. Rubén would get really wound up! During one of those races, in the final chicane, we hit each other and I can still remember seeing him fall off to one side, in slow motion. And the bastard threw his hand out and pushed me so that I'd fall too! Things like that helped to create that winning instinct within me – that competitive edge that I have.'

As well as lending her unconditional support to the passion shared by her husband and son, from the very beginning María was also the voice of reason and she insisted that Jorge should have what she considered to be a 'normal' childhood, away from motorcycles. 'I could see that my son wasn't playing with his friends much and his father would always say that he had something more important to do with the bike.' María felt, on more than one occasion, that motorcycling was playing too big a role in her son's life. Jorge's first crashes and the protective instinct any mother would feel in that situation certainly had a huge impact on her viewpoint. Jorge was so happy training and riding that he often needed reminding that there were other things to do than ride, although personally he felt there weren't enough hours in the day for his favourite hobby.

Chicho was always the soul and the brains behind Jorge's progress, but there is no doubt that the whole family took part. María recalls that all the money that came into the house went towards something to do with motorcycling: clothing, licences, championship entry fees, spare parts ... the list goes on. 'All our money went on it, nothing was bought for the house. For example, if we needed a new sofa it would have to go on the back burner – the most important thing was a new van to get to the motocross in Menorca. Everything we earned, which wasn't much, was spent on racing.' There's a hint of sadness in María's voice, because she can't help but be reminded of certain bitter suggestions that she never did anything for Jorge. 'If it was down to you, the boy would have never amounted to anything,' Chicho once told her. She didn't get to spend as much time with Jorge as his father did because she spent all day working – first as a courier and then as a cook in a hotel – and all to try and help finance Chicho's project with Jorge. In racing, money is more than important, it is fundamental.

At five Jorge was joined by a sister, Laura, a playmate and soon the object of an intense sense of responsibility and protectiveness that was already beginning to develop. 'When I went to collect them from school they were always waiting together,' remembers María with a smile. 'Jorge used to carry both of their bags and he didn't want anybody to speak to his sister. He always held her by the hand – he was very protective.'

'I've always had a rather distant relationship with my sister, although it is changing now,' contests Jorge, who invited Laura to move from Mallorca to London to live with him and their mother during 2008. 'Mainly it's because she is even more shy than I am! She has the same imagination as me, she draws well, she is very artistic, but she is quite hard to get to know because of this shyness and she has always seen me as the big brother who was always getting at her. I suppose there's a certain embarrassment when it comes to us communicating with each other.' At the age of four Laura used to ride with Jorge and Chicho on their off-road excursions. Her father taught her well, but she never liked riding at the track. The off-road stuff was one thing but when she rode at the circuit she would get scared and throw herself to the ground, crashing on purpose so that her father wouldn't encourage her to ride any more.

By the age of six Jorge was able to start competing with an official licence and he soon started to win almost every event he entered: minicross, motocross, trials, minibikes, supermoto and scooter races.

By the age of ten he had won eight Balearic titles and made his debut at national level in the 50cc Copa Aprilia. In the meantime he would continue enjoying his weekends off at Aquacity, especially if there was a Grand Prix on television. 'When I was watching the races on television and they came to an end I'd get so depressed. It meant that Sunday was coming to an end and it was almost time to go back to school. For me Friday was the best day of the week and when the 500cc race ended on a Sunday, that was the worst moment.'

Jorge was a good student and he applied himself from his earliest years at school. His teachers at La Milagrosa remember him fondly as a bright, intuitive child, with a love of reading and talent for drawing and the visual arts. Along with the sense of responsibility and the work ethic he was acquiring, Jorge also began to tap into his inherent winning mentality and competitive edge. 'He wanted to win at everything,' says María. 'For example, some weekends the whole family would get together at a sports centre and go to the pool, then play ping-pong afterwards. He always wanted to win and I had to let him because if not he'd get angry and have a go at me, saying I didn't know how to play properly.' For a kid who won virtually every race or event he entered, and who was getting used to the applause and admiration of the public, it became normal for him to enjoy the taste of victory and celebration. Even Jorge's look as a youngster was a reflection of the combative character and the born winner he was proving himself to be at every opportunity. That cute Mohican and the stars on either side ... every picture tells a story.

'My childhood was happy, although I'm sure I missed out on a lot of things – as I guess will have been the case for [Rafa] Nadal and hundreds of other kids they call "prodigies". They dedicate their lives to a sport and that's how they reach the top. I'm sure we all missed out on a bit of family loving. Personally I would have preferred for my parents to have been together at that time and to have spent more time with my mum. I would like to have been able to spend more time with my friends too. But now I'm making up for lost time – during the day and at night!' he laughs.

BIKES, BIKES, BIKES ... IT WASN'T ALL FUN

'My father used to say that riding a motorcycle wasn't for fun, that the philosophy of 'go out and enjoy yourself' was not the right one. I've heard it said to Dani Pedrosa too. But I completely disagree. If you are focused you can have fun and enjoy yourself.'

Jorge and his father continued to train, every day, every weekend. Little Jorge was like a sponge and he was learning fast, to the amazement of anybody who watched him. Both his parents recall that 'people couldn't believe how well and how fast he rode. At Aquacity there were people who would stay and watch Jorge ride instead of going for a swim. If the go-kart track was empty Jorge would get on his bike and before long it was full again, with everybody following him around.'

Hand in hand with those early successes came his first crashes and his first injuries. His mother struggled more than anybody to deal with them: father and son would hide his cuts and bruises from her, coming up with plausible excuses if she spotted them. 'That's just María going a little crazy' is Chicho's way of skimming over the white lies he told at the time. María recalls that when Jorge was hurt they would never admit that it had happened on the bike. Strangely, he always seemed to hurt himself playing with his friends, but never by falling off his bike. 'We used to take him to ride motocross at a circuit owned by a man who let us ride for free and one day my son came back with a nasty cut on his nose, which he still has a scar from actually. He told me that he'd done it playing with Rubén...' She can't remember the excuse he came up with when the brake lever punctured his stomach, but with an imagination like Jorge's you can only begin to imagine what it was.

'The thing was, you were against me riding,' Jorge interrupts his mother as the three of us chat at his London home.

'Yes, because I was worried you would crash,' answers María. 'And it's not that I was totally against it, because in the end you and your father did whatever you pleased anyway. But I was scared! When you crashed and came home injured you always had an excuse. Your father would tell me that Rubén had thrown a can of pop at you, or some other rubbish, and that's how you broke your tooth.'

'I've broken three!' grins Jorge.

'Three teeth!'

'And a few from the bottom too,' he bursts out laughing.

'Now you tell me. I once turned on the television to see him in hospital.' She's talking to me now. 'He was racing in the European Championship, he'd crashed and nobody told me anything. Then I saw him in the hospital! Can you believe that? But he'd better not think he had me fooled all the time. I know that scar was from jumping a motorcycle and not running into a branch.'

Jorge was approaching his tenth birthday when he started to outgrow the circuit at Aquacity. His sporting successes were becoming so regular and so impressive that his father had begun to realise his own dedication and good work were not enough; Jorge's career was going to need help apart from that provided by his family and the sponsors they had cobbled together in Palma. It was time to leave their island.

Nobody can deny the scale of the efforts and sacrifices made by the whole Lorenzo-Guerrero family, and particularly by his father and mentor, to make ten-year-old Jorge one of the brightest prospects in Spanish motorcycle racing. It was then that the moment came – as it comes to every motorsport hopeful – to find a manager and a team who were prepared to back the youngster. That was precisely what they were working towards at the Caja Madrid 50cc Copa Aprilia in Jerez, when Dani Amatriaín saw Jorge for the first time. He was bowled over.

The period that saw the turning point in Jorge's sporting life proved to be a defining one in his personal life too, when the first of a series of shattering experiences took place that were to have a major impact on his character. When he was ten his parents separated, and even though they shared custody, young Lorenzo spent the majority of his time with his father while his sister, Laura, stayed with her mother.

The day-to day-changes that came with the separation, the fact that every spare minute of Jorge's life was now completely dedicated to motorcycles, meant that Chicho became his only point of reference on a personal, professional and sporting level. Jorge had followed his father's example, inheriting not only his skills on a motorcycle but also certain aspects of his character – many of them positive, others less so. Shy, unsociable, serious and proud, he was a chip off the old block. 'Chicho is a good person but he is very proud and that has worked against him on many occasions,' says María, adding that he could have taught his son a few lessons apart from riding motorcycles – the kind that only a father's example can give. He was never short of lessons on how to ride motorcycles, but maybe Jorge's life away from them would have benefited from a little more attention.

Jorge recalls that his father would use any tactic he could to put pressure on him. 'Sometimes, with the Derbi, he used to say, "You always do the same thing. You start the championship badly, improve by the halfway stage, get to the point where you're doing really well and then back off for the last two races and do badly again." So when we'd get to the last two races he'd say, "Now you're going to do badly." I'd think he was talking nonsense but at the same time I'd make a massive effort to ensure I finished the season well. And it worked! Other times he'd say, "You never win from pole position, so you might as well not set pole." And I'd be thinking, "One day I'll change that!" In 2007 I won nine 250cc races from pole.'

Jorge knew how to drag his knee on the tarmac but he didn't know how to raise his hand and greet people, how important it was to say 'please', 'thank you' or 'goodbye'. Chicho's training methods had been tough and effective, but there was plenty of room for the teaching of good manners. 'Chicho was really harsh on Jorge when he didn't do well', says María. 'I remember being at a circuit one day when he was training and after one bad lap his father said: "What a shit lap that was!" That kind of attitude always wound Jorge up. He got back on the bike and rode a perfect lap.' For every action, a reaction. María couldn't understand why Chicho would say such things to a small child because she could see that he was getting on the bike angry, desperate to show his father that he could do better, and the risk of falling was much greater. 'Now what?' Jorge would retort. 'What about the time I just did?'

More and more, his mother became a spectator. 'I was still his mother, but I couldn't act like a mother.' Motorcycles were now the most important thing in his life and the pivot around which everything revolved. Before long she became isolated and she was forced to respect her son's career choice while maintaining the protective instinct and concern that she still displays. Over the next few years she was prevented from being as close to her son as she would have liked, and she had no say in the decisions taken by his father, but she continued in her role as the patient and obliging mother. Eventually, her attitude and temperament would pay dividends and she would return to her rightful place, living with Jorge and looking after him in London. 'I just want the best for him and I want him to appreciate things,' she says.

Jerez 1997 to MotoGP 2008
A NEW MEMBER OF THE FAMILY

Following those first sessions at the Copa Aprilia in Jerez, in 1997, where Jorge had crossed paths for the first time with Dani Amatriaín, the man who would become a 'new member of the family', his career took the turn on to what would prove to be its definitive path. 'When my father introduced me to Dani,' recalls Jorge, 'he said, "This is Dani Amatriaín." And I thought, "What about me? I'm Jorge Lorenzo!" I was a little shit, to be honest! I also remember being at Cartagena, when I was around ten years old, and somebody said, "Look, there's Alberto Puig! Why don't you ask him for an autograph?" And I said, "Tell him to ask me for one!" I was daft, and ignorant, but because I was so small everybody fell about laughing. If I'd have said that at 15 it wouldn't have been quite so funny!'

Amatriaín had been bowled over by Lorenzo's riding at Jerez, and the deal had been sealed when Chicho handed Dani the video of Jorge training in Mallorca. Only a few years before his father had been dropping him outside his classroom door for his first day at school; soon he would be accompanying him to Barcelona to start his new career. (They moved there as soon as Jorge finished his second year of ESO, when he had just turned 14.) Getting Dani to take Jorge on as one of his protégés had been no easy task, because at that time he already had several riders under his tutelage. However, it didn't take long for Jorge to confirm that special talent Dani had spotted for the first time at Jerez. 'The first time I raced for Dani was at Calafat,' recalls Jorge. 'I can remember thinking that the Catalans were totally different to Mallorcans and I felt a bit strange in the team. The main man was Iván Silva and I was like the spoilt brat.'

During that period, Chicho's own methods began to be mixed with the highly professional structure of Monlau. They had to work on developing an understanding, joining forces and making concessions on both sides so that Jorge could continue to grow. Cheni Martínez remembers: 'When Jorge was competing in the Copa Aprilia, his dad would stand alongside us on pit wall and make gestures to Jorge. They had their own little system of communicating race information. It was like sign language! Finally one day Dani said: "Chicho, we don't work like this. We have a pit board." Chicho was in his own little world, although you have to admit that if he wasn't like that then maybe Jorge would have never ended up where he is now. If you're not taught from the time you're very small it is very difficult to make it.'

When you think about it, maybe the sign language issue hasn't been completely resolved because Jorge still struggles with pit boards, as Juanito Llansá can confirm. 'It's a touchy subject, but he never looks at the pit board. He doesn't even want to! Not unless there is something that interests him. For example, if he wants to know if the gap to the guy behind has increased – if not, he doesn't bother. I always say to him, "When you go out on your first lap have a good look where the pit board is. Find a point of reference." We use a huge board and we've tried all sorts of brightly coloured numbers – red, green, yellow … and then every shade – lemon, luminous, black background, white background. We've had all sorts of issues with the pit board. We went from using something 1m high to 1m 70. I'm not sure if he can't see it or just doesn't want to!'

After his first year with Amatriaín, when he won virtually every round of the Copa Aprilia, Jorge signed a long-term contract with his manager. The kid had found his benefactor, and Dani had discovered the rough diamond he'd been waiting for. Before making the final move to Barcelona, Jorge's last couple of years in Mallorca were full of intense training and constant trips across the Mediterranean to compete in the Copa Aprilia. Despite such a hectic lifestyle he maintained a keen interest in his education and, according to his mother, 'Jorge got great results.' Even during his final year of school in Mallorca, driven by his enjoyment of reading and drawing, he took a keen interest in a very different kind of career to the one he would end up in: journalism. In fact, in his final year he was made editor of the school newspaper. 'He did every kind of work for the newspaper and he loved it. They always asked him to do the drawings,' recalls his mother.

Dani Palau, Jorge's closest friend from those days in Mallorca, has a slightly different memory of the young student. 'Was he a good student? Well, he got the grades and that was about it. He used to say that if he wasn't a racer he'd have become a footballer or a painter. In class he used to draw pictures of us – him and me. He used to draw pictures of our races at his dad's track. He used to draw himself with the number 1 plate, winning the race, and me almost a lap behind, stretching my neck … losing, basically! Only he was allowed to win, even in his drawings!' Jorge was a talented artist and used to sell his classmates portraits of themselves for a hundred pesetas. He won a host of young artist competitions and in 2007 he designed the winged number 1 that featured on his helmet. He also designed the number 48 on his Yamaha for his debut season in MotoGP, as well as the 'X-fuera' logo, which he developed over time with the help of Palau. He still takes a prominent role in the designs that feature on any of his official merchandise.

While María and Laura stayed in Palma, father and son continued their professional journey together, across the sea in Barcelona, but now they had the support of a well-organised team and the guidance of a personal manager. His old family had been split in half, but his new one grew as the Monlau school became his daily environment. Practically and theoretically, his education was now all about motorcycles. His relationship with Dani and the rest of the team was close from the first day and Jorge went about things in his usual manner, immediately starting to create expectation.

FACING UP TO BOTH SIDES OF SUCCESS

'He has always been like a grown-up, like a professional inside the body of a child,' recalls Dani. 'He stepped onto the World Championship stage and, despite missing the first two races of the season because he was too young, and injured, he wasn't even nervous on the night before his debut at Jerez. The only thing that distracted him a little was the television, the radio and the press in general because they all wanted to know about him. But all you had to say was, 'Hey, amigo! Don't get distracted!' Having spent his whole life around motorcycles, the pace of the things that were going on around him, which would have overawed any other kid, seemed normal to him. Since he was very small his mind was set on his job and everybody made him feel as though what was happening was completely normal.'

Jorge's father followed his progress very closely and formed part of the team. Success came quickly and, at the beginning, there were no major clashes of interest between himself and Dani when it came to making decisions. Chicho remained in charge of Jorge's personal development, and he also had a major say in anything relating to his career. He had formed Jorge and brought him up, he was a successful coach and, generally speaking, he saw eye to eye with Dani on all the decisions that were made. They were virtually partners. 'When my father and Dani were still getting on well we had some great times together,' recalls Jorge. 'I remember being at Jerez in 2002. On the circuit infield, by the back straight, there was a huge parking area, with a helicopter pad and a go-kart track. At five in the evening, when there was nobody about, we used to take the scooters over there and race, the three of us mixing it up! It was close because I would usually win but my dad had practised a lot there and Dani had been a professional racer. But Dani was really rough. He didn't wear a helmet but he'd dive into every gap, with my dad shouting, "¡Estás loco, estás loco!" ["You're crazy, you're crazy!"]. They were great days.'

Dani's recollection is that they had to work on Jorge from the start – in every area, but in particular the personal aspect. 'He was a difficult and tough character,' he says, citing it as the biggest obstacle to Lorenzo's professional development. Jorge had appeared out of nowhere, with huge talent and a technique that was way beyond his years, but there needed to be some order to his working methods and it was the team who had to lay down the rules. 'He didn't like going to the gym so we had to put somebody in charge of taking him there [Cheni], making sure he trained and trying to make him understand how important it was,' says Dani.

So it was no longer just Chicho and Jorge. Now there was a professional structure to his career and what lay behind some of the decisions was different to the interests they'd had when they were on their own. As a result, a conflict of those interests – on both a sporting and a personal level – was simply a matter of time. The first issue was personal, when Jorge had to choose whether to go on studying. Even though he would have been able to continue his ESO studies at the Monlau school in Barcelona, the best and most natural place to combine racing with studying, his father decided that he wouldn't be attending any more classes. Dani Amatriaín and the rest of the team were against the decision, but it was his father's to make and they could do nothing but accept it. 'Back then we had a good understanding with Chicho,' says Amatriaín. 'We usually agreed on everything. Apart from that! I wanted him to see his studies through, at least until the end of his fourth year of ESO. But at the end of the day Chicho was his father.'

María bitterly recalls a decision she was also fiercely against. 'Chicho could see that his vocation was to race motorcycles and that he wasn't going to earn a living out of studying. You couldn't even discuss it with Chicho, he didn't even allow me to have an opinion. I really suffered over this because I felt like the mother that never was. He pushed me aside yet again.' Jorge's father had it clear in his mind that his son's future would not be decided by reading books and that it was going to be difficult for him to train, travel and race when, for example, he had an exam to come back to on a Monday. As with all the decisions taken for him in his life up to then, Jorge accepted it as normal and was even thankful for it. However, his later preoccupation with books, reading and his insatiable hunger for learning are a clear example of the intellectual potential he possesses, which could have taken him in a completely different direction.

The team made sure that, even though he was to leave school, his education didn't stop completely and they arranged for extra tuition. 'It took a lot of effort to make him realise that it was important to keep studying, to learn English for example, but eventually it is his own willpower that has made him into such a hard worker,' explains Dani. 'It wasn't long before he demonstrated a huge will and need to learn, which is why he goes through so many books now. He makes a massive effort to develop himself through reading. He tries to learn from everything.'

The following years saw Jorge exclusively dedicated to motorcycles, aided by his father and a team that were slowly beginning to earn his friendship and affection. Dani had carefully planned each step to be taken, and he made sure that everything ran smoothly so that Jorge and his family didn't have to worry about a thing. Dani had to play every kind of role in his life, occasionally even that of a father. 'I always had a lot of respect for Dani,' says Jorge. 'He has a very dry character and over ten years together we kind of had a set role together. We went through a lot together. Motorcycles were the focal point of our relationship but gradually we started to discuss other things outside racing.'

Being so involved in his life meant that Dani would often be the one Jorge turned to over issues that his father did not look on with much sympathy. 'Chicho and my son spent a lot of time together when he was little, but as he grew older he started to form his own ideas, as every child of that age does,' says María. 'That's when the problems with his father started.'

Jorge was not a child any more, and his family were no longer the be all and end all of his life. There were other people involved in his daily routine now, and with them came different ways of viewing the world. Like any teenager at 15 or 16 years of age, his character and personality began to change. 'Sometimes Dani and I would take the supermoto bikes out and go on enduro rides in the mountains near Alella,' recalls Jorge. 'Back then he was still much faster than me on an off-road bike and even though I tried everything to stay with him he would blow me away! Dani would have to get off his bike, prop it against a tree and start my bike up for me because my legs weren't strong enough. He'd say, "Don't you dare fall off again!" Then a kilometre later I'd come off again and we'd be getting nowhere.'

His father must have realised that he was being removed from the front line in his son's life, and he didn't know the best way to take it. Chicho had always had very clear ideas and whatever he said went. Now things weren't working like that because Jorge's career was also in the hands of his manager and his team. The strict professional guidelines a young sportsman has to follow were in conflict with his father's desire to hang on to the reins of Jorge's future – and to make matters worse for Chicho, Jorge began to have his own ideas about what he wanted, when and how he wanted it, and he took a dim view of many of his father's actions. On Chicho and Jorge, María says, 'They had a lot of good times together but a lot of bad times too. He always had to do whatever his father said and there came a point when he didn't like it any more.'

Jorge made the leap up to the 250cc class in 2005, a season full of nerves and excitement. According to Dani, it was a campaign that showed up a lack of the experience required to handle situations at that level. The general consensus was that maybe if he'd won a title during his three years in the 125cc class he could have stepped up to 250cc from a more stable base. On top of that, the problems that began to build up around him, that weren't always his fault but which he took on his shoulders, and the continual comparisons with Pedrosa throughout the season ended up distracting him from the job at hand. 'I don't think we were as obsessed with Pedrosa as the media liked to make out,' insists Jorge, but at 18 years of age he was certainly not at peace either on the track or off it, and the arguments with his father began to escalate.

The differences of opinion between Jorge, his father and his sporting 'family' seemed to multiply with every victory. It is fair to say that Jorge's team began to take precedence over his family, and in particular his father, as the first world title came into view. Chicho remained firm in his beliefs about his working methods, which it could not be denied had created a winning rider, and he didn't agree with certain decisions that were made. He felt he was right, and that the team should respect him, but it was one thing to recognise who had created Jorge Lorenzo and another to act on his 'suggestions'. Many factors come into play when deciding on the direction of a team. The crisis that was developing with his father left Jorge without a close member of his family to turn to and the team, Dani Amatriaín in particular, surrounded him with the friendship and support that he needed.

By that time Marcos Hirsch, Jorge's physical trainer, had also become an important figure in the young racer's life and they built up a particularly strong professional and personal relationship. Together, Dani and Marcos formed Jorge's strongest pillars of support during the worst of the conflict, but there had been happier times in the gym for both Lorenzos with Marcos. In fact, one of Jorge's more amusing anecdotes comes from those days: 'My dad used to say that Rossi was a clown. He said he was a great rider but that he always had the best bike and that was why he won. So when Rossi moved to Yamaha he said, "Pah! He's not even going to finish in the top six. There are too many factory Hondas and the Yamaha is nowhere near as good." Marcos and I said that Rossi would win races. Not only that, but that he would finish in the top three in the championship. So we made a bet. My dad had just come back from Thailand and he'd bought this ridiculous Thai hat, with little balls dangling from it on strings. We said that if Valentino finished in the top three at the end of the season, he'd have to wear the hat for a whole week. Of course, Valentino won the title and my dad turned up at the gym wearing the hat. He looked so stupid that we felt sorry for him and after a couple of days we told him he could take it off.'

Marcos and Chicho got on well and while Jorge trained they chatted and told jokes. 'They used to talk about sports psychology,' remembers Jorge. 'They wanted to start a riders' school together. They were like peas in a pod!' Marcos used to call Chicho 'Jimmy Foss'. Why? Jorge laughs at the mere thought of it. 'One day my dad walked in, taking the piss like he does, strutting around saying he was like Jimmy Foss. He says, "Marcos, do you know who Jimmy Foss is?" Marcos says no, so my dad says, "Of course you do! Jimmy Foss, the guy who went around the world in 80 days." Marcos cracked up laughing. "You mean Phileas Fogg, Chicho!" Since that day he's always called him Jimmy Foss. We used to laugh so much!' But the smiles fade when Marcos recalls how things started to change. 'The three of us used to have a great time together but the older Jorge got, the more tension there was and the more their characters collided. A lot of times they turned up at the gym and they'd already been arguing. And we trained first thing in a morning! I told Chicho that if it was going to continue like this, it would be better that he didn't come anymore. You could tell it wasn't going to end well.'

MAN TO MAN, FATHER AND SON

The friction between father and son, and consequently between Chicho and the team that worked for and with his son, reached its climax during the 2006 season, shortly before Jorge's 19th birthday. Following his second 250cc victory in Qatar, the team decided to dispense with the services of the sports psychologist who worked with Jorge, Joaquín Dosil, who had been suggested by Chicho. An avalanche of accusations followed, which turned Jorge's world upside down. One of the keys to Dani's success with Lorenzo was surrounding him with people who all worked with him to achieve set objectives. 'People can be useful one day and no use the next. I've had to get rid of people when I could see that they weren't of any use and I've had to put up with a lot of criticism for that,' said Dani at the end of 2007. 'But I am in charge and I have to make sure that the people around him bring only positive things.' His judgement was vindicated when he introduced Alex Debón into Jorge's life during the worst period of the conflict. 'Alex is a wonderful person, a really good guy, and when I thought about how much good he could do for Jorge I immediately brought him into the team.'

'His father isn't a bad person and he wasn't acting like one, he just got extremely tense ... and it's his son, of course. He didn't do things as he should have, but he didn't do anything bad intentionally, things just slipped out of his hands and his tongue got loose!' That's María's description of a statement made by Chicho in the newspaper *Diario de Mallorca* at the beginning of June 2006, when he accused the team, and especially Dani Amatriaín, of manipulating his son. Chicho insisted that the kid needed a psychologist, his psychologist, and he blamed the absence of one for a run of bad form and crashes that Jorge suffered between the Turkish and Italian GPs.

María remembers being at home in Mallorca watching the Turkish GP on television with Chicho and a group of friends. 'He said then that he thought Jorge was crashing because the psychologist wasn't there. He felt that the focus Joaquín Dosil had given him was missing and if he had it, he would have got a better start and not crashed.' Chicho was furious about it all and María could see that he wouldn't be content just sounding off about it in front of friends. Perhaps this was the point where Chicho felt that his 'Giorgio' had been taken away from him. 'Maybe when he handed him over to Amatriaín he thought it would be just for a while and that later he would retake 100 per cent control of his career ... I don't know,' says María.

What is true is that a run of crashes and bad results sparked a flurry of unfortunate statements and actions. His father told Jorge that he needed to get the psychologist back on board, that he was the key to recovering his lost focus. His girlfriend at the time, Eva, had been frightened by seeing him constantly crashing and, convinced by Chicho's version of the story, called Jorge to tell him the same thing. His mother didn't know what to think or who to believe. The psychologist didn't seem like such a bad idea. She saw her son crash and knew something was wrong, but didn't agree with the way Chicho was stirring things up and was convinced that the comments being thrown around and the different advice he was being given could only confuse Jorge and make him even more tense when what he needed to feel was calm.

'Jorge called me, saying, "Eva is telling me one thing, my dad another," ' says María. 'He must have been going crazy. I told them "Please, leave him alone." He was risking his life out there.' It was even more difficult for his mother, who had to deal with the crisis from afar, at home with her daughter in Palma. 'I used to hear things on the radio and I was concerned because I felt my son needed to concentrate on his job. Chicho should have thought about that too. There was still a long way to go in the championship.'

María remains convinced that Chicho didn't launch into his tirade with any ill intentions; he just got wound up and lost his head. 'In Chicho's eyes everybody was taking advantage of his son, everybody was bad.' But one way or another Jorge needed to get out of that hole and the people who held out their hands to help him were Dani and Marcos. According to Dani, 'The problems he was having away from the track were affecting him a lot. He had too many things in his head, too many thing poisoning his mind, and he was picking up some really strange habits. He was confused, his thoughts were blocked and he didn't know who to trust.' The situation continued to deteriorate to the point that there was only one feasible way out: 'If you want us to work things out for you then you are going to have to separate yourself from your father and your girlfriend for a while and forget the psychologist forever.' Dani also reassured Jorge that he wouldn't allow any member of the team to do him harm, but warned that if he continued to race in his current mental state he was putting himself at great risk. This all made Jorge think, giving him the opportunity to step out of the firing line and consider his position. Jorge decided this was the advice he had been looking for and, since the team had been looking after him for some time now anyway, he would put himself body and soul into their hands while he focused on recovering his form on the track and found the mental tranquillity he needed to tackle his personal problems.

Jorge's determined reaction at this time of great tension was ironic, fruit of the example set by his own father. In effect, Chicho had fallen on his own sword. 'Jorge has picked up certain things from Chicho that I'd rather he hadn't,' says María. 'After so much time together it's to be expected that he'd take on some of his father's bad habits, and reacting impulsively is one of them.' However, his mother believes that this particular impulsive reaction was the right one and events have proved that beyond doubt. She believes it was time for father and son to go their separate ways because things had got so mixed up. 'Jorge loves him a lot and Chicho likewise, but those two just don't work together,' she reflects, eyes closed and with a shake of the head.

María rarely gets the chance to speak to Jorge about such delicate matters. 'He doesn't like to talk to me about things like that,' she says. 'He only tells me what he wants to.' She respected Jorge personally but as a first-hand witness believed that the vicious circle of crashes and disasters occurred because the chaos all around him made him anxious. 'I think Jorge became desperate to win just to prove a point to Chicho, but as a result he wasn't riding as he knew how. He was riding with a lot of anxiety.'

WIPING THE SLATE CLEAN

The key to Jorge climbing out of the mire was Dani and Marcos's calm and confident handling of the situation, in particular, and the help of the team in general. Little things like taking his mobile phone away during a Grand Prix weekend shielded him from any disputes and reinstated the calm he needed to ride as well as he knew how, like a potential champion. His mother has only ever had one piece of sporting advice for him: 'I have never told him to go faster, I only tell him to ride like he knows he can. In MotoGP I told him to go little by little, not to rush because he had nothing to lose. The worst that can happen is that he crashes and breaks something. Other than that, just enjoy it.'

In 2006 he won his first world title. The transition from family support to professional guidance had produced his first major success after a rollercoaster journey of glory, challenges and difficult personal circumstances. The day he won his first title, Dani noticed that Jorge was nervous on the grid, which was unusual. 'I saw him get really nervous. I know him really well and I knew how to make him react. I shouted "¡Jorge corre!" ["Jorge, race!"] to snap him out of it. Since he was still so young, whenever he was tense you just had to shout at him to get a reaction, to get him under control. I felt him bristle and I knew he was ready.' It was a tactic only Dani could have used and one that he had already employed on several occasions, shouting at Jorge so that he 'switched on' into serious, aggressive mode. That first title was an important moment for everybody involved in his career, proving to be the turning point from which they could review the past and look ahead to the future with more composure. 'I have known every minute of his life from the age of ten and if anybody deserves to be World Champion it is him, because he has sacrificed so much,' said an emotional Dani at the time.

The Jorge Lorenzo who started the 2007 season looking to defend his 250cc World Championship title was no longer a child but a young man with experience of overcoming adversity both on and off the track. Just as important as his successful defence of the title was the moment he put pen to paper, signing a contract with Yamaha to take the step up to MotoGP. Once again it was his manager who ensured that Jorge would have all the necessary tools to join the premier class in style: a factory team, well-planned pre-season tests, top-level technical staff and a good wage. Yamaha agreed to all these stipulations.

His 'sporting family' endured the intensity of two title-winning seasons together, overcoming the usual challenges and frictions of sharing such a close environment. His real family have also come through the crisis, his nearest and dearest repositioned and somewhat rearranged – his mother now taking over the role formerly played by his father. The mother who was unable to act like one for so many years is now devoted to being just that, taking huge pleasure in his successes but living in constant fear of the risks that life as a racer involve for a young man of 21.

Her emotional highs and lows, lived through her son, are typical of any family of a successful racer. 'I'm always worried – when he races, when he goes out on the town … like any mother, but especially a mother in this sport. I don't ever watch the races – I try to but I can't. I used to watch the 125cc ones occasionally but I hate to see the crashes in those races too. I try not to stay at home on the Sundays there's a race. I go out with friends knowing I can come back within an hour, when everybody will be calling to say congratulations. I ask them not to call me for an hour. Then they call to say how Jorge has got on.'

María couldn't even watch the races where Jorge won his championships. 'In 2006, in the race where he won his first title, at Valencia, I was there but I was wearing headphones, listening to music and walking around the paddock so that I didn't know what was happening.' She can't handle the fear of knowing that Jorge could severely injure himself at any moment and it takes huge willpower for her to overcome her anxiety. She gave up smoking three years ago and is racked by nerves. In 2006 she decided to channel her nervous energy into an objective, promising that if Jorge won the title, or at least if everything went well, she would go and give thanks at the Monasterio de Lluc in Mallorca. It is traditional on the island to make the pilgrimage from Palma to the monastery on foot, in August, if you have a wish that you want to come true. That year she did it on a bicycle, with friends, but in 2008 she kept her promise and walked there, in accordance with tradition.

María is proud of her son and of everything he has achieved up to now. She lives with him but does not get involved in his work and is grateful for every moment and every experience she gets to share with him. 'All I want is the best for my son and for him to appreciate things.' She is just as nervy as Jorge and cannot keep still for a minute, so ever since her son asked her to give up work and live with him, she helps him out in every way she can. 'I don't care about money and I've never asked my son for anything. I'm not used to anybody earning so much money – I've been bringing in 1000 euros a month for years and I know how to live off that. I could go back to work if I wanted, because I know a lot of people in Mallorca, but Jorge wants me with him.' Her words are laced with gratitude but not because she no longer has to work – she is still exactly the same hard-working woman who had to give up her son to keep the family going and help Jorge's career. She is grateful because ten years on she's reunited with him and now spends as much time as possible with him between races.

María loves to cook and even ran a ready-meal business for a while in Palma, so she is the perfect person to ensure Jorge maintains the strict diet prepared for him by Marcos. It's a diet he follows to the letter. 'Jorge eats terribly. Put that in the book!' she says with a wide smile. 'Seriously, though, he has great willpower and is very methodical. He has learnt to be like that from Marcos. When he was little he liked to eat buns and cakes, like any kid, but now he doesn't, he takes great care: vegetables and grilled chicken or fish. I sometimes say to him, "But son, don't you get bored with eating that?" ' She has also taken on the typical mother's role around the house, chivvying him, pestering him to be tidy and making sure he doesn't get used to having other people do things for him. 'He's got used to leaving things lying around because he knows somebody will come after him to pick them up. He's really untidy – he leaves things thrown all over the sofa and then spends hours trying to find things. He gets that from his father,' smiles María. Dani Palau backs her up. 'When we used to live together I was always clearing up empty yoghurt pots from beside the computer.'

While he used to be shy and needed to be told to go out with his friends and have fun, nowadays he needs to be reminded to come home. His mother also reminds him how he should behave in front of others, constantly telling him to be himself and not try to be somebody else, because the real Jorge is an incredible person. 'This cocky thing of his covers up who Jorge really is because he wants people to like him. I think people see him as arrogant because of the way he acts sometimes, the way he celebrates his victories. It means some people love him and some can't bear to look at him. There's nothing in between! At the end of the day, if you get to know him you become very attached. He never says no to anybody.' María is a staunch protector of her son, and while she is not slow to recognise that he can occasionally step out of line she insists: 'He is a very good person. I can be very naïve and a lot of things go over my head – my son used to be a bit like that too – but he is changing and little by little he is starting to understand things and developing a more mature approach. I also think he is quite modest – he wants to show off but this arrogance is not real. He has a lot of heart.'

Jorge, in advance of his years in many respects, is rebuilding his relationship with his mother at an age where most people are learning to be independent. Despite his experience of all kinds of situations, a lot of what has happened recently, within his family, is new to him. 'I'm definitely not the best son. I need to be more affectionate with my mother.' Jorge speaks in a whisper, clearly bothered by María's presence. He is even shy about talking in front of her.

'Mum! If you're right here I'm embarrassed to talk.'
'Okay, okay. I'm going.'

Jorge waits until her footsteps have reached the bottom of the stairs and doesn't speak again until he hears the door of his London apartment close. 'The problem is that our roles were established a long time ago and I find it difficult to change them or improve them. That's the way I am and she knows it. I have never been affectionate with my mother and to be so now kind of makes me feel embarrassed. It sounds stupid but I can't just suddenly be that way. Sometimes I don't look after her like I should, because she is doing a lot for me. She left Mallorca, her island! She even left Laura behind and they are like peas in a pod.' So why now, I can't help but ask. Why did a 20-year-old double World Champion suddenly need the mother he'd been without for so many years? 'Because I asked for her. I wanted to know that I have a mother. I needed one. To buy food, clothes ... but most importantly to look after me, to act like a mother. And I am really happy that she is with me.'

Dani Amatriaín had an alternative perspective on this sensitive and increasingly mature side of Jorge – and a different explanation for the 'cocky rebel' reputation he'd picked up over the years. Dani believed that his initial successes came before he'd been taught any manners and the criticisms he received for his attitude were too much for such a young man to take on board. Jorge still harbours constant doubts about how to respond to criticism and the reactions he provokes in people who cannot accept his character. He cares a lot about public opinion and even though he is changing, and improving – as many people who previously disliked him have been forced to admit – he must still learn to accept that he is never going to be to everybody's taste.

Now he thinks hard about what he says and does because he has also started to think about his future, after his racing career is over. Among other things, he'd like to try his hand at acting and even started taking classes during 2008, although he was forced to stop when he was injured. Dani also believes that the rebel streak that is still evident is because Jorge is a thoroughbred racer. 'He tries to cover it up by putting on a big show but when he is 100 per cent focused he is like a machine that is programmed only to win. That is why he says things that sometimes come across as aggressive. Winning is in his blood and he can't stop the fury coming out when he is totally concentrated. Even so, even in the heat of the moment, he has toned things down a little bit recently.'

'I think I'm starting to say more sensible things but at the same time I'm losing a bit of the spark I had a few years ago,' Jorge says, to my surprise. He can tell from my expression that I want to know more. 'I'm concerned because I read recent interviews of mine and there's nothing in them – no "juice" – they sound like the comments any other rider would make. But the thing is that I'm starting to see that there are other ways of making an interview interesting. You don't have to be outrageous, like saying "I'm going to win this race" or "So and so is a whatever…" There are other ways to be different. By being ironic, for example. Trying to express myself with a different kind of discourse, saying things nobody has said before. There are plenty of ways to be different! Finding them out is a challenge for me and little by little I'm getting there, but I have to find the right balance. There has been a big change in me. People didn't believe me when I started saying that in MotoGP I was going to need two years to learn, that I would need to tread carefully, that I was going to try and learn from everybody. They didn't believe me! But that is the most realistic way to be. It is a way of not being egotistical, of recognising that today things can be going well but tomorrow everything can go wrong, you can get injured and the whole year can be ruined.'

It has always been important for Jorge to feel comfortable and for there to be harmony around him, and now he has achieved that he has been able to start rebuilding his relationship with his father. They are slowly re-establishing their bond but, as María reflects, 'Chicho still has the same character and he doesn't always help things along as much as he could or probably should.' Chicho was and still is very demanding, and his intransigent attitude towards his son's career has not helped Jorge get the credit his mother feels he deserves back home in Mallorca. 'In Mallorca he is still well liked but probably not as much as before the fallout with his father. Our friends really sided with Chicho and I think there is quite a lot of jealousy towards Jorge.' Life will gradually fall back into place, given time and maturity on all sides. Jorge is now a calm and reflective young man who has a better grasp of how to navigate stormy waters and ensure they don't affect his work any more than is necessary. On 20 November 2007 his grandfather passed away, but Jorge was able to cope with it maturely, sticking with the professional commitments he had made for the day.

3

THROUGH THE CHICANE

The fears of a champion

'WHAT IF...'

It is not unusual to hear people class Jorge Lorenzo as a 'natural'. His God-given talent combined with a knack for being in the right place at the right time, and with the right material, are all ingredients necessary for a true champion. The facts suggest that there is much more to the story, however, because along with his talent there has been a lot of hard work and an almost religious dedication, as well as a group of people who have helped him develop and placed him in the right environment. They have been an important factor in the Lorenzo phenomenon, sometimes even the determining factor.

However, despite having been closely monitored from his earliest excursions on a motorcycle by Chicho, before Dani Amatriaín picked up the baton, Jorge has never quite got used to listening to others. His words and actions have sometimes seemed to be at odds with the reality of his career. Perhaps it is his impetuous character or the distance he seems to put between himself and the things that have gone on around him that have created the enfant terrible tag that has dogged him. He's had to listen to a lot of advice over the years, as well as being reprimanded and reproached, and perhaps he's not always taken on board what is being said. He's no ordinary pupil, though, and has needed special teachers to make him feel like a racer in body as well as in spirit. In that respect, the work done by Marcos Hirsch and Alex Debón has been priceless, and their dedication to Jorge when times have been difficult is an example of true perseverance and resolve. Marcos Hirsch has been his personal trainer since 2002, but the job title does not do him justice. He is the man who taught Jorge to work hard and come back even stronger from the pain. Alex Debón, his Sporting Director in 2006 and 2007, brought the perspective that was missing from both his career and his life, something nobody had been able to help him with previously.

A career as successful as Jorge's needed a background of calmness and stability and it was Marcos, a studious Brazilian, well read in the latest methods of physical training, and Alex, a Spanish racer battle-scarred and seasoned by life on two wheels, who provided that. They added polish to Jorge X-fuera (on the outside) and strengthened him X-dentro (on the inside). They talked to him at his own level, in language he understood, because that was the only way to get through to him. They were full-time friends and confidantes in times of adversity – and while it may not always have been obvious, there was adversity by the bucket load.

22 April 2007. A hotel in Istanbul, sometime in the early hours
Letter from Alex Debón to Jorge Lorenzo
ACCEPTING DEFEAT LIKE A TRUE NUMBER ONE

Good evening partner. It has been a really difficult weekend, especially for me, because as you know I have been in a lot of pain and I have not slept much. But, like you, I have shown my strength during difficult times, and that makes me look back and see that my future is much brighter. I am happy for you and so is Dani [Amatriaín] – not just for the result, which as you know is neither here nor there – but because in my eyes at the GP of Turkey I saw a Jorge Lorenzo with confidence in himself. I saw a calculating rider working at full power … a rider who can think when he is on a motorcycle and for me that is the most important thing.

You're making it really difficult for me to be able to beat you in any race this season but don't forget that I'm just one of many sons of bitches out on the track! Ha! I think the lecture I gave you on Saturday night and the visualisation we did in the hotel room were not only remembered word for word but also put into practice lap after lap on the track. In the end you came up with a little touch that the whole world witnessed, including Juanito and Valeriano [his mechanics].

I told you in our hotel room, 'Remember to congratulate your rival at the end. If you finish second, congratulate Dovi because he will have played his cards better than we played ours. If he beats us it's because he did something better than us.' It was something that the whole world saw, something you'd never done before. Back in the garage I almost cried when I saw Juanito say to you: 'Jorge, what you did today was priceless. You have no idea what you just achieved simply by congratulating your closest rival.'

That filled me with inner happiness. In that tiny gesture I was able to see my work reflected. And that was a great feeling for me. I still have a lot of things to learn about this game. I need to study the time sheets more, like Dani said the other day. There are other small details too but I'm convinced that one day I can reach his level because he knows a lot about this business. I'll find it hard, it will be tough, but as with everything I do I'll give everything I have. Like you do, big nose. And in the end I'll be rewarded with that moment of personal satisfaction that gives meaning to life.

I know that everything is going well now but like you I know, we know, that we have to be prepared for a defeat if and when one comes along. You have matured and you are the true number one but that doesn't just mean winning. It also means knowing how to lose because we can learn from our mistakes. We can learn a lot. Take note partner. Everything in this life happens for a reason, nothing is coincidence, and that is why you're going to show me, Dani and everybody else that you are no fucking junior. Like the other day, big nose. You are an animal on the track and in the garage you're an animal with your people. Remember that between the 'no use' and the no. 1 we have come a long way.

To finish off, before I go to sleep, I just want to say congratulations. You made me very happy this weekend. Thank you, Pixie.

The letter is signed 'Dixie', which is what Alex Debón called himself in a lot of his correspondence with Jorge, whom he referred to as 'Pixie' (referring to the Spanish cartoon mice). When Jorge was proofreading the original version of this book, back in 2007, and he read this letter again, he cried. 'You can't choose your emotions,' he said. 'You can break down in tears for all kinds of reasons, different circumstances. The stupidest thing can make me cry. I can cry listening to a song. When I read the draft of this book on a plane I started crying as soon as I read Alex's comments about Juanito.'

Alex wrote that letter just a few hours after the end of the Turkish GP in 2007, following a year that had gone full circle. The previous season, in 2006, Jorge was knocked off his bike in the first corner of the race at Istanbul Park, when he was T-boned by former 250cc rider Shuhei Aoyama, brother of Hiroshi. It wasn't long before he realised this wasn't just any old crash. The notoriously unpredictable Japanese rider had knocked him to the floor and, without realising it, into a bottomless pit. It was at that precise moment that Jorge's season, and potentially his career, went into freefall.

Like any fictional superhero Jorge had to hit the bottom before he could bounce back to the top and, like those superheroes, he had a faithful sidekick to help him on his way. In fact, he had two. His walk through the valley of crashes and bad results would not be in vain, and he had no intention of staying on the dark side. In 2007, the Jorge Lorenzo who threw his leg over his Aprilia was a completely new person. It was no longer 'all or nothing'.

Many things had happened to him since that crash in 2006 which is why, twelve months later, he knew how to accept second place behind his main rival, Andrea Dovizioso, collecting 20 points more than he'd done in the same race the previous season. The old Lorenzo would have been angry that he'd lost – he would have stormed into the garage, thrown his gloves onto the floor and moaned about his bike. Worse still, he would have thrown himself to the ground. But this time he knew how to accept second place, he knew how to congratulate Dovizioso, and he knew that second place was another step towards being number one. His outlook of 'nothing is ever enough' had been swapped for 'it's never too late'.

30 April–3 June 2006
THE YELLOW SUBMARINE

It is time to retrace our steps, back to 2006, with spring giving way to summer and the MotoGP World Championship in full flight, from

Turkey to Italy via China and France. Four races that would prove to be critical in the life of Jorge Lorenzo took place in the space of just 35 days. Jorge was going through a very tough time in his personal life, with the feud between his father, Chicho Lorenzo, and his second 'father', Dani Amatriaín, about to explode (although this was kept from him until after the Mugello race). His crash in Turkey had been followed by a fourth place in China and a French Grand Prix to forget, with three crashes in three days and another DNF. Things were not looking good. Five races into the season and Jorge was fifth in the championship, trailing Andrea Dovizioso by 29 points. Worse still, the number of crashes he was having was putting him at risk of serious injury.

After his sensational start to the season it was impossible to understand why his results had taken such a dramatic dip, unless you were aware of what was going on behind the scenes. 'It's true. I'd won the first two races and I was euphoric. We got to Turkey and I set pole by a full second. I thought, "This is easy! I'm going to have them for breakfast. I'm going to win a load of races this year." But I got a bad start and disaster struck in the first turn. I hit the deck; I couldn't believe it! I thought it was a bad dream, that this couldn't happen to me. It hadn't even entered my head. Shuhei Aoyama came to apologise but I was so fired up, I just couldn't accept it. I felt so frustrated, so powerless, and from then on I was in bad mental shape, I just couldn't get motivated.'

Jorge doesn't have many hang-ups, although there is one he can't shake. 'I always like things to be complete, for everything to work out perfectly. If it doesn't, that affects me a lot. It's silly, but the crash in Turkey ruined my plans. I began to have doubts. I went to Shanghai, didn't manage to set pole and was third for the entire race. There were two riders following me and on the last lap they both passed me. In the end I was lucky to finish fourth. I thought: "I'm going to lose this championship!" I was so annoyed. Dovizioso took over the lead [in the championship] and to make things worse my team-mate won the race. I remember I wouldn't speak to the press, I threw my helmet across the garage ... what a palaver! When things are going badly for you, you can find problems in everything, you start looking for excuses. You think your team-mate is being treated better than you. Silly childishness like that that doesn't get you anywhere!'

There was an extra reason for Jorge's frustration at being beaten by his team-mate, Héctor Barberá, with whom he shared a garage for two seasons, in 2005 and 2006. 'We actually didn't get on that badly at first. My father liked to talk with other riders and he wasn't bothered about talking to anybody, even if they were rivals, so he got to know most of them. In the CEV we got on well and when Barberá finished fifth at Brno in 2003 we went to congratulate him. The relationship between us was quite good – until 2004. I had a bust-up with him at Mugello after he barged me in a corner. In the next round, at Montmeló, I went to his box to see him and tell him that you shouldn't do things like that, that he shouldn't continue in that way. "Make it the last time," I told him. Then in 2005 Dani signed him as my team-mate. There was competition between us even in pre-season. We were young and we didn't get on. I didn't like him and he didn't like me. At the time I was very direct. He'd never done anything serious to me but I didn't like his attitude, he always had this little smirk on his face. The thing that really wound me up, though, was that he'd follow me in practice. He was always waiting for me and I didn't like it at all. I complained to Dani and Massimo Capanna, the crew chief, but he carried on – in fact I think he did it even more to try and wind me up! So in Turkey 2005 I decided not to even say hello to him any more, just to see what happened. Nothing! He was told to follow somebody else but it went in one ear and out of the other. So between Turkey 2005 and Japan 2006 we never spoke. The truth is that I was wrong to state publicly that I didn't like him because all it did was create publicity for him. I can't say he's a bad guy either, because he's been good to me on a couple of occasions. But really he's one of those guys you just don't understand.

'As a rider he's got real talent, but he hasn't lived for racing and that's why he has never achieved the results that would truly reflect his ability. For example, we once went to the gym in Malaysia to train. He did 15 minutes on the bike and then went off to play squash. I was there punishing myself for three hours! Physical strength is not the most important aspect for a rider but if you are pushing towards an objective you become stronger. That's just an example of why he's so inconsistent.'

Let's return to the 2006 French Grand Prix at Le Mans, where Chicho was insisting Jorge worked with sports psychologist, Joaquin Dosíl, who'd been introduced to him at the end of 2005. 'My father kept saying, "Dosil, Dosil! You have to work with him. Dosil is God!" He thought that psychology was the future of motorcycle racing, that nobody else had one so that's what I needed to gain an edge over everybody else. It's true that I learnt things from him, but it wasn't enough to justify the financial outlay. That's where the whole problem with my father started. They were friends, they used to chat on Messenger, they were both Gallegos [Galician] and they got on great. My father wanted me to continue with him, whatever the cost.'

With all this going on in the background, France proved to be his worst Grand Prix of the season, by some distance. 'When people predict that everything is going to go so badly, which is what my father was doing, it ends up going that way. During practice on Friday I was on my way to the fastest time of the session and then crashed trying to pass Poggiali. He was going slower than me, I passed him and then just lost the front. I was on another fast lap again on Saturday during qualifying and tried to go up the inside of a slower rider. I was two corners away from pole position but I got on the gas too early and I found myself back on the floor. From a potential pole I started eighth on the grid! The race got off to a fairly normal start, I was fifth but I knew that Dovizioso and [Yuki] Takahashi were getting away at the front and [Roberto] Locatelli was holding me up. The determination to get past makes you blind! You stop thinking about which could be the best corner to overtake in – you just go on a mad one and see what happens! I tried a pass on Locatelli in a corner where it is really difficult to overtake. I remember passing him in slow motion, praying we didn't touch and crash, but we did. Luckily, Takahashi passed Dovizioso and beat him across the line.'

Jorge seemed lost. He was losing his magic touch and his Achilles heel had been crudely exposed. His concentration was gone, and as a result so was his composure on a motorcycle. His results were a clear sign that something wasn't right and his life was starting to come under scrutiny too. It was time to make a choice. On one side were his father Chicho, his girlfriend Eva and his psychologist Joaquín Dosil. On the other were his colleagues and friends Dani Amatriaín and Marcos Hirsch. A group of people once united in the Jorge Lorenzo cause had been split down the middle by a clash of criteria. The unusual thing about cases like this is that both parties involved in the conflict had the common objective of Jorge's well-being but the crux of the matter was that there were many different ways to approach and achieve it. The approach, in particular, had to be one that suited the rider, who was no longer a child and needed to make his own decisions about how to solve dilemmas. He needed to make a choice with those closest to him – but who was closest to him? Which side should he go with?

It is important to remember that in the middle of this whole crisis was a rider in with the chance of a first world title and putting his life on the line on every lap. Jorge was trying his best to understand and assimilate what was happening to him. His father was passionately defending his only son's interests, as he saw them, insisting on the methods that had worked for him up to that point, including employing a psychologist whom he considered to be the key to Jorge's high levels of concentration in the run-up to Qatar.

'When this person [Dosil] was here, I was happy,' said Chicho in May 2006. 'Around 90 per cent of crashes are the rider's fault and if the rider is focused there is less risk. At Le Mans, without Dosil, he crashed three times. When he is with the psychologist, the statistics match up. But then he sacks him after Qatar and the crashes start. I can see that Jorge has problems and is not concentrating.'

Chicho also rounded on Marcos: 'I know him, and his method of mental preparation is nothing more than a rally cry. "Get out there and destroy them!" he'll say. He has grown up in a gym and he is stuffing my son with strange medication and products.'

Lorenzo senior was becoming further and further detached from the inner circle, so he decided to employ a new tactic to get through to his son, using his first and only girlfriend, Eva, as an innocent messenger. 'He used to call her and ask her to speak to me, to try and convince me to stick with the psychologist and promise not to quit.

My dad was trying to make me listen to him and he did it by using Eva as a tool. He got into her head.' Eva, who had been upset by seeing Jorge crash so much, and witnessing the day-to-day anguish he was going through, was unintentionally not helping matters by constantly calling him with advice.

'The girlfriend, Eva, had to go – she was giving him too many headaches,' says Marcos. 'He was like her little lap dog. "Your job is to race motorcycles every weekend," I told him. "When people go to work, they don't take their family to the office, do they? Well, your office is the circuit and you shouldn't take your girlfriend or your parents there anymore."'

'Marcos is the person who tells me things as they are,' reflects Jorge. 'He has everything I'm lacking, everything I'd like to have in terms of his social skills. God dished it out wrong – everything I want, he has! He has a personality that can really convince people and he talks straight.'

While these conflicts were taking place off the track, Jorge was constantly crashing on it. Marcos told him that things had to change. He couldn't stand back and watch while his friend was going head first into crash barriers. 'We are the yellow submarine,' Marcos said. 'We're on the sea bed, we've just touched the very bottom and we can't go any lower. So there's nothing left for us to do but start our journey back to the surface.'

The lowest point came after the French Grand Prix. Dani Amatriaín, the man who had guided him every step of the way since he was ten, was concerned and felt under mounting pressure. He told Jorge: 'I don't want to work with a rider who keeps falling off and is running the risk of hurting himself, seriously hurting himself. Stop for a moment, think, reflect. This cannot continue. I don't want you to kill yourself on the track.' Even Giampiero Sacchi, the man who had shown blind faith in Lorenzo from the start, made a rare interjection to back up Dani's assertion that things had to change. The problems had to be fixed and more crashes would not be looked on kindly.

Jorge was depressed. All he wanted was to continue to live his life as he'd done up to now – racing motorcycles and enjoying the company of his friends. It was time to use shock therapy and it was

Marcos, who couldn't bear to see Jorge looking so lost any longer, who took the initiative. He took him to Las Ramblas in Barcelona and sat him on a wooden bench in front of the famous El Liceo theatre. Whenever Marcos had felt down when he was younger he used to like sitting in the very same spot and thinking, watching the people walk by and imagining who they might be, what they did, where they were going. Actually, that's exactly what he wanted to find out about Jorge Lorenzo. Where were his life and career going?

'What are we going to do?' asked Jorge.

'What are you going to do? I'm just your personal trainer.'

'Okay then, what would you do?'

'I would get up from here, go and find Dani and close ranks. We can get out of this, we can fight back, but you have to do what we say. If you stray from the plan by a single step, that's where you'll stay. Don't ask me to run through walls with you and then apply the brakes. If we're going to hit something, we have to hit it together.'

Marcos could not have been clearer in his diagnosis or prescription. 'All three have to go, even Eva. At the end of the season you can go out with her again. But if you want to be World Champion you're going to have to cut your ties with your girlfriend. Forget the psychologist and forget your father. It's tough, I know, but at the end of the season you can talk things through and work it out with Chicho. Now is not the time for that. You need to get on the bike, get on the throttle and forget all of this other bollocks, Jorge.'

So Jorge made the decision to go with his friends. Everybody wanted the best for him, of course, but only Marcos Hirsch and Dani Amatriaín knew how to achieve it. 'I had no choice, I couldn't say no,' remembers Jorge. 'I had to cut myself free from everything. Only they could pull me out of the hole. "If you want to be World Champion, you have to leave everything behind," they told me. "Trust us." It was really hard because I loved my girlfriend like crazy! And my father, too.'

End of May 2006
ELIMINATING THE EXCESS BAGGAGE

Some people respond best to visual stimulation, others to auditory. They say Jorge Lorenzo is more proprioceptic – sensitive to the position, posture, movement and changes in equilibrium of his body tissue. In other words, he is affected more by feeling than he is by sight or sound. With his personal crisis now behind him, the Dani–Jorge–Marcos triangle introduced a new activity to their regime: film and debate, almost like a cinema club. *Rocky*, *Gladiator* and *300* were some of the movies of choice. Each had a similar message – free men fighting against injustice and adversity, who lived and died with honour, leaving their legacy behind.

They had realised how much more receptive Jorge was to emotion after they'd watched Russell Crowe as Maximus Decimus Meridius. Marcos told him: 'The World Championship is like a gladiators' arena. You are fighting for your life on the bike, just as they do in that arena. The public used to fill the Coliseum, now they pack out the circuits. Your survival depends on whether you win or lose, just like the warriors of old. The only thing you need to see is black bikes, you have to be colour blind, and see them as obstacles to overcome. You have to get past them and then go back to your cave to eat and rest before the next battle.' The idea began to get through. Jorge only needed to be concerned with the most important thing in his life – racing.

Then it was time to watch *Cinderella Man*. 'We wanted him to pick up on the moral of these films. We showed him characters who, supported by their friends, created an environment of strength and support. They also had a huge capacity for suffering and sacrifice. We wanted to make historical, realistic comparisons with what he had to do himself.' Jorge finally began to see the light.

Marcos didn't stop there. His affection for Jorge is so strong that he dedicated himself completely to help him in his hour of need. One of the causes, and at the same time consequences, of the crisis had been a complete loss of concentration and Marcos had to do whatever it took to get that back. He had heard of Ericksonian Therapy – a technique used for treating anxiety and recovering self-control – so he signed up for a course that he hoped would help Jorge. They got together in the gym where they usually trained and went into a side-room. Marcos told Jorge to stretch out on the floor and he turned out the lights. 'When a person is completely relaxed you can give them instructions and they will respond – in this case, it always has to be positive instruction. You couldn't give Jorge anything negative.'

Marcos made him visualise a Grand Prix. Jorge closed his eyes. 'Imagine that you are arriving at the circuit … how you go into the garage … get changed into your leathers … you throw your leg over the bike and head out on the track. Ready? Okay, now you're going to complete two warm-up laps and when you're on the grid, tap the palm of your hand on the floor.' Marcos spoke gently. Jorge rode each corner in his mind, shifting up and down through the gears, leaning left and right through the bends. He lined up in pole position and tapped his hand on the floor. 'When I tell you, set off and when you cross the line for the first time I want you to tap the floor again. Then again at the end of the next lap.' Marcos set him going and when Jorge crossed the line for the first time he started his stopwatch. What happened next was incredible. Jorge's 'mental' lap times were exactly the same as his real times in the Grand Prix! Give or take a tenth here or there, he had the circuit totally visualised and memorised. More importantly, he wasn't scared any more. In his head it was impossible to crash – he was back in control of the bike and he was not going to lose that control through lack of concentration or a moment's apprehension. It was only one problem less in a world where the risk of falling is not just in the hands of the rider, but it was a big step forward.

June 2006
ENTER A STRANGER

The moment of truth arrived: Mugello. Chicho had brought Jorge's personal problems into the public domain by talking about them on the radio and in the newspapers. Dani and Marcos did what they could to protect Jorge – Dani by asking journalists not to repeat any of Chicho's words in front of his rider and Marcos by spending four days glued to his side from sunrise to sunset. 'Now I look back and think I was so screwed up that if I'd found out what had happened before the race, what my father had said, I wouldn't have raced at all,' says Jorge. 'Physically I didn't feel scared but when you have crashed so many times in one weekend ... mentally you're obviously not in good shape. Having said that, I think other people saw things worse than I did because when I watched that race from Le Mans on video recently I was surprised by the look on my mechanics' faces when I crashed. I thought, "Shit! Things must have been bad!" '

With hindsight, Pere Gurt suggested that the foundations for Lorenzo's real success were laid in Italy – or maybe that should be re-laid. It was time to go back to basics, start again and return to the fundamentals that had been forgotten over time: organisation, professionalism and good timekeeping.

On top of the exercises in mental preparation, the relaxation and the late nights in Barcelona, chatting with Jorge to calm him and remove anxiety from his life, an important new rule was introduced into his routine at Mugello. Every Wednesday, when he arrived at the circuit, he would hand over his mobile phones to Dani Amatriaín – and he wouldn't get them back until Monday. There would be no laptop computer either. He would spend the five days of a Grand Prix completely detached from the outside world, where the racket had become so deafening and distracting. It was the final step towards blocking out any interference and it was then, and only then, that Alex Debón came on the scene, another voice of reason, with the right balance of professionalism and friendship, to help out the would-be champion.

Alex had known Jorge since the start of his professional career at Derbi, but they'd never talked. It had been five years since Jorge's debut season, so you could be forgiven for thinking that they didn't speak because they didn't get on, but that couldn't be further from the truth. They'd just never talked, because Jorge spent his time in the various pit garages that had been his home over the years, not speaking to many people at all and with little or no interest in anything that wasn't to do with bikes. To be fair, he'd been unaware that he could be interested in anything else, because nobody had opened that door to the outside world and he didn't know what he was missing.

Jorge and Alex had shared little more conversation than you would with a neighbour in a lift: in such an inherently individualistic and competitive sport, and with Jorge being as unsociable as he was, the only reason they even exchanged pleasantries was because they shared a manager. But one morning, apparently by coincidence, all that changed and from that moment on – the morning of the 2006 Italian Grand Prix at Mugello – Alex Debón became one of the most important influences on Jorge's career.

4 June 2006, 9.30am
Clinica Mobile, Mugello circuit, Italian GP
THE RETURN OF THE KING

Jorge was starting from pole position and he'd been fastest in the warm-up for the Italian Grand Prix, but something wasn't right. He was having problems with his race tyre and after the first free practice session he'd got off his bike and thrown a tantrum. His helmet had been flung to the ground, everything was 'shit' ... Dani Amatriaín had to reprimand him. At the end of the day, this was still a 19-year-old kid who had been programmed not to lose but hadn't been taught how to confront adversity, yet he found himself in the middle of the battlefield in a war that could not be won.

It was as he negotiated this shakiest of ground that Jorge crossed paths with Debón. Jorge has become a keen reader but he is not a fan of the classics. Nevertheless, he would no doubt agree with the words of the sixteenth-century Spanish poet and playwright, Miguel de Cervantes – 'A single word in time is worth more than a hundred too late' – at least in reference to what was said at that crucial moment in the Clinica Mobile, where Alex was having a massage. The warm-up had just finished and there were only two-and-a-half hours left until the start of the race.

Unusually, it was Jorge who made the first move. 'I said to Alex:

"How's it going? What do you reckon? Nervous?" I don't know why, I just did it. For the sake of speaking, for something to say, not for him to give me any particular answer. But he said, "I'm not nervous." I'm sure he was, because Debón is one of the riders who gets the most nervous. I'd actually seen him vomit before a race in 1998 because of nerves. Although it is true that the more nervous of the two on that day was definitely me. He asked me how I was and I said I wasn't good. I told him I was in the middle of a really shitty situation.'

'Jorge walked in and he looked fucked, pale … he could hardly speak,' recalls Alex. 'His arms were hurting because he was so tense. He couldn't loosen up and things clearly weren't going right for him.' Alex is no psychologist, but he saw something in that face which moved him. 'I told him he didn't look good. I told him he should think of the race as "The Return of the King", that it was the ideal race to start fighting back and that now was the time to start working towards his objective, recovering lost ground.'

Mentally, he was at rock bottom, 'surrounded by chaos' remembers Alex. He spoke to him because Alex is the kind of person who believes that there is a solution to everything – especially for a 19 year old. 'I told him not to worry about anything, that I was going to be in the race because it was one of the four I'd entered as a wildcard that season. "You push on and I'll cover your back," I told him, looking him straight in the eye. "I'll be behind you, like a bodyguard, and I'll help you." '

I still haven't got to the bottom of why Alex Debón decided to comfort Jorge with those words. In fact, he can't even explain it himself. Maybe it was simply because he's a good person, or because it takes a rider like him to understand what it is like to go through a situation like that. What is certain is that he couldn't stand and watch with his arms folded. And where did that phrase 'The Return of the King' come from? Cinema again? Did the *Lord of the Rings* trilogy change the recent history of the 250cc World Championship?

In fact, it was a situation more akin to *Sliding Doors*, with Jorge and Alex coinciding at what was, without doubt, the most important crossroads of Lorenzo's career so far. What would have happened if Alex had never found Jorge? Would he be a double World Champion right now? We'll never know. What we do know is that what happened next now forms part of his legend. Jorge looked him in the eyes for several seconds before his expression suddenly changed – not only his expression, but his state of mind. 'Is this guy for real?' he thought. 'What if he's right?' A lot has been written about Jorge's 'psychological reactions' at decisive moments in his career, and this would be one of the most definitive.

'I remember Alex saying, "When you get to the grid don't think of anything other than 'The Return of the King'. That you are back, that you will return again, and that I will be covering you all the way." But it wasn't as easy as that.' Jorge pauses. His expression is distant. 'It was easy for him to say that but not for him to do it. There were five riders with a chance of running up front and we would all have the knife between our teeth. He wasn't going to take me on, fine, but the others…'

Alex picks up the story. 'We lined up on the grid and looked at each other. Barberá burnt out his clutch. Jorge didn't get a good start but he quickly started to make up positions and I followed him. At about mid-distance he looked back and saw me there, right with him in the leading group.'

That leading group was made up of five riders: Dovizioso, Alex de Angelis, Takahashi, Jorge and Alex. 'I passed him in the second uphill chicane. I pushed on, moved into third place and looked at him,' says Alex. From inside his helmet Debón was trying to tell him to push. As well as his promise of help, there was another important factor which was that Debón, at the behest of his employers, could not finish ahead of Lorenzo. Mugello is an Aprilia circuit and Debón was still only a wildcard, a guest. The visual communication between the pair exploded into life with ten laps to go. 'That was when he reacted, because up to that point he wasn't sure whether to push or not,' says Alex. Jorge realised that he had an ally behind him and thought to himself that maybe what Alex had said to him in the Clinica Mobile was true. 'The guy spoke about "The Return of the King" but he also said he would be right here with me, and here he is.'

'Seeing another red bike there gave him strength,' remembers Alex. Jorge began to make up positions.

But there are two sides to every story and in this one, when Jorge noticed Alex passing him, he saw things very differently. 'I was annoyed when he passed me. I never thought that he would come from behind and make a pass. I had never viewed Alex as a particularly fast rider before. A good one, yes, but when he passed me it kind of dented my pride and I said to myself, "I need to get moving."' Up to that point Jorge had been riding tensely, but he suddenly loosened up. 'With my riding style, the more laps that go by the better I feel. I started passing people and then suddenly it started to spit with rain. That was key, because I realised I was going to have to get a move on or they'd stop the race with me in fifth. I got going and by the final lap I was challenging de Angelis for the win.'

Jorge recalls every move of the race with his hands – one in front of the other, re-enacting the choreography of that fateful day. 'I didn't think I was going to win. I was tucked in behind de Angelis and I'd decided the only way I could beat him was in a drag race to the line, but my bike wasn't fast enough. Luckily he ran wide in the final bend and I thought, "This is mine!" The way I went through that last corner, I don't know how I didn't fall off. If I was at 60 per cent lean on the previous laps, on that one I must have been at 70 per cent … and with more throttle. The bike was moving around all over the place. I took a gamble.'

When you think about it, that final bend at Mugello was also the moment Jorge Lorenzo's life turned a corner. It was all or nothing – the point of no return. He prefers not to think about it now. 'Sometimes I think, "How did I do it? How did I manage to ride so out of control, so loose?" In any case, if you pull off something like that it's because you know you can. I don't think it is a subconscious action. Sometimes I watch things back afterwards and say, "What was I doing? Am I mad?" But when you're on the bike you know what you are capable of. But if you end up crashing, boy do you end up crashing!' And if he had, maybe this story would never have been written.

Debón finished fifth in a race he could conceivably have won, although perhaps more importantly to him he won Jorge's confidence. Shortly after the race they bumped into each other in the team hospitality unit. 'He said "Thank you" and told me that he never imagined somebody would do something like that for him. It hadn't entered his head that a rival would be prepared to do what I had done. Not only encouraging him but actually helping him out on the track. Normally riders fight to the death, and at that time his relationship with [his team-mate] Héctor Barberá was non-existent.'

At the end of the race Jorge felt what he described as 'huge relief'. 'Sometimes when a rider wins they don't appreciate it enough. Maybe he'll say it was easy, forgetting some of the things that have happened or the hold-ups in the race, how hard he had to work to catch the leaders … When you've won a race and you watch it back on the video you can't remember most of that stuff that happened. You think to yourself that if they ran the race again you'd win it just the same because you were the better man, but the reality might be that you only won by a tenth and you have forgotten what you went through. But that day I remembered everything that had happened and I thought to myself that he saved me.'

The story has a happy epilogue, away from the centre of the action. As soon as the race was over, as Jorge crossed the line victorious, Dani Amatriaín jumped down from pit wall, ran across pit lane and charged into the garage, where Marcos had been quietly watching the race, hidden away in a corner. Dani jumped on him and threw his arms around him. 'You can see how big I am,' says Marcos. 'But I couldn't hold Dani up and we both fell into the tyres as we hugged.'

29 October 2006
Ricardo Tormo circuit, Valencia
'WE'VE DONE IT'

'After Italy my attitude completely changed because I could see that we had a chance of getting back on track and winning the championship. It wouldn't be easy, because we still hadn't recovered that many points on Dovizioso – I think we were still 20 or 21 behind – but it was conceivable. And I now had two things clear in my mind, without any shadow of a doubt: first, that I could win without a psychologist and second, that by listening to Dani and Marcos it was possible to turn the championship around.'

Strangely enough, at this point Jorge still wasn't clear what Alex Debón's role was, and it wasn't until two weeks later, at Montmeló, that it finally dawned on him that Alex hadn't spoken to him at Mugello just for the sake of making conversation. 'You know how I realised that he did what he did because he wanted to? Because he really meant it? Because at Catalunya he sacrificed his own race! I qualified second there and I had no pace in the race. I got a bad start and I lost touch with the leading group, but Alex stayed with me. He could have gone with them but he hung back and offered me a tow. Like a pack leader! It was then that I understood what he had been trying to say to me at Mugello.'

Jorge found this very strange because that kind of thing didn't tend to happen to him, but he had seen what kind of person Alex Debón was, how beneficial his influence had been and the evidence spoke for itself. If somebody is capable of thinking quickly and clearly at over 200km/h on a motorcycle, you can only imagine how many thoughts go through their head on the podium. Jorge had begun to mull things over the moment he crossed the finish line, and in the post-race debrief he made his thoughts clear to Amatriaín. 'We have to do something, but this guy has got to stay with me. I don't know what it is but there is something about him and we connect.'

Dani Amatriaín knew straight away what needed to be done. At this stage of the game it wasn't easy for anybody to get on with Jorge like that. 'He asked me to give him a hand because we needed to be World Champions,' remembers Alex. 'That was the priority. "This title simply must be ours," he said. I couldn't turn him down. When a friend asks a favour you have to step up to the plate. I was delighted to do so.'

From that moment the two of them, Jorge and Alex, worked together and spent many intense hours in each other's company. And from the first day the work was not limited to sport – Debón's personality interested Jorge just as much, if not more. They sent SMS messages, hand-written letters, and had online conversations. They traded affectionate insults, calling each other 'Caraburro'

['Donkeyface']. Dani asked Alex to come to all the races, including the ones outside Europe. They went from not knowing each other to sharing the same hotel room. The first time Debón took Amatriaín or Marcos Hirsch's place in the bed next to Jorge's was at Assen; the pair would talk for hours, often staying awake until the early hours of the morning. 'Some of the nicest moments in my life have been spent chatting with Alex in a hotel room somewhere in the middle of the night,' says Jorge.

The Lorenzo–Debón partnership was like a well-matched marriage. Not only did they share victories, and set-up and race strategies, but everything outside motorcycle racing too. Results on the track are often a reflection of a rider's personal life, so the package had to be complete. Alex was always there to listen and to say the right thing at the right time. 'I must admit that when we talked about racing I sometimes thought, "What is this guy going to be able to teach me? I've won seven races and he hasn't even had a podium!" But that thought lasted only a second because I soon saw how much he could teach me, and he really has.'

From Mugello onwards they put together a solid, structured plan. Jorge had already worked with a variety of sports psychologists, but nobody made as much of an impression on him as Marcos and then Alex. The proof was coming in the shape of good results; their challenge for the World Championship would be the acid test. It hadn't been easy but their first chance to clinch the title came in the 2006 Grand Prix of Portugal at Estoril. However, a tyre problem there meant that it would all go down to the wire, to the final round of the season at Valencia, where Alex Debón was again due to race as a wild card.

In practice and warm-up Jorge was okay because he still wasn't feeling the pressure. 'But as the race approached he started tensing up,' remembers Debón. 'I had a dilemma. I felt a responsibility towards Aprilia, to my team, to my sponsor Fortuna and to the team boss Gigi Dall'Igna, but I had to help Jorge.' The message from the factory was clear – do not even think about finishing ahead of Lorenzo. 'But only us riders know how easy it is to say that and how difficult it is to do, because there are another 36 riders out there just like Jorge and myself.'

ABOVE: *Lorenzo (48) en route to victory in the 2008 Grand Prix of Portugal, leading Valentino Rossi (46) and Dani Pedrosa (2) through the chicane at Estoril shortly after outrageously passing Rossi there for the lead.* (Simone Rosa)

BELOW: *With his victory at Estoril, Jorge became the 100th rider to win a premier-class race and the fifth youngest. He was also the youngest rider in MotoGP history to chalk up three premier-class podiums, taking the record from Dani Pedrosa by a single day.* (Simone Rosa)

ABOVE: *Jorge honed his skills on the wastelands of Palma de Mallorca, riding 'a mish-mash of a bike' built by his father.* (JL family collection)

BELOW: *Jorge wasn't even four years old when he competed, without a licence, in his first official race at Palma – a round of the Balearic Motocross Championship.* (JL family collection)

ABOVE: *At the family minibike circuit his father taught him how to stop without brakes by folding the front outwards.* (JL family collection)

BELOW: *Jorge lines up for a school photograph at La Milagrosa with his trademark Mohican.* (JL family collection)

ABOVE: *Dani Amatriaín spotted Jorge at the Jerez round of the 50cc Copa Aprilia in 1997 and was bowled over by his talent.* (JL family collection)

BELOW: *Jorge shakes hands with Giampiero Sacchi, Sporting Director of the Piaggio Group, after signing to contest the 125cc World Championship with Derbi in 2002. On his 15th birthday he qualified for the Spanish Grand Prix at Jerez, despite missing the opening day of practice because at 14 he was still too young.* (JL family collection)

ABOVE: *Jorge's career has always been a family affair and his father Chicho, mother María and sister Laura all sacrificed a lot. 'Everything we earned, which wasn't much, was spent on racing,' says María.* (JL family collection)

BELOW: *In 2002 Jorge felt the urge to reconnect with Mallorca and got in touch with some of his old friends from La Milagrosa, including Dani Palau (foreground)* (JL family collection)

ABOVE: *After winning the first two races of 2006, Jorge's personal problems began to transfer onto the track. He crashed three times in three days at Le Mans, including this collision in the race with Roberto Locatelli (15), which left him fifth in the championship – 29 points adrift of Andrea Dovizioso.* (Simone Rosa)

ABOVE: *With title rival Andrea Dovizioso only able to manage fourth, seventh place is enough for Jorge to clinch the 2006 250cc World Championship in the final round at Valencia, here his physical trainer Marcos Hirsch had dressed up as his 'double' along with Jorge's father Chicho.* (JL Family Collection)

ABOVE: *In order to improve his wet-weather skills, Jorge headed to California at the end of the 2006 season for some dirt-track training with three-times 500cc World Champion Kenny Roberts at his Modesto ranch.* (JL Family Collection)

BELOW: *Jorge celebrates victory at the Australian Grand Prix, although the title celebrations would have to wait another week.* (Simone Rosa)

ABOVE: *Up until 2008, riding in the wet had always been Jorge's Achilles heel and the 2007 British Grand Prix at Donington Park proved no exception as a promising race ended with a crash in front of title rival Dovizioso.* (Simone Rosa)

LEFT: *Jorge opened his title defence with back-to-back wins in Qatar and Spain.* (Simone Rosa)

ABOVE RIGHT: *Jorge combined business with pleasure at the 2007 US Grand Prix at Laguna Seca , working as a guest television commentator on the MotoGP race for TVE alongside Alex Crivillé and Ernest Riveras whilst behind the scenes the final touches were put on his contract with Yamaha for 2008.* (Simone Rosa)

RIGHT: *Having left Mallorca at a young age Jorge now takes every opportunity he can to get back there and relax, with or without company!*
(JL Family Collection)

Jorge hated working out in the gym during the early stages of his career but it is now one of his favourite parts of the job. His physical trainer Marcos Hirsch once told him, 'Don't worry, Jorge. If this whole racing thing doesn't work out, with the body I've given you, you can have a career in porn.'
(Emilio Pérez de Rozas collection)

2007 MotoGP World Champions

ABOVE: *Valencia 2007: Jorge celebrates his second consecutive 250cc title alongside 125cc and MotoGP World Champions Gabor Talmacsi and Casey Stoner.* (Simone Rosa)

LEFT: *The world's worst kept secret. Jorge signed a pre-contract agreement with Yamaha at Motegi on 24 September 2006 but the deal was not officially confirmed until 27 July 2007.*
(Yamaha Motor Racing)

BELOW: *A year on from his debacle at Le Mans in 2006, Jorge (1) leads Álvaro Bautista (19), Alex de Angelis (3), Thomas Lüthi (12), Mika Kallio (36), Andrea Dovizioso (34) and the rest of the 250cc field on his way to a fourth victory from the opening five races of a dominant campaign.* (Simone Rosa)

After a stunning start to his rookie MotoGP season, Jorge came back to earth with a bump in this sensational crash during practice for the 2008 Grand Prix of China. (Dorna)

Rookie rumble: Lorenzo had his hands full with James Toseland (52) and Andrea Dovizioso (4) in the battle for the Rookie of the Year title. Here they lead Shinya Nakano (56) at the Australian GP. (Andrew Northcott)

Above: *Jorge began preseason testing on the 2009 version Yamaha YZR-M1 at Sepang, Malaysia, wearing his new number 99 for the first time. His decision to switch from the number 48, given to him by his former manager Dani Amatriaín, was symbolic of his new-found freedom after an acrimonious split.* (Yamaha Motor Racing)

Below: *The preseason programme continued with a night test at Losail, Qatar, where Jorge finished second fastest behind Casey Stoner. Afterwards he commented: 'If I can stay injury-free and don't have bad luck, and if the bike goes well, then I can aspire to win races this season – more than just one.'* (Yamaha Motor Racing)

The tactics were planned in detail by Dani Amatriaín, as usual, and the message from him was simple: 'Block Dovizioso so that Jorge can win.' No more, no less. Debón got a good start but Jorge wasn't making progress. He wasn't passing anybody, he wasn't moving forward but he wasn't moving backwards either. Panic started to set in: 'Dovizioso passed two or three riders and the track opened up for him to escape.' It was the moment of truth. Alex passed Jorge, passed Dovi and tried to slow the Italian down.

The words rang out from the circuit's PA system: 'Debón tapón, Debón tapón, Debón carrerón, Debón que tapón!' ['Debón blocks, Debón blocks, what a race from Debón, what a block from Debón!'] 'The Honda was really fast and the only way to stop the guy [Dovizioso] was to brake in the corners.' Finally Jorge reacted. He came through the pack, passed Debón and made his escape. 'Meanwhile, I continued to block Dovi, the pair of us losing two or three tenths of a second a lap. By the end Jorge was a few seconds in front.' De Angelis won the race, Jorge was fourth, Debón fifth and Dovizioso seventh. Lorenzo was crowned 250cc World Champion! 'We've done it!' everybody shouted together.

December 2006, Badalona
DEFENDING THE TITLE

Working in Jorge's shadow Alex Debón won the respect of a lot of people, not least the new World Champion, while the esteem in which he was held by Dani Amatriaín went through the roof thanks to the contribution he had made to 'their' world title. Aprilia were also delighted to have such an effective and well-disciplined test rider. Debón finished the 2006 season as their talisman. 'In December 2006 I told Dani that for the next season I wanted to focus on development of the Aprilia RSA but Dani said no, he said I had to continue in my role with him, but this time working not only with Jorge but with Pol Espargaró too. I had wanted to quit working with one and ended up with two!'

'You've got balls, you're a worker – you can do it, you'll see,' Dani told him, and so Alex accepted. It's a well-known saying that it is relatively easy to get to the top; the difficult thing is staying there. So the challenge for Jorge, and Alex, couldn't have been any bigger and the sacrifices to be made were huge. Ahead of them was a season at full throttle, with no time for holidays and not a day without motorcycles. It was a major decision that came with a degree of responsibility only a man like Debón could assume. Alex decided to start 2007 with a letter to his friend, the new World Champion.

The year of the double begins
Letter from Alex Debón
THE NUMBER 1

The number 1 is not just the result of a job done. The number 1 is the result of a job WELL done. To wear the number 1 is a source of pride but at the same time it is something that can make us view life in a negative way if we don't stop to consider the change it has brought us. The number 1 should bring security, tranquillity, motivation. Achieving the number 1 represents a time of reflection for any rider. Every rider wants to see himself there and that's what everybody fights for every day. Some, like me, will never reach it.

You have achieved something massive but you are still not the number 1 in many things. In believing in yourself, in having confidence, in transmitting confidence, in assuming your responsibilities. In applying yourself fully to the job, assuming all of the risks that your chosen line of work involves – a line of work that has given you everything and in which you have nobody and nothing to fear – crashes and all … You are the icon of a society that changes over time, every single day, but you will never win anything on your own. Only good people – highly trained professionals – achieve the results you are aiming for.

You don't feed anybody but there are a lot of families who eat off the work that is done for you, putting up with you everyday. Because you're not exactly good looking!

Keep your feet on the ground. Today you are the champion but tomorrow you will still be Jorge. An ugly fellow with money and friends who are only interested for as long as the money lasts. Look after your people. Take an interest in how they feel, how they get up in the morning, how their families are, if they are well or are in pain. Look after the little details that make people get up in the morning ready to take on any challenge, however difficult it may be. That is when you see a person, when you see a champion. That is when you see the true number 1.

You are a person, champ, but to me you will still be Jorge, the same person you were in 2006. My friend, a great person, an ugly fellow. To me, your friend Alex, the most important thing is that you grow as a person. I couldn't give a shit if you set pole or win a race. As a person it gives me great personal satisfaction that you value every moment by my side, alongside your people, alongside the people who care for you on a daily basis. Because one day you will finish racing and as well as a great champion there will be a great person, with great friends, and when you need them they will be there.

This is the price of fame. The price you have to pay around here, one of the many sacrifices you have to make. But in the end you'll appreciate it and you'll see for yourself how special every moment can be and enjoy the personal satisfaction it brings.

Grateful ... being number 1 means being grateful. Being noble, to yourself and to those around you. It is getting up in the morning and thanking God for being who you are, for everything he has given you and that which is still to come. Thank the people who have made it possible for you to become number 1, who make the effort every day to ensure that you remain number 1. 'I'm the best and everybody can suck my dick,' is no good to me. That would be a mistake.

So what is number 1? Being number 1 is the fruit of a lot of hard work, ambition, recompense. We're going to work hard, non-stop. Trying to weigh up every little detail, every situation, and know how to control the things within our control even if that might not really be the case.

Pixie, I'll tell you what we're going to do, starting today. We're going to forget about girls. We're going to work flat out to get to the first race and start opening up clear ground. We're going to start dreaming about that number 1. That bastard number 1. We're going to look into each other's eyes and I'm going to see that gaze I love so much. We're going to set the bike up and have fun on it. We're going to thank the mechanics for their work. We're going to forget about designs, interviews, photos and other bullshit. We're going to be Jorge Lorenzo. We're going to wear the number 1 and accept the challenge. We're going to take our place and respect our rivals.

And remember. Between the no. 1 and the 'no use at all' we are World Champions. Between thinking we've won and going out defeated, we are close to our objective. We're ready to start. We're ready to do it all again.

Jorge Lorenzo knows that sitting in the front row at the cinema is the worst place from which to see a film. It took the Debón formula to convince him that occasionally seating yourself a few rows back in life can give you a better perspective on what is going on around you, and his achievements so far are a sign that he has taken things on board.

Once you have reached number one status you realise that what initially seemed like the ultimate objective is nothing but another step forward, because the job isn't finished. It is not a case of simply parading that number, because it is actually a number full of numbers: the hours of hard work, the bad times, thousands of right and wrong decisions, and many, many people. That number 1 plate provided a great opportunity to hand out another lesson to the champion, one that would allow him to continue to grow. It was the right time, the best time for a born winner like Jorge, to make him see that he didn't win on his own, he won thanks to his people, and thanks to his bike. It was time to make the switch from me to we.

Every word of Alex's letter must have struck a chord inside Jorge – it was purposeful and resonant, the key to the success of the Debón therapy. Before each message, each letter that he sent, Alex would spend a lot of time in deep thought, choosing the right terms. The system he used to work with Jorge was done in concurrence with Dani Amatriaín. 'During my life I have often skipped the chain of command,' says Debón. 'Here, each step has been discussed, deliberated over and perfected before being transmitted to the rider.'

Mugello, June 2007
BEFORE AND AFTER

During the education of a champion the phrase 'let him learn from his own mistakes' is applied with a regularity that is directly proportional to his success. In other words, the more Jorge matured as a rider and the more his confidence was reinforced by his victories, the more decisions Dani Amatriaín and the team allowed him to take for himself – even though they knew for certain, at times, that his decisions were the wrong ones.

One such instance came during qualifying practice for the Italian Grand Prix at Mugello in 2007. It is no secret that Jorge used not to be a fan of riding in the wet (that all changed at Indianapolis, in 2008, when he finished third and would almost certainly have passed Nicky Hayden for second if the red flags hadn't come out seven laps from the end). As black clouds began to form on the horizon in Italy he decided to gamble on it not raining and waited in his pit box for the skies to clear. The rest of the riders went flat out to post fast laps, with the television footage cutting back to an unflustered Jorge – smiling, confident, absolutely sure of himself. Provocative, even. Until the rain came. Then the panic set in.

2 June 2007
Extract from a text written by Jorge Lorenzo entitled:
'IN SEARCH OF GLORY'

It has been a difficult day. I find myself laid out on the bed in my hotel room. As I reflect on what has happened, my mind cannot escape thoughts of tomorrow. The hope of a possible miracle, a possible victory, lifts my sadness a little. Could I really still win or am I being too optimistic? In any case, I'm going to go to sleep thinking that tomorrow could be a great day for us…

It is Sunday, race day. On my arrival at the Clinica Mobile for my traditional back massage, I bump into Toni Elías. He tells me that a few years ago he went through a similar situation and he was so desperate to make up positions that he made some mistakes and it cost him a place on the podium. 'But is it possible to win?' I asked him. 'Yes, of course. But don't be too hasty at the start, it is a long race and if you have the pace you'll get there,' he answered. Will he be right?

Well, almost! Lorenzo started from 20th on the grid and he battled through into the lead until a crash on the final lap, following a collision with Álvaro Bautista, ruined what could have been the all-time greatest comeback in 250cc history. He didn't win, it's true, but what is equally certain is that he had changed his mindset and his approach. Alex's positive message had hit home. Debón wasn't with him at the track on that occasion, so he kept in touch by email.

2 June 2007, Mugello
MESSAGE FROM ALEX DEBÓN AFTER FIRST FREE PRACTICE

Today was a great day, Jorge. Finally I think we are closing in on the objective we set ourselves at Jerez in January, the one we made strides towards at Can Padró and at last we, or should I say you, have reached today at Mugello.

Today I have to congratulate you. Your people, your mechanics and the media have done the same and I think you have seen a change in yourself, in your confidence. I read in an interview that a World Champion is not a champion but a race winner in the wet. Today you showed why you are number 1.

This self-esteem and the will to improve, as well as the attitude we spoke about last Friday night, will give you strength through difficult times and it is then you will learn what it is to be WORLD CHAMPION.

I know that a lot of things worry you – about your environment and your people. I'm bringing everything I know to the table and trying to steer the ship to a calm port. Maybe I'm getting involved in things that aren't my responsibility but I promised Dani I would help him and I will see it through to the end. You continue to show everybody, including me, that you are on the right path, you are maturing and we will resolve the issues that worry you one by one. All I ask for is a little patience.

Today you showed that you are competitive in the wet and that is another blow to the other riders. More than one of them, as you know and as we have discussed, won't be able to sleep like I can, spending every second trying to improve. We have completed the first part of the season together. We're at the sixth round and in the perfect position. We put new batteries in some months ago and in Barcelona I will help you recharge them for the second half of the championship…

If you get a good start in the race then push over the first five laps, check your pit board and keep the men behind you under control. DOVI DOES NOT LIKE THIS CIRCUIT, we know that, but he will be going all out because this is his home race. Maybe if we push him he will slip up and we will leave here even stronger, but you don't have anything to prove to anybody.

REMEMBER:
Between number 1 and 'no use at all' we are still world champions. This is where your journey began. This is where we witnessed the return of the king. This is where we built what is now a strong team, a rider with motivation and attitude, a rider who transmits joy within his own box and cares for his own people. This is where we began a sex-free love affair, dickhead! This is where the future number 1 of Spanish motorcycle racing was born.

Be smart, play your cards right and above all do not drop your guard. It is the others who have to take risks to overturn the number 1. Our job is to keep building and that is what allows you to think about what you are doing on the bike. Positioning yourself on the handlebars, shifting your weight across the tank and on the footpegs. That is what riding is all about and that is what you know how to do best, big nose…

Dovi is going to show you the wheels of his Honda and try to make you nervous over the first few laps so that you make a mistake. But you have the bike and the pace to fight back. Remember China and France. Arrive, get ready and get through it without taking unnecessary risks. Waiting to see what happens would be a mistake.

Get to the final lap with an advantage and remember that if Dovi is anywhere near he will close his eyes and go for you like he did in France, where he did the last lap without using his brakes and set a 38.5. That's

199

called 'going for victory'. Watch out for de Angelis but if you can break free from the start and put some ground between yourself and them they will fight it out with Barberá and Bautista.

If you have a problem and there is something up with the bike do not panic and just finish the race with as many points as possible, which is the best thing for the championship. And when you get back, don't kick off with the mechanics. They give their best and racing is racing.

With this I want to remind you of how much you have matured and of how much of a professional Jorge Lorenzo is when it comes to his job. He knows all too well, as we have said so many times, that when everything is in its place then we are in ours. That is what you call being ready for (god willing it won't happen) defeat.

The last thing I will say is that I'm sorry I'm not at this race. On Sunday my best friend gets married and the best present I could offer him was to be there for him, since I missed his stag party and a second party held for friends. From here I want to thank you and assure you of this: JUST BECAUSE YOU CAN'T SEE ME DOES NOT MEAN I AM NOT THERE.

I will be watching on the television and on the Internet. I'll call you in the evening and we can speak. My phone is always on and if you have any doubt or worry then call me any time. If not, then good luck buddy. At least now at night you'll be able to knock a couple out without having to wait for your room-mate to fall asleep, ha, ha!

HALA. A KISS, BIG NOOOOOOOOOOOOOOOOOOOOOOOOOOSE

2007 season
'HAVE YOU SEEN MY CRYSTAL BALL?'

Jorge has got used to listening to Alex. 'Now, if I don't say something to him he thinks everything has gone badly. He needs to see a reaction from me so that he knows he's not on his own. But you can't hand everything to him on a plate either. He needs to mature and make his own mistakes. Otherwise, he won't appreciate each moment.' Jorge went from not listening to, or confiding in, virtually anybody to valuing the opinions and assurances of professionals and people he respected.

'Alex helped me a lot. He brought me a lot of calm, especially in terms of second-guessing what will happen in a race. He'd say things like, "Dovizioso is really strong here and I think he's going to try and escape" or "Dovizioso is looking good but I think he'll try and follow you. De Angelis has no rhythm so he'll put a soft tyre on to try and escape over the first five laps but then he'll slow down." Or he might say, "So-and-so is good on the brakes, so-and-so isn't, but you'll be able to leave them over the last five laps." He'd basically tell me what he thought was going to happen in a race and he was always right! The first time was at Assen. He said, "Today you've got to try and escape and nobody will stay with you." That's exactly what happened!'

Jorge had had to wait until the end of the 2007 season for Alex to get it wrong. 'I wanted to throw it back in his face, he couldn't be infallible, but the bastard always got it right. He'd sometimes say, "Tomorrow you're going to surprise yourself" and I'd rub my hands thinking, "Yeah, right, I'll have you this time." I'd say, "OK, let's see!" but then the next day I won with a far bigger advantage than I'd expected. It was pretty impressive.'

Some Saturday nights, on the eve of a race, Alex would switch roles from psychologist to veteran rider, handing out advice to his young charge. It was this flexibility that set him apart from any of Jorge's other advisers. 'Alex also helped me from a technical point of view, as a rider,' recalls Jorge. 'He showed me how to prepare to overtake. I used to get up behind somebody and didn't know how to wait for the right corner, the right moment. He used to say, "If you get a bad start and you're fourth, take it easy. At the end of the back straight, prepare yourself, get in the slipstream and then as you brake for the corner, bang! Pull to his right, stick the bike in there and take his line so that he can't fight back. And if you have to, get your elbow out…" ' Jorge laughs heartily. 'He always used to say that – "Get your elbow out." I didn't do it, though. Alex used to do it, but I didn't dare.'

Alex's predictions would turn into self-fulfilling prophecies. The more accurate his guesses, the more Jorge believed them and the more confident and well prepared he would be for the races. And the more confident he became, the more daring Alex would be with his predictions. 'When you have already experienced something in your mind, already visualised it, it becomes more easy to carry out in reality. It's like you've already been there, you know what to do, what you are capable of. Improvisation doesn't tend to work out well, especially in sport.'

But the day Alex Debón left Jorge absolutely and completely amazed was before the San Marino GP in 2007. 'Now this is heavy. Alex told me that sooner or later Dovizioso was going to break down. "If you ask me, Dovizioso has got to slip up sometime," he told me. "And I think it will be here." And it happened, at San Marino! After that he used to say, "Have you seen my crystal ball? What do you think to the crystal ball?" '

September 2007
LETTER FROM ALEX TO JORGE BEFORE THE SAN MARINO GP

Now it's time to get down to business, we've got a lot of work to do and I think you're stronger than ever. We have six races left until the end of term – six exams to pass and since you're such a good student you won't want to have to repeat a year because if you do TEACHER ALEX WILL CHOP YOUR BALLS OFF! So listen up.

30 points to Dovi
40 to de Angelis
89 to Bautista
113 to Barberá

Now we're going to a track which is home to the Italian gayboys chasing us in the championship. De Angelis fucked it up last time out at Brno and he's going to want to win. According to what he said in an interview recently he's out of the championship now but he wants to win races and that means he'll be giving everything. And he'll probably screw it up ... like in Germany, Brno and England, where he screwed it up.

Dovi could be more dangerous but I still think he'll slip up before the end of the season and since I think it so much it won't be long before it happens … without wishing bad things on anybody.

We're going to stick to the goal we set ourselves back in December with Dani, which I think is the best way and it hasn't exactly turned out badly so far. Your bike has been working well in the last few races and that's the way it will stay until the end of the year.

I don't want to think about the title yet, or next season, because we still have these exams to get out of the way and we are going to pass them all with flying colours, I'm sure of that. But we cannot afford to let our guard down and we have to keep working as we have done up to now to make sure Dani and yourself get your just rewards.

I think it is the right path to follow because from now on they're going to start with the same old stories. About winning the title here or there, the number of poles or wins, about Bautista's new bike … anything to put you off your game.

We have a title-winning bike that is running well, a dedicated and devoted team of staff and a kid who continues to surprise his boss. SO FROM HERE, FROM THE TOWN OF LA VALLLLLL, I'M TELLING YOU TO CONTINUE TO ENJOY WHAT YOU DO, WHICH IS WINNNNNNNNNNNN, BIG NOSE!

Love

Alex

Forecasting that de Angelis would have a bad race, even at his home track, was nothing out of the ordinary considering that he had won just one race in nine years of World Championship competition. However, the Dovizioso prediction was unlikely, to say the least. 125cc World Champion in 2004, and stepping up to 250s at the same time as Jorge, in 2005, Andrea had recently completed a consecutive run of 31 points-scoring races. Only Luca Cadalora had a longer record in the 58-year history of the category. But Alex was convinced Dovi, Lorenzo's greatest rival, would break down in San Marino, and he did. That crystal ball…

German GP, Sachsenring circuit
'ISIDISI' ['AC/DC']

Over the course of the 2007 season Jorge Lorenzo scored 12 podiums from 17 races, including 9 victories from pole position. He was crowned World Champion before the end of the season and in general everything went well, if not perfectly. However, there were some bad moments, such as the collision with Álvaro Bautista at Mugello, the crash at Donington when he was having the best race of his life, and the tyre problem in Japan. Oh, and Germany!

We have been strong during difficult times and that is how we will be World Champions again. The evidence was at the German GP, where I was very concerned about the situation and where we could have come away defeated and badly damaged. Because your rider was not in good shape – neither concentrated nor convinced. And the bike, as you know, was not running at 100 per cent. But in the end we were strong and we will stay strong in search of our objective. (Extract from a letter from Alex Debón to Dani Amatriaín, shortly after the 2007 German GP)

Jorge finished fourth in the 2007 German GP. At any other time that would have been considered a bad result, but not this time. It wasn't just because his great rival, Dovizioso, finished behind him but also because Jorge had started to really understand that certain battles have to be sacrificed in order to win the war. Above all, he had stopped thinking: 'What if?'

'I like to have my own ideas and discuss them. To know the reason behind things and to be sure that I am not wrong.' It was a statement of intent from Jorge and it serves to take us back to the 2006 German GP, exactly one year before. Jorge's recurring fear had been that they would get the race strategy wrong. Each of his biggest worries started with the words 'What if…?' 'What if we do this instead of that? What if we do that instead of this? What if I crash, what if I don't have a good race pace, what if Dovizioso chooses different tyres, what if they are better than me, what if it rains…?' Alex had had enough of his insecurities. With so many 'What ifs', he never had anything clear in his mind. 'I was relying on chance,' recalls Jorge. 'That's why I had so many doubts over whether we were doing the right thing; because I thought everything happened by chance.'

'I got so fed up with it,' says Alex, his eyes as big as Valencian oranges. 'There were so many nights when we were awake until two in the morning speculating about what might happen that I said to myself, "That's it. As of tomorrow this guy is not going to say, 'What if' ['Y si', in Spanish] ever again." I decided to buy myself an AC/DC [pronounced 'Isidisi'] in Spain) T-shirt and pin badge. I said to Dani, "Today I'm not wearing a Fortuna shirt or any team uniform. This has to be done! The sponsors shouldn't mind but if there's a fine I'll pay it, don't worry." '

Alex turned up in the team's garage dressed as Angus Young, the singer from AC/DC, and smiled at Jorge. 'He cracked up laughing but I handed him an identical T-shirt and badge. He said I'd gone totally crazy but I told him, if you want to lose the "Y si", then have some "Isidisi"! ' Jorge put the T-shirt on and as the pair laughed together the atmosphere in the garage relaxed. When they took the shirts off, Alex insisted that Jorge keep the badge on for the rest of the weekend.

That way, whenever he thought 'Y si', it would be there to remind him to have faith. 'After four days he stopped doubting himself and after that if I told him something was white he believed it was white – but because it was white, not because I said so. I totally won his confidence that day and after that my opinion was more important to him than any other. I taught him only to worry about the things he could control. Everything else, he just has to put up with.'

4 November 2007, 13.00pm
Ricardo Tormo circuit, Valencia
WHAT GOES AROUND

Alex Debón arrived at Valencia, his home circuit, ready to make the final race of the 2007 season his own. He was entering as a wild card. Since Jorge had already been crowned 2007 World Champion there were no team orders of any kind, unlike the previous year. It was time to round off the season and achieve the last of the five targets he had set himself at the start of the year. The first four were already in the bag: to become a fast rider respected by Aprilia; to develop the RSA into a race-winning bike; for Pol Espargaró to finish on the 125cc podium (third place in Portugal); and for Jorge to win his second title.

His first four targets had been successfully accomplished, but the most difficult and, for a perfectionist like him, the most important was still to come. Alex wanted to finish on the podium for the first time in his career and, at the age of 31, he achieved it, clinching third place ahead of Dovizioso in one of those strange coincidences that life throws up. The rider he'd blocked in 2006 to help out his friend was also the rider he beat for his first rostrum – the highlight of a race that saw Jorge finish seventh in his final 250cc appearance.

The pillars of the Alex–Jorge relationship are built on solid foundations. 'Firstly, I have always been straight with him. Secondly, whether he wins races or sets pole, as a fellow rider I couldn't care less. "I am your friend and I am not looking to benefit from you," I told him. "I'm here because I'm here and I'm here to do you a favour. But I'm a rider and I don't care if you win because if I could I would beat you." '

Debón's competitive spirit was in full flow at Valencia, where he almost took the stickers off Jorge's bike with one of his more aggressive passes. It was easy to see what they were both up to. Alex was desperate to earn himself a ride for 2008 and he was baring his teeth, while Jorge knew at exactly what time he'd be making his MotoGP debut on the following day and had been more concerned about whether he had enough passes for his friends, which hotel they could stay in and how they'd get into the track than today's race.

In a way, everything ended as it had started the year before – decided by fate. After the race Jorge went to congratulate Alex and at the podium ceremony their traditional roles were reversed. Alex stood beneath his country's flag with tears in his eyes as the World Champion stood below, applauding alongside the mechanics.

'Several things dawned on Jorge at that moment,' reflects Alex.

'He was applauding a guy who had given up a lot for him and he realised how the story had changed ... how you see a podium one way from the inside and another way from the outside. That applause at Valencia, and the hug he'd given me in Malaysia after winning the World Championship, were the best form of payback for me and the icing on the cake after our two-year "project". They meant much more than words.'

December 2007
THE END OF THE ROAD?

The Debón–Lorenzo project had been a meticulous, elaborate operation, and it took hours and hours of work behind the scenes to produce those spectacular results. Writing, talking ... Alex was not just any old psychologist whom Jorge would visit for an hour and sit on a couch. There was no 'Let's meet from four until five and talk it over.' 'My job was to be with him 24 hours a day, talking about anything that came up and trying to get messages across. Messages that a rider can understand. It worked well for me because all I did was try to apply my own life experiences.'

'I have won races without Alex,' adds Jorge. 'Nobody could say that I wouldn't have won if it wasn't for him, because I had already won at Jerez and Qatar before we met. But he was fundamental in several things: my race strategy, visualising the race on the day before, preparing overtaking moves, keeping me company and making accurate predictions. He is also a very optimistic person. In a lot of races he was shitting himself, he didn't have a clue. But he never told me, he never let me doubt myself. Even though he would admit it afterwards!'

On the way back from the trip to Australia and Malaysia, with the second title in the bag, Alex had a conversation with Dani Amatriaín. Jorge had spent the whole trip asking, 'What about next year? I'm going to be in MotoGP and I want Alex with me. He calms me down and opens me up to different perspectives. How are we going to do it?' But Debón had a huge dilemma. He had been given the opportunity of a lifetime – the chance to join the front line had arrived with the offer of a full-time factory ride in 2008. 'The opportunity had come late and I wanted to put everything I had into taking it. I don't want anybody to be able to say that I didn't try. I will give everything I have and if somebody beats me it will be because he is the better man, not because I haven't given my all.'

As it turned out, Alex won two 250cc races in 2008 and finished fourth in the championship.

Text written by Jorge Lorenzo entitled:
'TO MY SUCCESSOR'

I have wanted to write this down for some time now but for one reason or another – whether I have come up with a more simple subject or because I simply didn't know how to start – I have put it off and put it off. But I think the time has arrived. This letter is dedicated to my adviser, my confidant and my friend, Alex Debón, a man with one of the biggest hearts in the paddock to whom I owe much more than this column. An extrovert like few others, he has natural charisma. A charm and natural self-confidence that allows him to easily win you over and gain your confidence. A Don Juan who had to cut off his own ponytail for love. How touching!

AN EXPERIENCE THAT WILL BE TWO SIZES TOO BIG FOR US
As you know, next year we both start a new adventure. At the age of 31 the opportunity of your lifetime has finally arrived. It's a little late, that is true, but as they say, 'Better late than never...' How a certain somebody we both know would love to have the bike you have for next season! A new experience is laid out before our eyes. A difficult experience. An experience that at the start will be two sizes too big for us. An experience we yearn for and fear in equal measures. An experience full of risks and complications but at the same time an experience that, like a tree, will bear fruit if it is properly watered. And, my dear friend Alex, you know a lot about that. Not literally, caraburro ... you know what I mean.

BE GENTLE WITH MY BIKE

Ah! A piece of advice: be gentle with 'my bike', she works best that way. Let her take you. Don't force her, don't try to dominate her, she's not Japanese...

I FEEL NOSTALGIC

Anyway ... I know it is not normal for a kid ten years younger than you to be dishing out advice, but you have to understand that I only have four races left with my 'beloved Italian' and the truth is that I feel a little ... nostalgic? Yes, that's the word. We've had too many unforgettable times together not to feel that way.

I'LL BE YOUR NUMBER ONE FAN

If we are lucky and we take the title beforehand, Cheste will be our final battle as rivals. From then on I will be your number one fan. A fan who will never ask for an autograph (not because I don't admire you but because I have never done it before) but who hopes that sooner rather than later your dream will become reality.

From a friend who loves you. Jorge.

Marcos Hirsch and Alex Debón admit that Jorge was a different man before 2006 – he was unfriendly and he didn't even trust his own shadow. Clearly it is in great part thanks to both of them that the Jorge Lorenzo of 2008 became a star both on and off the track – 'X-fuera y 'X-dentro' ['around the outside and on the inside'] – or, at the very least, a star with nothing to fear.

4

OPENING THE THROTTLE

It's 'LorenShow' time

Not all of Jorge Lorenzo's objectives for 2007 were as obvious and as public as winning his second World Championship. He also wanted to share the joy of winning with his team and with his fans.

The season started for him at the Auditorio de la Casa de América de Madrid. It was 30 January 2007, the presentation of the Fortuna Aprilia Team, when the new RSW250 would be unveiled, adorned with the golden-winged number 1 designed by Jorge himself. As well as changing a paper number 48 into a number 1, the magician Lucas Di Giacomo made the bike appear out of a wooden box to the tune of 'Final Countdown' by Europe. The presentation was a sign of things to come...

In March Jorge's media coach, Miguel Ángel Violán, organised a conference with students from the Barcelona Business Administration School (EAE). It would be an important part of Lorenzo's media training with Violán, who wanted his charge to face an audience he didn't know, who might catch him out. Jorge obviously had a lot of faith in his coach by this point, and for his part Violán felt the racer's image as an uncommunicative loner was already deceptive. It was time to widen his horizons and step things up a notch. 'You'll be speaking in front of a select audience, different from what you're used to. It is a business school and it won't be a small group.'

'Sounds great. How many will there be? Four hundred, five hundred?'

'Jorge! There'll be fifty!'

In a discussion entitled 'Why I like to race', Jorge won over a responsive audience with answers like, 'Smiling is fundamental', 'I try to be a different rider, special, and I would like to be unique' and 'My dream is to be the best rider in history. I want to continue giving the fans something to celebrate, like in my last race.' It would obviously be unfair to take phrases out of context, because they don't make as much sense when removed from the situation and ambience in which they were spoken, at the conference, but they do at least serve as an example of Jorge's approach and his intentions at the start of the 2007 season, and they were certainly a reflection of how different his preparations had been compared to any previous campaign. At the end of the discussion, Oscar Coduras, Director of the MBA Sport Management course at EAE, dubbed him Dr 'Velocitatis Causa' [a person who has a mission for speed] and Jorge was more than happy to put on the cap and gown and accept his honorary degree.

'He's very much a "Let's get on with it" kind of person,' recalls Miguel Ángel. 'He was lively, fun, daring and displaying that touch of aggressiveness that he always has. The kids left there delighted, with a really good image of Jorge aside from his sporting success. If he put his mind to it, he could be a snake charmer! And when they dressed him in the gown and cap I saw real happiness on his face.' It was only a small detail, but for Jorge, who had left school at the age of 14, it was recognition that he was starting to make up for lost time.

The 2007 season was edging nearer and Lorenzo's plans for it were starting to emerge. Jorge's spontaneous reactions to his previous successes and failures had made him a few enemies, and he wasn't convinced by the negative view that 'You can't please everybody', as he'd been told on many occasions. All he wanted was to have some fun and for people to join in that fun. He had a new take on racing now, and his attitude was more focused, but he wanted people not to judge him harshly when he was just behaving like any happy, excitable young 20 year old.

When he pulls off one of his trademark 'X-fuera' ['around the outside'] moves, or any other of the equally spectacular stunts that set him apart from his rivals, he wants his skill to be recognised – 'like they used to with Kevin Schwantz'. But the only recognition that comes Jorge's way tends to be negative, purely because of who he is. 'If you were Swedish, for instance, everyone in your country would be sucking up to you,' somebody once told him. 'But here anybody who admits to having feelings and who is prepared to do things differently is frowned upon. People need to side with and against somebody.' Jorge is a born fighter, though, and he wanted and needed to win over the public. If his achievements on the track weren't enough to do that, then he would try to make up for it with some fun celebrations that would let everybody know that, more than anything else, Jorge Lorenzo was a witty and entertaining young man.

Jordi Pérez, Fortuna Aprilia team co-ordinator at the time, said: 'Some people say: "Look how funny that footballer is playing the bongos!" The next minute they're saying: "It's about time he stopped playing the bongos and started scoring goals." ' Jorge was well aware of the risk he was running in putting on a show after each win, but while it has been said of him that he is shy, never let it be said that he is scared.

'MY ONLY RIVAL LAST YEAR WORE NUMBER 48 AND THIS YEAR HE'S WEARING NUMBER 1'

During his career, Jorge Lorenzo has come out with enough pearls of wisdom in front of the microphones to make a necklace. The above statement is just one example of the headlines he constantly offers to journalists. Jorge and his advisers actually believe that he has more media pull in Italy than in Spain, because it is not easy to be a prophet in your own land. Despite all his best efforts and intentions, this is something with which Lorenzo has had to come to terms. He is often misunderstood but doesn't want things to remain that way, so he will continue to fight on, and more especially off, the track, in order to change people's perceptions of him.

Jorge is fiercely determined both in his racing and his life. Nobody knows if he was born with that quality or learnt to be that way, but he refuses to be beaten by the intolerance of his critics. In trying to be accepted by everybody, he is constantly looking for new ways to achieve that recognition. He has taken classes in public speaking to try and improve his relationship with the media and the public, even going as far as employing his own media coach. Maybe what happened to Jorge is that he didn't know how to sell himself properly, and that's surprising for somebody who is concerned about every aspect of their image, but he has had to try hard to reveal his 'true self' and he works tirelessly to prove himself to his critics and the general public.

Now he wants to go a step further, and he has already taken some acting classes. He doesn't want a big deal to be made out of his shyness – and he's always said that he would like to be an actor – but in this case there is no doubt that acting would help him to conquer some of his few remaining fears, at least in a social sense. All this is in the name of progress, of improvement, of reaching a stage that is really important for him: to be truly unconcerned about what people say about him. In other words, nobody has forced Jorge into this. As he once said: 'I'm no yokel, so I don't want to look like one when I speak in public.'

12 December 2007
Laver Street, London
LOOKING BACK

Jorge is talking, hardly stopping for breath. 'Valentino arrived on the scene and revolutionised everything,' he says. 'He brought radical change. I remember that at school, on the day after a race, everybody would be talking about the battle between Doohan and Crivillé ... and then about Valentino Rossi! It wasn't normal for us to be interested in the winner of the 125cc race! But he did things differently, he started to improvise. There was a group of us who used to get together to watch the races at my father's track at the waterpark. There was my dad, his assistant Toni, my friend Rubén ... we used to watch the races and then exchange opinions. Everybody said Rossi was a clown ... Rubén and I were Max Biaggi fans ... we used to criticise Rossi because we liked Biaggi and I suppose it was jealousy. If you don't like somebody you find it hard to admit when they do something well. It's human nature, especially when you're a kid. But we had to admit that this guy was totally original. He did things that nobody had ever done before. He was different from everything and everybody, he worked really hard and he was really fun.'

This youthful, envious disapproval aside, Jorge has always enjoyed Valentino Rossi's celebrations, so why not give them a try himself? Once again it's that same old story, the desire to be genuinely original. In fact, his favourite phrase is, 'You have to be different.' He wanted to celebrate his victories, he didn't want to let his fans and his critics down – or himself – but clearly Valentino had been there first.

'When Jorge was little I used to think that Rossi was a bit of a clown too,' Maria suddenly interjects. 'It wasn't until I became involved in this business that I realised how wrong I was.' With that, she snapped us both out of our trance. We had been at their London flat for several hours, working on this book, and Jorge quickly picked up on what an interesting comment his mother had just made. Everything looks different from the inside. 'The thing is that Rossi has the ideal character to do what he does,' Jorge concludes.

'Ever since he was little, whenever he finished on the podium, Jorge would celebrate differently from everybody else. He jumped differently,' says María.

Jorge looks at her, surprised. 'I used to jump on the podium?'

'You would shout, "Bieeeen!" and jump in the air,' she replies. 'I watch you at races now and it's exactly the same. You have the same face, the same expression. You are euphoric. You look exactly the same as when you were little.'

'I have always been very expressive, in victory and defeat. I used to go crazy when I lost…'

'And when you won!' María interjects. Now she looks at me. 'I remember being at a circuit once, at one of the first races he did. In fact I think it was his first race, in San Juan. He was only three years old and it was raining. He kept having to stop and poke the mud off his rear wheel with a stick. And because he couldn't see anybody, because the race was over, he looked at his dad and said, "Have I won? Have I won?" The race had finished! The poor little beggar – everybody was laughing at him and he just kept riding.'

'I got lapped two or three times,' remembers Jorge. 'I was racing against much older kids – 10 and 15 year olds. There was so much mud that the rear wheel kept locking up against the mudguard. But what's that got to do with my celebrations, Mum?'

'Because, Jorge, ever since the beginning, all you ever thought about was winning. It was all about winning, winning and winning. Celebrating it, sharing it, have developed naturally.'

Strangely enough, Jorge's first notable celebration didn't come in a motorcycle race but during a school football match in the playground of La Milagrosa when he was ten years old. 'I don't know if you remember when Valentino Rossi won at Jerez and parked the bike up before running into one of those portable toilets that they have at the Grands Prix. I can honestly say that I can't remember if I did it first or if I'd seen Valentino do it … I think I did it first,' he says, gazing into the distance. 'Anyway, the fact is that I'd planned it. I decided that if I scored a penalty I would run off and lock myself inside the school toilets. Sure enough, I scored and off I ran. My friends fell around laughing. I've always been a terrible footballer, but I enjoyed that!'

His first celebration of note at a racetrack came in the 50cc Copa Aprilia at Montmeló in 1998. 'I won, stood up on the bike and raised my hand, then raised one finger. It seems such a normal thing to do nowadays, but people didn't tend to do it back then.' It also became normal to see Jorge on the podium sucking on a Chupa Chups, the famous brand of Spanish lollipops that have been long-term sponsors of Dani Amatriaín's teams and riders. 'It wasn't long after the time when Johan Cruyff used to do something similar [on the bench, as manager of F.C. Barcelona].' In Brazil, when Jorge won his first Grand Prix, back in 2003, he mimed the action of firing a gun. Then, in 2004, he pretended to play the guitar after beating Dovizioso at Brno. 'In the end it looked like it was supposed to be a Spanish guitar but I'd wanted it to be an electric one!'

All these early celebrations were merely a hint of what was to come. Over the years they have made plenty of people smile, but perhaps none more than Juan Llansá. 'I find them really funny,' he smiles. 'Even though I am almost 50 years old now, I enjoy them as much as if I were 20! I get involved whenever I can. At the British GP in 2006 I wore a Dutch hat and glasses. I really like the fact Jorge does these things, because they're intended as a present to his fans.

That gets me going, it gives me energy, because if you switch off you may as well not bother. You have to enjoy life. The day I stop enjoying being with Jorge, it's time to pack up and go home!'

Summer 2006, some time during his four-hour daily training routine
Hotel Barceló-Sants gym, Barcelona
LET THE 'LORENSHOW' BEGIN!

Mens sana in corpore sano. While Jorge dedicates time and effort to training his mind, it's as nothing compared to the dedication he puts into his body. Hour upon hour is spent in the gym, using weights and in front of the mirror, but it's not a question of vanity. It is a matter of necessity because nowadays, more than ever before, world-class motorcycle racers have to be world-class athletes too. Having said that, Jorge certainly enjoys the fact that his clothes hang right and he's happy to take any opportunity to show off his washboard stomach. 'Wherever there's a mirror, he'll be in front of it,' laughs Cheni Martínez. 'He gets it from Chicho,' adds Marcos Hirsch.

The body he has now is a gift from Marcos, his physical trainer and one of the few people happy to tell him things straight. A motorcycle racer doesn't necessarily need the muscle definition that Jorge has, in terms of shape and proportion. Marcos sets him specific routines for preparing his body for the rigours of riding, but at the same time achieving as much aesthetic improvement as possible. In this respect Marcos was smart, because he reeled Jorge in and got him hooked on training. 'Don't worry, Jorge. If this whole racing thing doesn't work out, with the body I've given you, you can have a career in porn.'

Maybe it was on the day he said this, or maybe not, it doesn't matter, but it was certainly within the four walls of that gym, between rep after rep on different muscle groups, that the 'LorenShow' was born. There was a time when only Rossi used to put on a show, but even that has become a rare event. 'Now he only does it on certain occasions,' says Jorge. 'The World Championship was losing a bit of sparkle. Other riders were trying things but they weren't funny, especially in 125cc. There was a time when Melandri tried to imitate Rossi but he never managed to make it as funny.'

Jorge had been thinking for a long time about how he could offer his fans something extra after a win. A lot of people saw him as too serious, but he wanted to show that he cared about them, that he enjoyed what he did and that he was affable and good-humoured, as well as imaginative. He needed an ingenious plan because he had a clear objective: to celebrate the World Championship title in style. 'We wanted to do it in style, go mad,' recalls Dani Palau. That seemed a long way off, back in the summer of 2006, but once the crises of Turkey, Shanghai and Le Mans were behind him the dream of beating Andrea Dovizioso was alive again.

Strictly speaking, the first episode of the 'LorenShow' was at the Spanish GP in 2006. It was his first victory in the 250cc class and Jorge got off his bike, took off his helmet and started shouting at the fans. 'It was pretty spectacular and it was the first time we used the word "LorenShow",' he recalls. 'Palau and I used to put together a ten-page magazine of our own after each Grand Prix and on the front cover of that particular edition we put a photo of my celebrations and the headline [in English] "Welcome to the LorenShow!" That was awesome, really different. I have always been creative and I fancied doing something special after I won, so I decided to give it a try!' The design of the magazine, by the way, was similar to *GQ*. 'Well, not similar exactly. We kind of copied it! We were worried about getting into trouble for copying it but I hope they don't hit us with a lawsuit now … it was only for us!' he laughs.

With Marcos, passing the time between sets of weights with endless discussions 'about anything and everything', according to Cheni, 'they had plenty of hours in the gym to turn things over in their minds. Also, Marcos has a gift for getting Jorge to talk. For him to loosen up, say things, get things wrong! Because he knew everything would stay between those four walls.'

That was how Jorge's confidence began to grow – and when he was at his most relaxed one of his favourite topics was girls. Learning the art of seduction was a subject he was desperate to pass with flying colours, especially at the age of 19 – and what better school than the cinema? Marcos introduced Jorge to the art of nightclub pulling, American style. Not by taking him out on the tiles or by trips overseas, but by making him watch *Saturday Night Fever*, because Marcos is both a film buff and an expert on 1970s music. John Travolta's role in that film is iconic for any teenager of that era: Tony Manero was just like Jorge, arrogant but charming, but Manero's character also carried a more subliminal message for Jorge, as a romantic who couldn't live without his friends. He simply loved the scene where Travolta gets dressed in front of the mirror, and he could think of no better way to celebrate his first title at the Ricardo Tormo circuit in Cheste, Valencia, on 29 October 2006. The moment Jorge crossed the line to take the title, coming in fourth in a race won by Alex de Angelis, it was showtime.

It wasn't really a particularly memorable effort. Marcos appeared, dressed as Jorge, with a ghetto blaster on his shoulder that Tony Manero himself would have been proud of. The 'Staying Alive' dance routine was short and not particularly well choreographed, but at the very least it was an indication of what the fans could expect in the future. 'There were only two dance steps, to be fair,' says Jorge. 'But the funniest thing about it was seeing Marcos, who is 1.85m tall and weighs 140kg, squashed into a set of leathers.' The seed had been planted for the 'LorenShow' to blossom the following season.

The props they'd used for the Valencia celebration weren't easy to come by, and the process had started two weeks earlier in Portugal. 'The radio wasn't a problem, but it wasn't easy to get hold of a set of leathers in Marcos's size,' laughs Palau. In the end, Garibaldi agreed to custom make a set in XXXL just for him. The joke quickly swept around the Fortuna Aprilia hospitality area: 'Have you heard that the price of steak has gone up?'

'Oh? Why's that?'

'Because you have no idea how many cows they had to kill to make Marcos's leathers.'

All joking aside, with Marcos turning up as a bigger version of Jorge, the message to the world was clear. 'Today, I grew up.'

6 March 2007
Hotel Ritz-Carlton, Doha
THE EYE OF THE TIGER

Back in 2006 there'd been no plans to celebrate race victories, only the world title. In theory, 2007 was going to be no different. Apart from anything else, Jorge had enough on his plate trying to get himself together in time for the first race in Qatar. Pre-season work had not gone well, and after the official test in Barcelona he claimed: 'They are all trying to intimidate me, making risky passes as soon as I leave the pits … I tried that too when I was 16 but now it seems ridiculous. Let them try an X-fuera down Craner Curves at Donington, if they're up to it.' Were Jorge's rivals beginning to sense a weakness?

Lorenzo and his people were tense. Life changes as a World Champion; it comes with extras: gala openings, award ceremonies, advertisements … all this had distracted him from the most important thing – racing. For everything to make sense again, for life to be bearable, he needed to feel the thrill of victory once more. He knew that, but as hard as he tried things just weren't happening. After three months away from his beloved Aprilia the lap times weren't coming and he was a second off his normal pace. The new chassis was proving to be a headache, yet the moment when he would defend that number 1 plate for the first time, in the opening race of the season at the Losail circuit, was fast approaching. Dani Amatriaín was sure he knew what the problem was. 'The eye of the tiger', the attitude that had pulled him through the crisis of 2006, had been lost.

Making that clear to him seemed like the best way to get it back, and by watching *Rocky* films Jorge slowly began to recover his own self-confidence. Simply by closing his eyes and visualising himself stepping into the boots of the 'Italian stallion', who came from nothing to be World Champion, had a positive effect on him.

Jorge Lorenzo and Dani Amatriaín checked into the Ritz-Carlton Hotel in Doha a week before the MotoGP circus landed in Qatar. Jorge was feeling strong, the job done by Marcos Hirsch was blatantly obvious – you only had to look at his abdominal muscles to see that – but on his arrival in Qatar he was 3kg overweight. 'I'd done the muscle mass work properly but with so many media and commercial commitments, as well as some medication I'd been taking for my spots, I wasn't able to do enough cardiovascular work or stick strictly to my diet. That's why I wasn't as skinny as the other riders.'

In the hotel, isolated from the rest of the world, Jorge hit the gym hard, morning, afternoon and evening. A quick-thinking production team from Televisión Española, who were staying in the hotel, suggested filming a piece in which Jorge would play the role of Sylvester Stallone, with Dani Amatriaín as Apollo Creed, the man who'd helped him recover that killer instinct. The title song from *Rocky III*, 'Eye of the Tiger' by the band Survivor, played over and over. It was 6 March 2007. Just four days remained before Jorge would begin his title defence. Four days of chicken salad and soup.

10 March 2007, Doha
Text written by Jorge Lorenzo entitled:
'SIGHTING LAP'

It's the sighting lap. As we warm up our tyres I feel a bead of sweat trickle down my face. We're in Qatar, gentlemen! Inside, Lorenzo is already throwing punches and in a few minutes he'll be throwing them on the outside too.

OK. My mechanic is waiting for me on the starting grid. I turn off the engine, remove my helmet and gloves, put on my team cap and MP3 Oakley shades.

I switch on and the first thing I hear is that familiar rock beat of the Red Hot Chili Peppers. But this isn't the right moment to be listening to 'my' band. I need something different, something that brings an image into my head as soon as I hear it. Something that gives me a little extra kick of motivation, and allows me to go out with total confidence. Next song. It's 'Eye of the Tiger', from Rocky III … perfect.

I don't know, but the older I get, the more I notice how my maturity helps me to fight back the nerves. I'll never lose those pre-race butterflies completely. What can you do about them?

While my mechanic reminds me who is the number 1, I take the opportunity to have one final swig of my mineral drink. The bike is fired up, there are no excuses now. This is the moment where 25 gladiators go into battle.

Just as the red lights go out, my engine drops revs. It's a bad start but two corners later I pull off one of the riskiest overtaking manoeuvres you can attempt on a motorcycle and I pass four riders in one move. It was dangerous but it came off and within a kilometre I was past bike number 12 and with clear track in front of me. So how did the race go? I think it went well. At the end my mechanics were happy anyway...

'It seemed impossible to make up a second per lap, but I managed two!' remembers Jorge. It had all worked out, but the Lorenzo/*Rocky III* feature he filmed with TVE, training and running on the beach, had been a huge gamble. It was broadcast at primetime, just before the race, and was watched by several million viewers in his home country. Jorge met his side of the deal by winning the race, but with the criticism he got for doing the piece, you can only imagine how bad it would have been had he lost. But the gamble had paid off and, critics, fears and phobias aside, he'd achieved his goal. He had recovered 'the eye of the tiger'.

Two weeks later, March 2007
FLYING THE FLAG

After his victory at Losail Jorge pretended to skip like a boxer, as he'd done for so many hours in the gym with Marcos. It was a spontaneous, intuitive celebration and an early turning point for his season. After such a morale-boosting performance during and after the race, why not celebrate all his victories from now on? 'In Qatar I did the skipping-rope thing but I never thought that in the future I'd be using props to celebrate my victories!'

The preparation that went into each episode of 'LorenShow' was a simple but elaborate process. Generally the original idea would come from Jorge and, often with the help of his computer, Palau would fill in the details. It became something of a team effort at Motorsport48, where almost everybody began to join in the fun. Everybody except the boss: Dani Amatriaín kept his distance. He didn't like or dislike the celebrations but he preferred to leave them to Jorge as a bit of innocent fun.

Out of the blue came another idea, this time from Marcos. Once again, it was an idea born in the gym. 'You are a warrior. You have to reclaim the championship, right? But what kind of a conqueror doesn't have a flag?' Jorge's eyes began to twinkle.

'It has to be something really visual,' Jorge told Palau, taking on the idea. 'Imagine that in each race I stick a flag into the ground, as if I have conquered that land. Like Christopher Columbus when he arrived in America!' The design process was short, with Jorge's X-fuera logo the obvious choice, set on a black background – the colour used by pirates. And written in English, so that it would be understood all over the world, not just in Spain, would be those now famous words: 'Lorenzo's Land'.

The day of its first unfurling soon arrived. It was the Spanish Grand Prix at Jerez, known as 'The Cathedral' by local fans. Dani Palau headed for partisan territory – the section of track that features the 'Ángel Nieto' and 'Peluqui' corners, where he would meet his friend if he won the race. 'I had goosebumps. You should have heard the noise from the crowd when Jorge stopped!' he recalls. There were 140,000 people packed into the grandstands at Jerez that day and they had been treated to an outstanding 250cc race: 'la carrera de los cuarenta y dos adelantamientos' ['the race with forty-two overtakes'].

Jorge Lorenzo savoured the moment. As he had done in 2006, he removed his helmet, got off his bike and punched the air to celebrate his second victory at Jerez. Then the flag appeared by his side. He took it and drove it deep into the gravel. Jerez had been conquered, the first circuit to be claimed as 'Lorenzo's Land'. A few weeks later he won again, in China, and again he planted the flag. However, unlike Jerez, this victory was his first in Shanghai. Nobody was going to stop him now.

Final week of April 2007, shortly after the GP of China
INSPIRATION AT 170BPM

The long hours spent in the gym were tough and often tedious. It is difficult to find new ways to summon up the energy and motivation to keep coming back day after day, for ever harder punishment. Jorge gets through it by locking himself in his own little world, lost in his own thoughts – especially during cardiovascular exercise. 'I spend over an hour at full tilt on the cross-trainer, working my arms, legs and heart. It gets really tedious.' Music helps him to drift into another world and his mind takes flight. He thinks about being on his bike, 'But I don't imagine myself racing – I just imagine myself after the race, celebrating victory. That's when I come up with my celebrations.

'That is where my inspiration comes from. Envisioning the vented emotion that comes pouring out when I win. It almost feels real. And I'm on a cross-trainer with my heart rate at 170bpm! I think most of my ideas have come to me on that machine!' Jorge smiles. It is strange that what motivates him is not the process but the end result, not the excitement of passing riders but the thrill of crossing the line with nobody ahead of him, not the racing but the winning. And it is on the cross-trainer, sweating away like he would during a race in Malaysia, at the peak of exhaustion, heart thumping as fast as it will go, that he sees things most clearly.

The French GP was not long away and he needed to come up with something new. 'I couldn't think of anything. We travelled to Le Mans without a plan.' As usual, on the Thursday, Jorge and Dani Palau completed a lap of the circuit on a scooter. Suddenly, in the middle of a corner, he stopped. 'You know what Valentino has never done? Bring out a double.'

Palau was hooked: when Jorge gets an idea in his head it is difficult to get him to change his mind and this was a really good one. He made Dani try on his race leathers and almost fell over laughing. 'You look just like me!' It wasn't unusual for Palau to try on Jorge's leathers because since they were a similar size he often acted as his official tester when new ones arrived – 'To give them the okay.' Incidentally, I should correct myself here. Jorge obviously does allow people to change his mind occasionally, because his original idea was for his double to try to steal his motorbike. Jorge would chase him,

223

tackle him and throw him to the ground. 'We even rehearsed it!' But it was deemed to be too violent and he was talked out of it.

Another coincidence ended up becoming significant for Jorge's season, but this unexpected incident could have brought that – and his celebrations – to an early end. On Friday morning there was nothing to suggest that this Grand Prix would be different from any other. Jorge arrived at the pit box, said 'Hi' to everybody, talked to his mechanics – Giovanni Sandi, Juanito, Vale, Ivano, Luciano, Carlos, Loris ... the usual; or at least that's how it seemed. Jorge put on his helmet, and threw his leg over his Aprilia. But unlike most practice sessions, Dani Amatriaín wasn't there to watch him go out. And unlike most practice sessions, this one would not go smoothly.

'The weather forecast was predicting rain so I wanted to get a fast lap in before it started and the track got wet. I wanted to be the only one to get a dry lap in so I went flat out from the start, pushing like an animal.' But the tyre wasn't up to temperature, and neither was the track, and in one of the first corners he was thrown over the handlebars. It was a massive highside, Jorge travelling about three metres into the air before coming down hard on the cold French tarmac. Dani arrived in the garage in time to see the replay on the television screens. 'What the hell were you trying to do?' he barked at the mechanics. 'Set pole position at eleven o'clock in the morning?'

It was a big crash of the worst kind – it was unexpected – and more typical of an old 500 bike than a 250. As Jorge lay prone on the ground, everybody feared the worst. A broken femur? Injured pelvis? Planning Sunday's celebration was the last thing on anybody's mind. The ambulance brought Jorge back to the garage, where he was greeted by one of the Italian doctors from the Clinica Mobile. Amatriaín, Gurt and Llansá looked on anxiously. 'What's he saying? What's he saying?' Dani shouted at Pere. Dani spoke Italian well but he was so nervous that he couldn't understand the doctor. 'He says he's okay, calm down Dani.' Somehow he had escaped with nothing more than a broken toe on his left foot. It wouldn't be enough to prevent him from racing. 'I went straight back onto the track,' recalls Jorge. 'And miraculously I ended the session second fastest, just 0.001 seconds off first place!'

After practice on Friday they returned to the corner of choice to rehearse their celebration routine. 'We were rumbled by the German rider Dirk Heidolf. You should have seen his face when he saw us rolling around fighting. He couldn't believe what he was seeing. I think he thought he'd gone mad!'

Despite the injury Jorge won the race as planned and, as planned, his double ran onto the track. He tried to rob him of his leathers, his flag, his applause and glory, but Jorge sent him packing. When he got back to parc fermé he was interviewed, as usual, by TVE reporter Marc Martín.

'What did that celebration mean?' asked Marc. 'Who was it and why the clone?'

'The Jorge who ran out wasn't me,' came the reply. 'That was the Jorge that crashed on Friday, but he has gone now. This is the real Lorenzo, the winner.' Somehow Jorge had turned a crash in his favour and he had done it on the hop, literally. It was only after the race had finished that this explanation had occurred to him.

3 June 2007, 13.00pm
Mugello circuit, Italy
'AT MY SIGNAL, UNLEASH HELL'

Jorge was coming up with more ideas for celebrations than he could use, and that was probably a good thing because some of them would have got him into more trouble than they were worth. Like the one that involved him wearing an Andrea Dovizioso mask. 'We've still got the mask but Andrea would have had to do something really bad to me to warrant getting it out ... though he'd better watch it!' smiles Jorge. Another one that failed to get past the ideas stage was for Valencia, the final race of 2007. Jorge had already claimed the title and, after being criticised all year for using the 'Lorenzo's Land' flag instead of the Spanish one, planned to go completely over the top, using not only the Spanish flag but dressing up as a bullfighter. Maybe it was a good thing he only managed seventh.

The celebrations he did get to use became ever more elaborate and meticulously planned. He would scour the circuit for the best corner, with the best camera angle and the best view for the fans. Jorge had decided that each celebration should have something to do with the country he was in, and in Italy a friend, Jordi Oliva, who worked for Dorna [the commercial and television rights holders for MotoGP] gave him an idea.

'In Italy they've nicknamed you "Spaniard". The commentator on Italian television has started calling you that.'
' "Spaniard"? Why?'
Because you are like a gladiator and that's what they call the main character played by Russell Crowe in the movie Gladiator.'

Maximus Decimus Meridius was a Roman general born in Mérida, Spain. He lived in the second century and since this was the second year of domination by a Spaniard in the 250cc class then what better way for Lorenzo to celebrate victory in the Italian GP than by dressing up as his namesake?

'In fact, the idea of doing something historical came after watching *300* with Marcos,' explains Jorge, 'We watched the film again with Palau, the three of us talked about it and we decided we wanted to do something related to the Battle of Thermopylae. It was while we were looking for a King Leonidas suit that we came across a Gladiator outfit. That coincided with me finding out what [Italian television commentator] Guido Meda was calling me.'

The wheels were quickly put in motion. Like any good media relations manager, Pere Gurt sourced an exact replica of the costume worn by Russell Crowe in the film, which was owned by an agency in Madrid. It cost 600 euros a week to rent and the sword was extra. It was kept in a corner of the garage at Mugello, where Dani Palau devoutly guarded it from the inquisitive eyes of journalists who were already wondering what Lorenzo had up his sleeve if he won this one.

On race day Palau headed for the corner where they'd agreed to meet if a miracle should happen. Jorge was starting from 20th on the grid, but he still had his sights set on victory. Everybody knows what happened next. On the big screens around the circuit, Palau watched his friend slide into the gravel after colliding with Bautista. He jumped onto his scooter and raced to fetch him, sword, breastplate, helmet, 'Lorenzo's Land' flag and all. The Italian fans spotted the props and, despite Jorge's popularity there, Dani could hear them laughing and shouting insults.

The mediocre can be unforgiving when a winner falls from his perch. 'The preparations were perfect, but unfortunately the race wasn't!'

Text written by Jorge Lorenzo entitled:
'LET'S TALK CINEMA'

Like any kid, the cinema has always represented something magical and mysterious to me. It is a really powerful way of grasping your imagination. Not just the cinema, but also the television. 'What's behind that little screen?' you wonder. Are they all inside that little box with the aerial on top? There are a lot of films that have had an impact on me. I must have been four or five years old when I saw Steven Spielberg's 'E.T.' for the first time. It had been out for a good few years by then and repeated a million times on the television but when you see a film like that for the first time at five years of age there's this little fear that creeps inside you every time you open your bedroom door, or the wardrobe, or when you look under the bed. Who can say for sure that we're alone on this planet? If they were to exist, would they be pleasant-looking, well-meaning beings or would they be Machiavellian aliens with bad intentions?

As I'm sure you did, when I was little I used to soak up Disney films. Who hasn't seen 'Beauty and the Beast', 'The Little Mermaid', 'Pocahontas', 'The Hunchback of Notre Dame', 'Toy Story' or 'George of the Jungle?' Who has never wanted to be like the lead characters and possess some of their magic powers?

Even though he wasn't exactly an actor, I went through a period when I was really into Michael Jackson, the 'King of Pop' in the 1980s and 90s. The way he danced really fascinated me. I remember when all my class-mates used to encourage me to do impressions of him over and over again.

More than the film I'm watching, I tend to focus more on the characters. Their personalities, their way of speaking and interacting with other people. Not long ago I watched 'As Good As It Gets', with Jack Nicholson. It is a great comedy about a neurotic grouch, who is also a successful novelist, and his relationships with a local waitress and his gay neighbour. It really struck me how such an obsessive, rude and obnoxious person can still come across as charming. Other actors who have inspired me were John Travolta in 'Saturday Night Fever', Brad Pitt in 'Legends of the Fall' and Tom Cruise in 'Top Gun', among others.

My latest celebration was inspired by 'Gladiator' (the armour and sword were the ones used by Russell Crowe's double in the film) and the more recent film '300'. They are films about honour, respect and courage – values I share. So when they told me that the Italian television commentator Guido Meda had started to call me 'Spaniard' during their race broadcasts, I didn't think about it twice. I had to get hold of that outfit any way I could and bring it to Mugello. It was the perfect opportunity because as well as being in Italy, the chance to win a race from so far back on the grid was a real acid test, a huge battle that had to be won. You already know what happened next, but later at Misano I finally got chance to wear the suit.

The next films I want to see are Woody Allen's 'Play It Again, Sam' and 'Studio 54'. But that's another story…

2 September 2007, 13.10pm, San Marino GP, Misano
'SOMETIMES I DO WHAT I WANT TO DO, THE REST OF THE TIME I DO WHAT I HAVE TO DO'

Jorge toyed with the idea of wearing his new outfit if he won at the GP of Catalunya but eventually decided that revenge is a dish best served cold and it was better to wait. The season would give him plenty of opportunities to settle the score and the Italian fans would have no choice but to bow down before him like a Roman general. Every great film has unforgettable lines that are often repeated by film buffs. This one from *Gladiator* suited Jorge down to the ground.

My name is Maximus Decimus Meridius … commander of the armies of the north … general of the Felix Legions … loyal servant to the true emperor, Marcus Aurelius … father to a murdered son … husband to a murdered wife … and I will have my vengeance, in this life or the next.

'What a well-chosen phrase!' Lorenzo must have thought. Italy owed him one and he was going back to collect his dues. It wasn't to be in that first race on Italian soil, but he was determined to get his revenge in the second. He rented the outfit again, waving goodbye to another 600 euros, but this wasn't about the money. This was a question of honour. He didn't know the circuit, because there hadn't been a GP there since 1993, and although he had visited Misano once, when he'd signed for Derbi in 2002, he was only 15 then and not old enough to actually ride.

None of that mattered now, because he went out and won. And on top of that, Dovizioso broke down. Jordi Pérez and Cheni Martinez raced out onto the track to dress their man. They'd already discussed with Race Direction and the television directors where the best place would be for the celebration in terms of safety and maximum exposure.

Jorge didn't want to take the outfit off – not when he stepped on to the podium, or when he sprayed the champagne. He even kept it on for the press conference. He clearly wanted to recoup his investment, but above all he wanted to enjoy the moment. He felt like the king of the world. ' "Now THAT was legendary," Guido Meda told me.'

Cinema has always been important to Jorge – to inspire him, to escape reality, and to help him out of a crisis. Marcos has always insisted on the importance of the 'seventh art' and since the age of 16 Jorge has watched films recommended by his trainer, writing comments about them in their famous notebook. However, not all of them were to his taste:

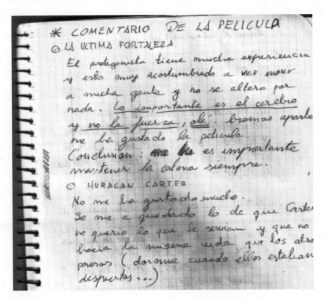

THE LAST CASTLE

The main character is very experienced and used to seeing a lot of people die, so it doesn't upset him at all. The most important thing is the brain, not strength, olé! Joking aside, I like the film. Conclusion: it is important to always keep your cool.

THE HURRICANE

I didn't like it much. The thing that stuck with me was that [Hurricane] Carter sent back the food they gave him and he didn't have the same routine as other people (he slept when they were awake).

Remainder of the 2007 season
FROM CATALUNYA TO THE TITLE

The Gladiator celebration at Misano was the tip of the 'LorenShow 2007' iceberg. At the GP of Catalunya, Dani Palau dressed up as Lorenzo again, this time joined by a third lookalike – Jorge's good friend and Spanish Championship rider, Ricky Cardús, for a rock concert with a difference.

The trio completed a recce of Montmeló on Thursday and Friday and performed a rehearsal at the corner of choice, in front of the stadium section. 'I told them, "When we're playing here, I want you to jump around like the Red Hot Chili Peppers. Go on YouTube, have a look at the videos and learn the dance moves," ' recalls Jorge. 'But the bastards ignored me!' For one magic moment Jorge, Dani and Ricky were no longer Lorenzo, Palau and Cardús. They weren't even three Lorenzos, dancing and singing like maniacs in front of 100,000 people. They were Anthony Kiedis, Flea and John Frusciante. Only Chad Smith was missing on drums, otherwise they would have been the real Chilis. 'I wanted there to be four of us, like the real Chilis, and I was going to ask Ricky's older brother Jordi to join in but there weren't any more leathers in my size. Also, getting a drum kit onto the track would have been a nightmare!'

After Catalunya came the British GP and before travelling there they went to dinner with a racing friend, Xavi Ledesma – the owner of the Fortuna Team hospitality unit and one of Jorge's closest friends in 2005, as well as being the organiser of the Copa Aprilia when he first started racing Xavi told them that the tradition in England was to drink tea in the afternoon. No sooner said than done. They went out and bought a tea tray, complete with teapot, cups and spoons. Palau planned to sit at a table at the Melbourne Loop, dressed as a waiter in a tuxedo and crash helmet. All Jorge had to do was turn up, rest his feet and have a drink. Oh, and win the race.

Unfortunately, the final and most crucial part of the plan started to go wrong in the warm-up because, as is well known, rain is as traditional at Donington as tea. Despite the heavy downpour, Jorge produced a great performance – he was having the best wet race of his career. 'Shall I go out or not?' thought Dani halfway through the race. His buddy was running in second place behind Dovizioso. He had to have faith. 'If you have any doubt, something is bound to go wrong,' says Jorge. 'Whenever I have felt sure I would win I have won, but if there has been any kind of doubt I've lost, come second, or something has happened. That is what the brain is like.' And just as Palau made his mind up and went to load up the scooter with props, Jorge hit the deck. That was one cuppa that was hard to swallow.

Jorge's next celebration was enjoyed by the Spanish fans, although it was on a Saturday rather than a Sunday. The Dutch are a bit different in everything, even their racing, and since 1949 the TT at Assen has always taken place on a Saturday. Jorge knew exactly what he was going to do if he won. He wanted to copy the thousands of locals by riding a pushbike.

They rehearsed their routine at two or three different corners. 'This place is best. How far will you ride the bike? Will you be able to cycle in boots?' Every minute detail was taken care of. 'We'd practised in that area where Valentino sat when he won the MotoGP race, the bit that looks like a target. I was going to leave my Aprilia and the pushbike would be in the middle of the circle. We thought of it before Rossi!' Suddenly, he changed his mind. On his return to the pit garage he realised that there was a stage, all set up right next to the track, because just by the final chicane that leads into the start-finish straight there is a VIP terrace. It was the perfect place – and not only that, there was a television camera directly opposite.

'We could sit down and have a drink,' Jorge told Dani. The fact he'd missed out on his cup of tea at Donington a few days earlier still irked him, so it was all hands on deck. The owners of the terrace had to be consulted and asked for permission. Initially they weren't too keen because there are no fences there and it is easy for people to get out and access pit lane. For that reason, a huge deposit has to be paid to hire the area, which the circuit organisers retain if there are any problems.

In the end they realised it was a Lorenzo celebration and they went along with it. This time Jorge backed up his plans with a dominant victory. However, having left his bike propped against the fence before climbing over the tyre wall and on to the terrace, he was swamped by punters taking photographs and the television cameras lost him in the mêlée. 'On top of that, the bar owner was a complete opportunist and he got a bunch of people to hold up an advertisement! It was a disaster.'

Even though not much could be seen on the television, it was clear that Jorge's double had returned and that they'd gone to have a drink together. But why? Jorge was happy to provide the answer in parc fermé. 'After the crash at Donington, somebody [Dovizioso] had suggested I was getting nervous. So I sipped on a herbal tea.' Some time later Dani Palau insisted that the initial idea was to drink a glass of water but, as at Le Mans, Jorge was thinking on his feet and he was eager to hit back at Dovizioso. 'Sometimes that happens to me. I get really good ideas on the spur of the moment. Other times I really have to think things through for them to work out. But sometimes I get a flash of inspiration.'

Jorge finished fourth in Germany but there were no plans for a celebration even if he'd won. He was worried about the joke wearing thin. 'You have to keep people guessing. It is good to have an element of the unexpected. If we did it every time it wouldn't be funny any more. The truth is that I like things to be complete and maybe I would have continued the celebrations race after race but I let them convince me. It was good to have a break.' The summer holidays were approaching and they wanted to leave the fans gagging for more. 'To be fair, I have to say that I can't always put on a big celebration because I need helpers and Palau didn't come to every race. For the ones outside Europe we had a much smaller group.'

There were no celebrations in the Czech Republic either, but this time for a different reason. Nobody at Motorsport48 was in the mood for a party. Dani Amatriaín's assistant, Esther Serra, had just lost her brother, Marc. Jorge won but conducted a silent parade of his now obligatory 'Lorenzo's Land' flag in honour of the family.

'The problem with the celebrations is that it gets harder and harder to come up with something original, with meaning, that isn't just plain stupid,' says Jorge. 'Ideas are finite. We had something planned for Portugal but I'd prefer to keep it to myself – I might use it in the future. We also wanted to do something with animals but are they allowed on the track? We planned to get Datil, my mum's dog, a set of made-to-measure leathers but imagine if we brought him out and he had a shit on the track! That'd cause a scene!' Jorge fell about laughing as his imagination took over. 'It's a shame Marcos doesn't come to more races because we could dress him up as Shrek! Ha, ha!'

21 October 2007, 13.00pm
Sepang circuit, Malaysian GP
THE GRAND FINALE

We are approaching the closing scenes of 2007. A second world title waited on the other side of the world, where a tightly sealed box sat in the corner of the Fortuna Aprilia garage. Everybody knew what it meant, but nobody knew exactly what it contained. Jorge had his first chance to clinch the title at Phillip Island but it was a long shot and that, in turn, created a dilemma. If he was crowned World Champion there it was obvious – the box would be opened and the celebrations would begin. But what if he won the race and not the title? Would he have to think of another celebration? 'I'll come up with something,' Jorge mused.

And boy did he come up with something. Riding at a second per lap quicker than anybody else on the track, Jorge produced his most convincing performance of the season. Unfortunately, with Dovizioso finishing third, it wasn't enough. Jorge still had the bicycle celebration up his sleeve and in lieu of a better idea he borrowed Giovanni Sandi's fold-up bike, painted in team colours, and pedalled to parc fermé.

On this occasion, most people failed to see the funny side. 'Anybody who wants to understand it can understand it,' Jorge said at the time. But when you're going a second a lap faster and then come back on a bicycle, some people are clearly going to take offence. Maybe he realised his mistake, but he probably also thought that feeding his cocky reputation from time to time wasn't such a bad thing either. In any case, Jorge won in such style that he had licence to celebrate in any way he wanted – and he chose 'Lorenzo style'.

Jorge won his second 250cc World Championship at the Malaysian Grand Prix with one race to spare, to top off an outstanding 2007 season. And what better way to celebrate in style than by looking way back to the very first race of the year in Qatar, when Jorge recovered the 'eye of the tiger'? His antics in 2007 had made him the leading contender for the title of paddock showman left vacant by Valentino Rossi in a season when the Italian had little to celebrate. It's clear by now that Jorge is up for a challenge and a second 250cc World Championship title was enough of an excuse for him to stake his claim as the leading heavyweight in 'motorshowbusiness'.

On this occasion it wasn't actually one of his own ideas, but he made it his own as soon as it left the lips of Marcos Hirsch. Having started the season training like Rocky Balboa and trying to recover the 'eye of the tiger', he took the title in Malaysia (coincidentally a country the famous Italian novelist Emilio Salgari referred to as the 'land of the tigers') and there was only one way to celebrate – as the new CHAMPION OF THE WOOOOOORLD!

That box in the corner of the garage at Phillip Island contained a story all of its own. Jorge and Marcos's initial idea was to set up a boxing match between the two of them, in which Jorge would knock Marcos out. 'The idea was that I had to beat a heavyweight. And boy is he heavy!' laughs Jorge.

'When I'd dressed as Jorge at Valencia the previous year, the message was that he had grown up,' explains Marcos. 'This time it was a case of demonstrating that he was capable of anything. Even knocking out somebody twice his height and weight, like me!' Another of Jorge's ideas was for Marcos to grow his hair like Don King, the world's most famous boxing promoter. In the end the celebration wasn't exactly as Jorge and Marcos had planned, partly because the Brazilian trainer was unable to make the trip to Malaysia.

The final idea came about after a conversation between Jorge and Marcos after which the 'celebration panel' of Jorge, Dani Palau and Pere Gurt set things in motion. They went on the Internet to download information about the Clint Eastwood film *Million Dollar Baby* and then researched other famous boxers like Mike Tyson, Evander Holyfield, Oscar De La Hoya and Julio César Chávez.

Once they had decided on a look they set about sourcing the outfit. Esther Serra was sent to a fabric shop in Barcelona, which is where they encountered their first setback. They didn't have any gold fabric for the hooded cloak – only black – and if that shop didn't have it, it was difficult to imagine anywhere else that would. But necessity is the mother of invention and somebody suddenly remembered that the covers used to unveil Jorge's Aprilia RSW250 at the start of the season had been gold. Problem solved!

Now it was a case of putting the whole outfit together. They'd found a blue cloak in a Barcelona boxing shop, and picked up a gum shield at the same time. There were some fruitless trips to fancy dress shops. It was time to get the family involved… Pere Gurt called his mother, Rosa Casas, and her friend, Carme Armengol. After much protest, which fell on deaf ears, the pair reluctantly accepted the assignment and, as a result, MotoGP ended up with two more avid fans – to the point where they would get up at 5am to watch Jorge race in Australia.

A world championship belt needed to be found at the same time, so the team got in touch with the Spanish Boxing Federation (FEB), who recommended 'Charlie's', a specialist shop in Madrid. Bingo! Not only did they have a belt, they also had a pair of golden gloves. The only problem was that the belt featured the Dutch flag, but Esther wasted no time in having the red, white and blue colours replaced with a logo designed by Dani PalaWeb that read: 'Loren Show II'.

In the end Jorge didn't use the gum shield, but there's a little story about that too. When Juan Llansá saw it he said there was no point: 'That is a shit gum shield. You need one made to measure!' Juanito knew what he was talking about – he'd not only seen plenty of riders use them over his 20 years in motorcycle racing, but also his daughter, Zaida Llansá, was the 2001 Kata [a form of martial arts] World Champion. As soon as he landed in Australia he looked on the Internet for a martial arts shop near Phillip Island. He bought the silicone, warmed it in boiling water and made Jorge bite it for a made-to-measure gum shield. Lorenzo still decided not to use it for the celebrations, but Juanito saved it just in case Jorge decided he needed one for MotoGP. 'He never wore one in 125cc and 250cc but I've saved it just in case he really needs to grit his teeth in MotoGP!' Llansá laughed.

Everything was prepared as quickly as possible because there wasn't much time. Jorge quickly became impatient: 'Pere, how's the cloak coming along?'

'Don't worry about it.'

'If it's going to be shit just leave it and we'll think of something else.'

'Trust me. I don't doubt your work, so don't doubt mine.'

It was almost time to leave and everything was ready. Cheni Martínez picked up the outfit and went to meet Jorge at the Hotel Barceló-Sants gym in Barcelona for a dress rehearsal. He had to try everything on before leaving for Melbourne. In the car on the way to the airport Jorge received a call. It was Pere. 'How is it?'

'Pffff. It's not bad.'

Pere Gurt hung up with a smile. 'We've done it,' he thought.

The box remained unopened in Australia, of course, but in Malaysia the surprise was unleashed. The hardest-hitting World Champion in racing was about to be crowned and the character of Rocky Balboa represented the strength he'd displayed to overcome his own limitations and fears. Jorge Lorenzo had not only clinched his second world title, he'd proved to himself and to the world that he could do anything, as a rider and as a person. And then he and the clan treated the public to their most memorable celebration yet.

His friends, headed by Juanito Llansá, waited for him with the boxer's outfit that Lorenzo wanted to wear to mirror his battling performances on the track that season – the cloak, gloves and belt of a World Champion, made out of gold fabric and with a logo on the back, hand sewn by Pere Gurt's mother and her neighbour. It simply read: *Loren Show II. World Champion 2007.*

The 'Lorenzo's Land' flag had fluttered at seven different circuits during the year, but this time it was the Spanish flag that an emotional Lorenzo drove into Malaysian soil, in the final turn of the Sepang International Circuit. The whole act had been Jorge's tribute to 'the eye of the tiger', the winning attitude of Rocky Balboa that he'd adopted as his own. All the knock-out blows to his rivals during the season had given him just cause for celebration.

Celebrations are often forgotten the following day, as soon as the outfits and props have been returned, but not this time. The World Championship gown and gloves will always remain part of Jorge's life. 'One day I returned home to find that my mother had prepared a surprise. She had redecorated my bedroom and there it was, my gold outfit, hung on the wall, looking magical.'

Some people think Jorge Lorenzo is simply copying Valentino Rossi, the originator of post-race victory celebrations, in order to enhance his own image. Others feel that perhaps he takes things too far, or they may view the Lorenzo antics rather more favourably. Jorge will continue to hope they're accepted for what they are: harmless, innocent fun but always with a moral to the 'story'. There's no doubt, though, that he will have something to say if other riders start copying him...

5

OVER THE LINE

Jorge Lorenzo: a champion in the making

Jorge Lorenzo's road to MotoGP began at Jerez, in the final round of the 50cc Copa Aprilia, in 1997. That was the year Dani Amatriaín first 'discovered' him, although the youngster had already collected a hatful of silverware in junior categories. Ten years later he would arrive in the elite class of world motorcycle racing with plenty more trophies.

A nudge in the right direction
FROM MOTOCROSS TO ROAD RACING

'My qualities? I think I am a rider who has great throttle control, good corner speed, I don't crash too often, my lap times are consistent, I produce strong finishes and I tend to be imaginative on the track. I'm not good on the brakes but I can be when the situation calls for it. I don't back down from a head to head and in the past I have tended to mentally 'sink' my team-mates. These are my qualities. My defects are that I start badly and I'm not fast in the wet. Maybe I also still lose my cool at moments of tension, although I am much calmer now than I used to be.'

Every story has a beginning and the Lorenzo one starts at the Copa Aprilia, in which Jorge was able to compete thanks to a helping hand from the Salom family. Moto Salom was the biggest Aprilia dealership on the Balearic Islands and the family, whose sons David and Toni were racing, provided Chicho with the first true race bike of Jorge's career. 'It was all thanks to the Salom brothers' grandfather, who was the real head of the family,' recalls Jorge. 'One day we went to visit him at the dealership and he told us that the Copa Aprilia organisers were looking for new riders. They only had 13 kids signed up so they'd asked all the dealers in Spain to try and come up with some more. Salom had sent the message out to all the most promising young riders in the Balearics, except us. They didn't think we'd be interested and I was still really young, I was only ten years old.'

One of the main reasons why the Saloms didn't get in touch with the Lorenzos was because, in Mallorca, everybody assumed that little 'Giorgio' was going to be a motocross racer. A career in road racing still hadn't figured in the Lorenzo family plan. 'My first "official" race was actually in the Mallorca round of the 80cc Spanish Motocross Championship. The level was really high and I wasn't ready, I was much younger than everybody else and I finished 16th. I'd always liked motocross. Somebody had lent me a video of the 500cc Motocross World Championship and I was a big fan of Joel Smets. Instead of liking Stefan Everts, I went for Smets. That has been a constant feature in my life because I always seemed to prefer the guy who finished second over the guy who won. It was the same with road racing. I preferred Biaggi to Rossi. Before that I used to support Doohan. My dad would shout for Alex Crivillé, but for the sake of being different I'd be shouting for Doohan.'

At this point Jorge's mother, María, interrupts. 'The thing was that to take part in the Copa Aprilia we had to buy a bike, which cost half a million pesetas [roughly £2500]. To tell the truth, the Saloms were really good to us because they allowed us to pay for it in instalments. It took us a whole year to pay it off! But if you compare it to what the house cost us, which was around five million pesetas, half a million for a motorcycle was a lot of money.'

Jorge picks up the story again. 'The first time we tried the bike was in the car park at the Llucmajor circuit. The following week we went to the track at Can Picafort and I tested for the first time with David and Toni Salom. I was pretty quick and lapped a second behind David, who ended up winning the championship. Three weeks after that I entered my first race at Cartagena but the organisers didn't want to let me race because I was still so small. I was 10 and the minimum age was 12. My father started talking to as many people as he could, he even called the Federation, trying to get them to allow us to race because we had paid to sign up and travelled a long way. In the end, to get around it, they made him sign a document that said he accepted full responsibility in the event anything should happen to me. And out I went! I did well from the start because there were kids as old as 18 out there. I was third fastest, ahead of Toni Salom! I remember that it rained in the warm-up and I was running road tyres. Back then they didn't change tyres even if it rained. I ran off the track and crashed on my second lap. The bike was completely full of mud and when they brought it back to the garage on the back of a truck my dad gave me a huge bollocking. "Why did you crash?" he shouted. "Now the bike might not be any use for the race!" He immediately started washing it down with a hose – the first one he could find! It was right outside the Copa Aprilia organisers' hospitality. They were all in there eating and my dad, right outside, was hosing the bike down. The hospitality boss, Xavi Ledesma, came out and shouted at my dad. "What do you think you're doing? Can't you see people are eating and you're splashing them with water?" They started arguing. Xavi is a great friend of ours now but back then … what a palaver! The important thing is that I was able to go out and race, eventually finishing sixth after spending the whole time in eighth, only for the two guys in front of me to crash. Then I went to Montmeló and finished eighth before competing in the final race of the season at Jerez, where I was spotted by Dani. I finished seventh there.'

THE FIRST GLIMPSE OF A WORLD CHAMPION?

'I always take the same line. I would say that is one of my most important qualities. During a race my line through any given corner might vary by a metre here or a metre there with each lap. Some riders take a certain line through a corner on one lap and then on the next one they're three metres off it. I can do ten straight laps within a tenth of a second of each other.'

In 1998, at the age of 11, Jorge Lorenzo was just another one of the kids at Monlau Competition but the time to prove to Amatriaín that he was the one worth taking a gamble on had arrived. It was time to step up to the big league, to national competition. The 50cc Copa Aprilia would be his learning ground and success came quickly, with victory in five of the six rounds, making him the youngest rider ever to claim a Spanish Championship title. The season started on 10 May 1998 at Cartagena and the only race he didn't win was at Jerez, where he finished third. 'I set pole position in practice but I didn't get a good start and a group of eight riders formed. We spent the whole race passing each other all over the place, it was amazing! I was leading on the last lap but two riders came past [Iñaki Aznar and Ángel Rodriguez] two corners from the end and I finished third. I was furious! I really went off on one.'

Jorge laughs at how angry he got that day, before his face lights up with the memory of another story from that season, also at Jerez. 'There were two rounds a season held at Jerez – the third and the last. I set pole by a couple of tenths but Joan Olivé was going really well. He'd just won the 50cc Catalunya Championship and he was ending the season in great form. In the race I just went flat out because at that point I didn't have a clue about race strategy. I started to pull away but Olivé was right there. My dad had always told me that Joan was really smart but as usual I went my own way, even though my dad always used to say: "If you have a rider behind you for more than five laps, let him pass and watch him."

'You have to have a really cool head to be able to do that, to let a rider past. A lot of riders are scared to do it because you think that you won't feel as comfortable behind him or you might not be able to get back in front. Some feel that fear more than others, and I felt it! I tried it a few times later in my career, signalling to another rider to pass me, and it didn't work out. Luckily, usually when I've been in front, I've ended up winning anyway. I still find it difficult to let another rider past because I haven't won many races from second place on the last lap.

'Anyway, back to the race. I decided to ignore my dad's advice and just kept pushing. And there was Olivé, tucked in behind me. In the first turn of the final lap he passed me. I got nervous and tried to follow him but he was in a really strong position because he'd been watching me for the whole race and he knew exactly where my weak points were. He opened up a gap of about 20 metres. Then we got to the last corner.' Jorge stops talking and starts laughing. Really laughing. And I start too – like when somebody is telling you a joke and you start laughing before the punch line because you know what's coming. 'I couldn't allow him to win that race, I just couldn't allow it! So I did the same thing to him that Loris Capirossi did to Tetsuya Harada in Argentina in 1998 and the exact same thing Valentino did to Sete at Jerez in 2005 – in the same corner! I just let off the brakes and ran him off the track! I came across the line gesturing as if to say, "What happened there?" I remember that they used to show highlights of the Copa Aprilia on TVE and after showing the footage of the podium they showed an interview with me claiming that it was nothing, just a racing incident. I said I hadn't touched him and that he'd crashed on his own. Valentín Requena [formerly the Grand Prix commentator on Spanish television] said, live on air: "Come on, Jorge, your nose is going to grow!" That night when we arrived back in Mallorca my dad got hold of the Olivés' home phone number and made me call him to apologise. Poor Joan said he forgave me, although he said it through gritted teeth. Both our dads found the whole thing hilarious.'

In 1998 Jorge Lorenzo made it a grand slam of pole, fastest lap and victory in virtually all of the Copa Aprilia rounds he entered. The following year, in 1999, he stepped up a level to 125cc and he cleaned up there too, winning four of the six races to take the title with a 21-point advantage over Javier Forés. The only races that slipped through his fingers were Jarama and Albacete.

That same season he tested a Grand Prix bike for the first time at Cartagena. The bike belonged to Max Sabbatani. 'He was really small, even smaller than Pedrosa, and very thin. He was virtually a midget! In fact, he still is because I've seen him a couple of times knocking about the paddock. Anyway, at that time I was about the same size as him so they let me test his bike over three days. Emilio Alzamora was also testing and he was three seconds quicker than me, but the most important thing was that I was setting similar times as [Lucio]

Cecchinello and [Nobby] Ueda and I was a second quicker than [Simone] Sanna. I was quicker than him and I was only 11!' It was also at Cartagena that Jorge first met Spain's famous '12+1' World Champion, Ángel Nieto. After watching him on track, Nieto was convinced. 'Amatriaín, this kid looks like a World Champion to me.'

From the national to the international stage
EARLY BATTLES WITH DOVIZIOSO

'Who am I like? I've been compared on many occasions to Kevin Schwantz, especially during 2005, but my riding style, the way I twist the throttle, is more like my idol, Max Biaggi. Like him, at first glance I don't look to be going fast. I could have something of Valentino Rossi in terms of my creativity on the track and mentally I think I am most similar to Wayne Rainey. I have the same desire he had to improve, to be a better rider. But I am Jorge Lorenzo.'

In 2000 Jorge left the promotional series behind and, at the age of 12, he made his debut in the 125cc Spanish Championship, commonly known as the CEV (Campeonato de España de Velocidad) with special permission from the Spanish Federation. It was the second time his young age would give the authorities a problem and it wouldn't be the last. He had a best result of sixth in the two races and finished 18th overall in the championship. 'I had a problem that season because racing a Grand Prix bike is very different from testing one. I was really small, so small that I couldn't reach the gear-shifter to change it properly. I was also scared about revving it too hard and destabilising the bike so I was shifting around 1000rpm too early. My technique allowed me to be really quick through the corners but I was losing a lot of time down the straights by not using the full rev range in each gear, so the bike was slow. It took me about a year to work it out. People kept saying to me, "Change later!" but my hand said no! I was still very young.

'In the first race at Jarama I was 17th in practice and in the race it rained. I got lapped by the guy in fifth! Ángel Rodríguez won the race, lapping six seconds a lap quicker than me! In the fourth race at Albacete Dani Amatriaín asked Toni Elías, who was my team-mate that season, to give me a hand. Toni offered me a tow in practice and I finished sixth, which I repeated in the race. Slowly I was starting to improve and in the next race at Valencia I was third fastest in practice – only Pedrosa and Olivé were ahead of me. There was a problem with the transponders and they actually told me I was fifth, which I was already really pleased about, so you can imagine how happy I was when they detected the problem and moved me up to third! I was on the front row! I got a decent start and spent the whole time in fifth, a long way behind fourth and a long way clear of sixth but with just three corners to go I suddenly got really nervous. I slowed right down and then fell off! I got back up and then fell again. I'd missed a golden opportunity and it is still one of the races I most regret. I thought I was going to finish fifth so to make sure I slowed down but then started to take a different line as a result. You should never drop your pace on a motorcycle and I never allowed it to happen again. That was the only time I've ever panicked at the prospect of a good result.'

The 2001 season saw Jorge record his first two podium finishes in the CEV and his first pole position. He finished fourth overall in the national championship and won his first race on the international stage with victory at Braga, Portugal, in the European Championship. He needed a special permit from the FIM to race in Europe because he was still only 13. He missed three European Championship races after breaking his collarbone at Cartagena. 'My first international race was at Hungaroring. It was a nightmare because the bike wasn't running well and I was more lost than an octopus in a garage. [Andrea] Ballerini won the race and Dovizioso was second. Then we went to Assen, legendary Assen, and things finally worked out. I was seventh in practice and in the race I had a battle with [Mika] Kallio and [Alex] Baldolini. I beat them both and finished fifth. The next round was at Most, in the Czech Republic. There were so many riders that practice was split into two groups. I set the fastest time in my group and I was sitting waiting for the other lot to finish. We all had our fingers crossed that Ballerini wouldn't snatch pole. Juanito Llansá was saying, "Don't worry, he's not going to take it from you." Ballerini was on a red helmet [on course for pole position] but he didn't manage to improve on my time. My father and I were on cloud nine. I'd set my first pole in the European Championship! I led the way at the start and Dovizioso and I escaped. It was our first head-to-head encounter, the first time we raced each other. My dad had heard that Dovi was a really clever rider and he warned me before the race. But just like in 1998 at Jerez, with Olivé, I acted like a dummy and pushed for the whole race. I kept looking behind me to see the bastard still there! It was impossible to shake him off, he was watching me the whole race until the last lap. Three corners from the end I could hear his engine getting closer and I saw his shadow to my left, but he didn't come past. I thought to myself "This guy is going to try something in a second!" I decided I had to run a tighter line and close the door. Sure enough, Dovi went wider through that corner and then dived up the inside. I didn't close the door in time and tried to get in his slipstream, desperately hoping I could get him the next corner, but I ran wide and he won. I came back in tears, I didn't even want to go to the podium, I felt so cheated. I'd been on the limit for the whole race and I felt like I deserved the win more than he did.'

That was the first battle between Jorge and the man who would prove to be his biggest nemesis during both his 250cc World Championship-winning seasons. Andrea Dovizioso was a name the team would not forget quickly. 'Jorge beat Dovi in Braga but in the previous race at Most, what a tantrum!' recalls Juanito, laughing. 'He didn't even want to go to the podium, he was crying like a baby! I can still see Dani (Amatriaín) talking to him, trying to convince him. In the end he went but he didn't want to look at anybody.'

Jorge has a lot of respect for Andrea Dovizioso and feels that his two 250cc world titles have even more prestige because he had to beat the Italian to win them. 'You wouldn't label Dovizioso as fast, particularly, but he's much faster than he looks. He doesn't set many pole positions but he is always up front in a race, fighting to win. He is very intelligent and you can't trust him an inch on the last lap. He has been faithful to Honda, he has great belief in them. His negative side is that he tends to play the victim too much. He'll say that if his bike had a better engine or if it was a bit faster he would win. He's even said that if he was on the same bike as me he'd give me a hiding. I think he looks for excuses too often sometimes, but as a rider and a person I don't have a bad word to say about him.'

In fact, the best description of the way Jorge was riding in 2007 came from Dovizioso himself. 'He is the only one who has understood how to ride the Aprilia – with sensitivity and not force, like de Angelis and Barberá.'

May 2002, Spanish GP, Jerez
GIVE YOUTH A CHANCE

'All I ask of my bike is to love me as much as I love her. I want her to be powerful when necessary but above all manoeuvrable, playful, effective. Circuits have more corners than straights so it is more important to have a good chassis, so that you can hold a good line, than it is to have sheer horsepower.'

Good results in the CEV and the European Championship opened the doors to Derbi for 2002. The opportunity to contest the 125cc World Championship on a factory bike at the age of just 14 had been unthinkable during the days he spent learning to ride on the wasteland in Palma de Mallorca. But, not for the first time, Jorge's precociousness worked against him and he missed the first two races of the season because he didn't meet the minimum age requirement.

Dani Amatriaín had taken care to convince the boss at Derbi, Giampiero Sacchi. 'We have got a pearl of a rider and you have to sign him. If you are patient, what I am offering you is a World Champion.'

In the CEV and European Championships Jorge had received special dispensation to ride, but this could not happen at Grand Prix level. Even if he had been old enough, though, he would have missed those opening two races of the 125cc World Championship, at Suzuka and Welkom, after breaking his collarbone and wrist at the IRTA test in Barcelona. 'Yeah, it's true I wouldn't have been able to race anyway. It was 2002, I was 14 years old, and in the final five minutes of the final day of the test everybody was pushing for a quick lap time. The guys put a qualifying tyre on and I was going well, but suddenly at around 150 or 160km/h, I opened the throttle and lost the rear. I took a terrible whack! I went flying. Apparently Cecchinello had crashed on the previous lap and there was oil or a piece of fairing on the track.'

And so it was that this potential World Champion arrived at Jerez, metaphorically speaking, through the back door. 'We turned up in our caravan and it was the smallest in the paddock,' remembers Jorge. 'My dad used to drive and I used to sit in the back. We arrived on the Thursday and the circuit was already packed with people! I'll never forget that.'

Extracts from a text written by Jorge Lorenzo entitled:
'MY FIRST GP'

On Friday 3 May I wasn't allowed to take part in practice. I was still a day short of my 15th birthday and the rules prevented anybody younger than that age from competing. They tried to convince the organisation but it was impossible. The only thing I was allowed to ride that day was a scooter that barely reached 45km/h. I spent the day watching from behind the walls that protect the riders – and sometimes break their legs – next to the photographers and their cameras, sitting on my 50cc scooter watching the likes of Poggiali, Pedrosa, Ui, Vincent and company fly past. If I remember correctly, I didn't feel any kind of frustration or annoyance that I wasn't allowed to ride. I was just so excited about what awaited me the next day...

The face of a young Jorge Lorenzo watching free practice for the Spanish GP from behind the protective barriers at Jerez already forms part of popular MotoGP legend. Jorge was in another world, walking on air. 'On the Friday the journalists started to interview me. Even the gossip magazines mentioned my debut – Hola [the Spanish, and incidentally the original, version of Hello], for example. There was a lot of expectation.'

Finally the big day arrived: Saturday 4 May 2002, the day of his

15th birthday. Jerez was bursting at the seams, with more than 100,000 people packed into the grandstands for the Spanish Grand Prix. 'They presented me with a surprise birthday cake at the Derbi hospitality. I didn't know what was going on, I couldn't focus on what I needed to focus on.

'My dad told me just to start slowly in practice and gradually pick my pace up, just to make sure of a place on the starting grid. We were worried about any kind of mechanical setback, or even a crash – scared the bike would break down and then I wouldn't be able to race on Sunday. I had two sessions to get myself together. It would be a massive achievement simply to qualify with such little time available but I went out and managed it. I was 33rd – third last and on the back row. But I was officially a Grand Prix rider.

'I'm sure I'm exaggerating when I say that, at that point, you could have counted on one hand – not including Dani and my dad – the people who really believed that green-eyed kid with a face suggesting he was at odds with the whole world would come back to the same circuit five years later as 250cc World Champion. Giampiero Sacchi would be one of the fingers on that wise hand, of course. He backed me when I was barely 14 years old and only had a single European Championship win to my name.

'The clearest image I have of that day is turning round on the grid to see my father and Giampiero Sacchi looking at me and smiling. Sacchi has a lot of love for me. I'm one hell of a rider as far as he's concerned and he appreciates me as a person, too. I have a lot of love for him as well. At the beginning, when I was small, I didn't really trust him – I thought it was all a façade. I remember thinking, "He's so Italian and a such a fake." But for many reasons I have since realised that he's a gentleman. He has never let me down and he has always had faith in me.

'I remember before the race I was a bag of nerves. It was normal. It was like sending a soldier to Iraq before he'd finished his training. I felt defenceless. Inside I knew I wasn't quite ready for the battle. Even so I gave my best. I knew I couldn't bottle out. And then the race started. As usual I started making up positions and caught a group that had been quicker than me in practice. I went a second quicker than I had managed in qualifying and I remember battling with Simón and Bautista, who were both in the group. I beat them and finished 22nd.

'But the important thing wasn't the result. The most important thing was that we'd started a cycle. I was an international rider now and from here onwards all we could do was improve. Day by day, practice by practice, race by race.'

On that day, 5 May 2002, Jorge became a 'motorcycle racer' in every sense: personal, professional and in the eyes of the media. It was the first time he had competed in a race that was screened live on television. 'People told me that I was riding with my legs wide open down the straights, that I wasn't tucking in properly. They said I had to close them tighter – my feet, too. My riding style was pretty ugly.' There was an extra birthday present in store for Jorge too, as he got to meet his idol, Max Biaggi. 'He invited me to his motorhome. It was through a friend of mine who was a waiter in the Derbi hospitality and also a friend of Max. We spoke for about five or ten minutes. He said: "So, you're a fan of mine, yeah? How come you're not a fan of Valentino?" "Because I have always followed you," I answered. And he said: "Valentino is a good rider, but his bike is very fast." I never met him again after that, and we never spoke, but Biaggi used to send messages to my chief mechanic, Giovanni Sandi, who used to work with him, telling him to wish me luck. He said he'd be watching me on the television.'

At the age of 15 years and 1 day Jorge Lorenzo became the youngest rider ever to compete in the World Championship – taking the record from Stefano Bianco, who was just a day older when he competed in the Australian Grand Prix in 2000. Other records quickly followed as he picked up his first points at the GP of Catalunya on 16 June 2002, when he finished 14th – 44 seconds behind the winner, Manuel Poggiali. In only his fourth race he became the youngest rider ever to score points in the World Championship. 'That record has since been broken but they'll never take the record of the youngest rider to compete in a Grand Prix from me!' says Jorge. 'Somebody could equal it, but never beat it. To compete in a race you have to take part in qualifying on the Saturday so unless the rules are changed I'll hold that record until the day I die.'

After Catalunya he scored points in three more races: in Great Britain, Brazil and at the Pacific GP in Motegi, Japan. His best result came in Rio, with seventh place at the Jacarepaguá circuit, on 21 September 2002, and he finished his first full season with equal 20th place overall in the 125cc World Championship, having scored 21 points.

The first victory ... 'X-fuera'
HER NAME WAS RIO!

'I have always adapted to my bike. I have never tried to make a bike adapt to me. In racing the only option is to do well because your livelihood depends on it.'

The 2003 season got off to a bad start, the highlights being sixth places at Catalunya and Portugal as he picked up points in just four races. 'If he had a Honda my boy would have won a race before Pedrosa,' Chicho Lorenzo famously declared at the time. Surprisingly, without a podium finish to his name, the first victory arrived in Brazil, towards the end of September.

Strictly speaking, that first World Championship victory was forged a month previously, at the end of August 2003, in a test session at Almería. Jorge had taken his first victory in the CEV at Jarama in June, beating Álvaro Bautista by the length of the front straight. Before returning to the reality of World Championship duty a private test was arranged at Almería, in which Ángel Rodríguez and Julián Simón would also take part. While Rodri and Julito battled it out to become Jorge's team-mate for 2004, Juan Llansá launched into one of his famous tirades. Jorge reacted with sixth place in Portugal and then victory in Rio.

Even more strictly, of course, it all began on 4 May 1987, the day Jorge was born, but in terms of his career it would be more accurate to suggest that everything started on 20 September 2003, on the other side of the world, at the Jacarepaguá circuit in Brazil, where Jorge claimed victory in the Rio GP ahead of Casey Stoner, Alex de Angelis and Dani Pedrosa.

'The first time I saw Stoner was in the CEV, back in 2000,' recalls Jorge. 'We looked down the entry list and spotted this really young Australian, riding a Honda. Since there were two groups we were able to take a look at him from the control tower at Albacete. He was really fast but at the same time he looked out of control. He was running wide but he kept on the throttle, giving it full gas, the bike swerving all over the place. He is aggressive, very brave and extremely talented, and he rides without fear of crashing. Having said that I think he could get a little more out of what he is doing if he was a bit more lively – if he was more in touch with the fans. He's like Doohan in that respect, but he's happy that way and each to his own, I guess.'

Now they were reunited in the World Championship, and Jorge's dream of joining Stoner as one of the best young riders in the minor category were turning into a reality. He was aged just 16 years and 139 days when he climbed onto the top step of the podium in Brazil – at that time the second-youngest Grand Prix winner of all time behind Marco Melandri. Obviously that made him the youngest ever Spanish winner, breaking the record held by Héctor Barberá by three months.

That first victory came without any prior warning, although it certainly wasn't unexpected – not for Jorge or for anybody close to him. 'Between 2001, when I first raced in the European Championship, and my first season with Derbi in 2003, I used to predict the result of a race half an hour before it started. It started at Assen in 2001. I used to say, "Today I'm going to finish fourth" or "Today I'm going to finish seventh..." Because I used to get so nervous before a race, I made up a ritual. I used to go to the bathroom and in order to relax I'd set targets that were reasonable or even below what I knew I was truly capable of, so that I wasn't disappointed. And most of the time I'd be proved right! Occasionally I'd be a position or two out, but mostly I got it bang on.'

The first time Jorge Lorenzo predicted a win for himself was in Brazil. His father Chicho was equally convinced, but since the kid had never won before, the challenge was huge. 'The Derbi wasn't the best bike in 2003 which is why what he did in Rio was so incredible,' recalls Juan Llansá. 'He came from behind, fought with everybody and then beat them. I think Jorge had realised in Portugal that he could win because at Estoril he'd finished sixth but he was only eight seconds off the leader. That was the key statistic. He'd had similar results before, like when he was sixth at Montmeló, but then he'd been over 22 seconds behind the winner, miles off. This time they were right in front of him, he could see them. From Portugal we went to Brazil … and this time he beat them.'

A previously unpublished text written by Jorge Lorenzo
Japarepaguá circuit, Brazil, 20 September 2003 at precisely 11.41am
'MY MOMENT'

A single droplet trickles down my face and explodes on the surface of the asphalt. The suffocating heat and humidity that dominate the atmosphere are not the main reason for it to escape my body. Rather, it is the palpable tension and anxiety of the moment. A droplet so small, so insignificant, that it has evaporated within seconds of hitting the ground, seconds in which a peloton of seven riders has roared past. All of them with their eye on victory. The stars of the championship are in there: Casey Stoner, Pedrosa, de Angelis, Talmacsi, Andrea Dovizioso … and me. Aged just 16 and hanging on to my Derbi, I surprisingly find myself in fourth place. I get ready to cross the line.

With my head tucked in behind the fairing and without breaking my concentration I throw a quick glance to my right. I can see the faces of excitement among my crew on pit wall. I don't need to see the 'L1' on my pit board, I'm perfectly aware of that. It's the last lap. There is just enough time to appreciate the look on some of their faces. They are shouting and screaming, trying to give me the 'final push'. They have every reason to, because in my hands is the opportunity to save all of their asses … The season has been going badly, really badly, if not disastrously. The omens were not good for a team aspiring to the title to have had a best result of sixth so far. As if that wasn't enough, the bike at that time had great top speed but in general terms it left a lot to be desired in comparison to the Honda and the Aprilia.

Right now I feel alone, very alone. Suddenly, I feel the weight of responsibility take over my whole body. How am I going to do this?

Here I am, alone with myself, my bike and my ability. Nothing else, nobody else. A podium finish is within touching distance but my people would be happy with fourth. Even a fifth or a sixth would be good, because behind us there are another four riders ready to do whatever it takes to steal a position. It won't be easy. Who am I kidding? I'd be happy with that. Logic tells me that I'm okay where I am, there is no need to take risks. But at the same time there is another voice inside me saying exactly the opposite.

In theory, what I have achieved up to this point is already impressive so I don't have anything to lose. Hang on a second. Could I be fooling myself here? Do I really have nothing to lose? If I make a mistake and don't finish the race this whole thing will be merely anecdotal. A great race without a finish. Sure, my team would congratulate me on a great performance and give me a round of applause, but we'd spend the rest of the season regretting what happened. On the other hand, if I finished on the podium I'd be their hero. Don't ask me why, but I knew that I had already achieved what I set out to do. I had managed to stick the pace with the guys who had been, for want of a better expression, my 'Gods' up to that time. Riders who I only ever raced alongside in my dreams. Now they were fighting with me for victory! 21 laps dicing with the biggest fish in the pond ... What a buzz! That was enough for me! Or at least that is what I had thought until the start of the final lap...

Now everything was different, everything had changed. The final lap was like another race altogether. It was time for 'the Grand Finale', the moment when I would show the whole world what I was capable of. I was ready to raise the stakes by double, or even treble...

I believe that sooner or later there comes a moment in a person's life when a star falls into their lap. What I'm trying to say is that the opportunity of a lifetime appears right in front of their nose. It is at this moment that a person has to close their eyes and go for it. Only the people who recognise that this is their moment and act upon it in time are able to make the most of it. Those who doubt it, those who are indecisive or think that more opportunities like this will come in the future, will fail. This was MY MOMENT and I had to do something about it.

I get myself ready. I transform. Did I say transform? Yes, I want to do something great and I am going to attempt the impossible. And so we arrive at the first corner of the final lap. It is a right-hander, where I had already noticed my great corner speed during practice. The previous day, during Saturday's free practice, I couldn't understand how I could be so much faster through that section than everybody else. That advantage had carried into the race and, if anything, it had increased. So at that very moment I decided to try something I'd already attempted, perhaps too tentatively, on a few previous laps – an overtake around the outside.

I went deep into the corner, thinking that I'd have to close the throttle to keep the bike on the right line, but it kept exactly the same level of grip around the outside that it had previously had on the inside. That gave me courage and I gradually opened the throttle more and more. To my surprise, my crazy idea was working and metre by metre I drew closer to Pedrosa, who was inside me in third position. He looked to his left, watching incredulously at the ease with which I passed him. At that point I just wanted the corner to end because I knew that sooner or later this was going to turn out badly. But no … it didn't turn out badly and the inertia and speed I was generating carried me past Stoner at the end of the corner! I'd just passed Pedrosa and Stoner around the outside in one go! Of course, I ran too hot into the next corner and the Australian got a position back on the brakes. I should have known it was too good to be true.

Even so, I was up to third place and there were only three-quarters of a lap remaining. Suddenly and momentarily my mind wandered from the race. I remembered what Emilio Alzamora (my team-mate) said to me the day before: 'If it is a group race tomorrow, whoever comes out second from the corner leading into the back straight will win. If you are in third place, even better.' If Emilio was right, my plan could not be going better. I found myself in a privileged position because my Derbi had always had great top speed and I felt sure I could hang on to my position until we arrived at the longest straight on the track. When we got there, it would be time to attack. So that is what I did. I closed every door through the next series of corners as best I could and we arrived at the back straight, which was almost a kilometre long.

I wasn't very close to Stoner and de Angelis as we came out of the corner but that actually helped because I was able to make use of the slipstream without them getting in my way. At the start of the straight I noticed that not only was the gap not decreasing, as I'd expected, but it was actually increasing as Stoner took advantage of the slipstream from de Angelis and pulled away from me. However, things quickly changed as my Derbi began to pick up speed (thanks also to a slightly longer gear ratio and more aerodynamic fairing to the other bikes) and while they hit top speed I continued to get faster and faster. In an attempt to try and block a pass on the inside, de Angelis had moved to the left, which was the direction of the next corner. Casey was right behind him, trying to stay in the slipstream, and even though there didn't appear to be enough room he tried to squeeze past Alex on the inside. I was drawing ever closer to them and I still had time to make a choice. There were two options – left or right. Down the right was the least risky option because there was more space but even if I managed to pass them I'd be in the worst position for the corner. If I went for the riskier option down their left I would take the lead and have the best position for the corner. There wasn't much time to think about it so in the end I went for the riskiest option and dived up their left side.

I was mere centimetres from the edge of the track but I was able to take advantage not only of a draft from Stoner but also from poor de Angelis, who could see victory slipping through his fingers once again. The San Marino man desperately tried to rescue the situation by running around the outside at the end of the straight but his efforts were in vain. Nobody was going to pass me now. I felt a shiver run down my whole body, similar to the one I had felt when I took the lead for the first time at mid-race distance. But this time the shiver was more intense because I knew I was about to touch the sky. With only a few metres to go, each metre was like a whole race of its own. I was cursing the final corner, thinking that somebody might try a kamikaze move, but it never happened. And that is where my story starts.

Some people think that, because of his physical and extravagant riding style, Lorenzo is the next Kevin Schwantz, the winner of 25 Grand Prix races between 1988 and 1994 and the 500cc World Champion in

1993. A good part of the reasoning behind this is Jorge's winning performance in Brazil in 2003. Rio, as well as being the scene of his first victory, was where his 'X-fuera' reputation was forged, thanks to that majestic double pass on Dani Pedrosa and Casey Stoner through a right-hander at the start of the final lap. The history books will say that his nickname was earned there, but few people know that he'd already 'patented' the move during the 2001 European Championship at Braga in Portugal.

'My first international victory was at Braga, in the European Championship. I did a 'por fuera' there but I didn't realise it at the time. I was on pole, got an average start and Mattia Angeloni passed me. We were both on a Honda and at the end of the straight I went around the outside of him into Turn 1. I went on to win the race but nobody knew that I'd made that pass or, more importantly, what it meant. Only me. Only I knew that I'd done something different.'

The 'X-fuera' move is now the stuff of legend, but it was actually born out of necessity. Jorge came up with it because the Derbi didn't pull until it got to the top of the rev range. As such, he had to take a wide line into the corners and keep his speed up, otherwise he would lose it on the exit. 'The Derbi didn't accelerate so to make sure I didn't lose my speed I had to go through the corners really quickly. I worked that out myself and realised that I had to sacrifice a little in braking, take a little off. For example, Alzamora used to brake exactly the same as he had on the Honda. But the Derbi didn't accelerate and it used to take about an hour to get out of the corner. I decided it was better to brake less, take a wide line and let it run. I developed a level of corner speed that was much, much faster than the others in certain places. I was losing out on the brakes and under acceleration but in certain corners, like at Brazil, it was an advantage. I was able to go quicker through the corners than my rivals, even if it meant going around the outside of them.'

Victory proved to be a huge weight off Jorge's shoulders. 'Winning changed him and Brazil was the key,' says Pere Gurt. 'The pictures from Rio were of a kid who was finally letting everything out.' Jorge finished in the points on three more occasions before the end of that season, picking up his first fastest race lap, at Motegi on 5 October, and his first pole at Sepang a week later. He finished 12th in the championship on 79 points.

The 2004 season would prove to be his last in the 125cc class and his last with Derbi. He was offered the chance to switch to Honda but he decided to stay faithful to the Spanish factory. 'I don't regret it at all,' insists Jorge. He finished the season fourth in the championship on 179 points, although he could easily have finished runner-up to Andrea Dovizioso. All he had to do was take three points off Roberto Locatelli at Valencia but he crashed out and, to make matters worse, his future team-mate, Héctor Barberá, with whom he was already starting to have problems, won the race and took the runner-up spot in the championship with it. However, before taking the step up to 250cc with Honda for 2005, Jorge celebrated victory on three more occasions, at Assen (26 June), Brno (22 August), and Losail (2 October). Lorenzo left his 125cc record at four wins, three poles, three fastest laps and nine podiums from 46 races across three seasons.

2005: A CRITICAL SEASON

'They say you are only as good as your last race. But I have never believed that. We all have a past.'

Jorge loves that phrase. Used in a different way from how he originally intended, you might say that his past started in 2005, his first season in the 250cc class. That was the season that he decided he no longer wanted to be a mere spectator to the battle between Dani Pedrosa and Casey Stoner. Yet despite chasing them both hard, Jorge didn't rack up a single victory.

On four occasions it was so close he could almost taste it. At Mugello he set pole, the youngest rider ever to do so in 250cc history, but in the race he was beaten to the line by Pedrosa. 'I was coming under a lot of pressure from the media,' remembers Jorge. 'They kept on reminding me that I could beat Dani Pedrosa's record as the youngest ever winner of a 250cc race. They started saying it at

Mugello, when I finished second. In fact, if I had won there I would have set a virtually unbreakable record because I still had almost a whole season to spare.'

The situation repeated itself at Brno, in the Czech Republic, where he also started from pole only to finish second to Dani once again. The jinx continued in the Grand Prix of Qatar at Losail, where again he set pole and again finished second, this time to Casey Stoner. There seemed only one way to finish the season at Valencia, with second place, again behind Pedrosa. Nevertheless, his debut 250cc season ended with an impressive tally of six podiums, four pole positions and fifth overall in the championship.

THE CRASHES

Another of Jorge's favourite phrases is: 'The only thing that scares me about racing is hurting myself.' Those who know him best say that the times they have seen Jorge at his lowest have been while he has been injured – firstly because of the physical pain, secondly because it means he is out of action, and thirdly because of the recovery process he must go through. During his time racing in the smaller categories Jorge rarely crashed, but he broke his wrist once and his collarbone five times. 'The right one once and the left one four times,' Jorge points out.

'The first time I crashed was in 1997 at Muro, the only circuit in Mallorca that hosts a round of the Spanish Motocross Championship. We usually used to train at Sant Joan and Muro. I started racing on an 80cc bike built in 1988 – it was ancient! People used to laugh at us because of that bike. It was slow, the suspension was crap ... eventually my dad decided to buy a new one. We were really excited so we went to give it its first run out. On the way from Palma to Muro, which is about a 50-minute drive, I was saying to myself: "Jorge, this is a special day, it is not every day you get to ride a brand new motorcycle so be careful, you don't know what it is going to do. It is a day for having fun, enjoying yourself and above all not crashing!" I went out on the bike, did a couple of laps and came back in. During my second run my dad took his eye off me and I got passed by a 250. Some guy aged about 35 or 40 on a 250, and I was on a little 80. But I thought, "This guy's not getting away!" I got behind him and I was going really well, riding really fast, but the bike was out of control. Suddenly I saw the guy on the 250 hit a jump. I gave it a bit more gas and when I hit the jump I realised I was going too quickly. I hit the brake but I was already in the air, and it was the rear brake! The momentum of the bike made it turn in the air and I landed upside down, with the handlebar against my arm, and bounced along the ground. It was a monster crash and my dad heard it from almost 500 metres away. He came running over and rushed me to casualty. I'd broken my collarbone but worse than that I'd destroyed my new bike!

'The first time I broke my collarbone in a road race was at Cartagena in 2001. I'd just won in the European Championship at Braga and I was so confident that I was going to win again. Just when you think you're the king of the jungle, when you have that cocky swagger about you, that's when you crash. Any time I have been careless, I've had a big one. My dad warned me but... During afternoon practice on the Saturday I ran straight at a right-hander. The run-offs were a mess and on a road racing bike if you hit a bump you get sent flying. That's what happened. I was invited to watch the races from the control tower at Cartagena and people dropped in to see me. But all I could ask myself was, "What am I doing here?" '

Every crash he's had has hurt him. Physically, obviously, but for Jorge it damages his morale even more. Like at the GP of Catalunya in 2005. 'I remember being fastest in every session, except in qualifying when Pedrosa beat me to pole position. We could tell that Pedrosa's people and even Dani himself were worried because I had a consistent and quick pace. Pedrosa even got so nervous that he made a mistake with the clutch on the grid and he was way back on the first lap – eighth or tenth or something, I can't remember. I got a good start but it was really hot and I wasn't getting much feel from the tyres. My pace was slow, about three seconds off what I'd been doing in practice. The race pace in general was slow but mine was even slower and I was struggling to stay with the group. Barberá, who had qualified seventh, was ahead of me and on the sixth lap Pedrosa came past and tried to push his way to the front. I realised I was too relaxed. Pedrosa tried to stretch it out and at that point I got nervous. I tried to make it all back in just a couple of corners. I got up behind de Angelis, who was running third, and when I tried to pass him I got it all wrong. I thought de Angelis was quicker through the corners than he was and I let the bike run off the brakes, only to hit his rear tyre. We both went flying and I broke my collarbone.

'That was one of the worst moments of my career. I couldn't believe I'd wasted such a good opportunity. I don't know if I could have won but I know I could have fought for victory. I remember seeing the television pictures – me with my face full of dark brown dirt, screaming with pain. I walked over to the tyre wall to get away from the track but there was no sign of an ambulance. I went crazy! I started kicking the side of a car and when the ambulance did turn up I started kicking that too, cursing everything. The marshals tried to calm me down, the doctors too, but I was hysterical because I couldn't accept the situation. They took me to the Clinica and the ambulance was bouncing around all over the place. Every time it hit a bump I'd start shouting and swearing at the driver. When we got there and they unzipped my leathers you could see that the collarbone was broken. Dani, my dad and Palau turned up and Palau started crying. That started me laughing! It was really comical. My whole family had come to the race – my mum, my girlfriend and my sister – and instead of celebrating a podium they had to spend the week with me in hospital. Whenever I get injured I just try to go to sleep so that it's over quicker.'

In 2007 Jorge came close to doing himself serious damage at Le Mans. It led him to write about a subject that clearly caused him concern.

Le Mans, French GP
Text written by Jorge Lorenzo entitled:
'FLYING IS NOT IMPOSSIBLE'

Suddenly, within a millisecond, your heart rate shoots up to 200bpm. You know what's going to happen next. You have abused the throttle and the rear tyre is lodging its complaint in a show of unexpected betrayal. You take one last loving look at the dash of your Aprilia and brace yourself to make the landing as pain-free as possible. Whoever said it was impossible to fly?

Now you're flying. What a wonderful feeling … right? Actually, no. Not at all. As you sail through the air, long enough to look down on the French tarmac from the viewpoint of Pau Gasol, panic takes over your body and you fear the worst. The landing is hard and now you're rolling across the scenery like tumbleweed across the Wild West. Except flesh and bone weighs more than straw and gravity is quick to remind you of that fact.

You want the nightmare to be over as soon as possible so that you can check if you've been lucky or if your guardian angel is on a coffee break … The left foot burns and starts to hurt, and you start to fear the worst. Is it broken? Is that the championship down the drain? These are just a couple of the many thoughts that flash through your head during the six seconds that the whole episode lasts. You try to stand up in the gravel but your instinct tells you to stop. Two marshals come to the rescue and stretcher you to safety, away from the battleground full of soldiers that is the circuit (hey, some soldiers shoot you from behind, you know!).

Once you get your boot and sock off you can see that the foot is not broken, despite the pain. Another marshal invites you onto his motorcycle and takes you back to your refuge, commonly known as the 'box'. Your team anxiously awaits your arrival. They were scared – maybe even more than you were – but once they know that there is no major injury their only concern is to repair a bike which, I decide, if ridden before it is ready, could result in reduced performance and the consequent disappointment of the rider in question.

The decision is made. You will try and ride your second bike, a bike so similar yet so different in the way it feels to a rider. You have 25 minutes to pull off a miracle. Can you make provisional pole after everything that has happened? Not this time, but you weren't far off. Not far off at all.

This time Jorge escaped, although for a moment Dani Amatriaín felt inside that the season had ended right there, in that corner at Le Mans.

The strangest in a catalogue of accidents that resulted in a broken collarbone came at Valencia in 2005. 'We still can't work out why he crashed there but he was going very fast through the second corner,' explains Juanito Llansá with an air of resignation. 'Maybe he went over the painted line in the chicane or even touched the dirt on the outside of the track. But what a trip that was from Valencia to Barcelona! Three hundred kilometres of swearing and shouting. "It hurts! Stop the ambulance! Give me something for the pain!" Four hours that you had to experience to believe. Because when Jorge is in a good mood he's great, but when he gets something into his head, there isn't a person who can make him see sense! He wanted them to give him something but they'd already given him anti-inflammatories before we set off.'

That crash in the post-season test sent Jorge into a mini-crisis, having only just made the switch from Honda to Aprilia. 'I felt everything was fantastic. The first time I rode the Aprilia I thought it was the dog's bollocks. I'd spent the whole season struggling to tuck in behind the fairing on the Honda and on the Aprilia I had room to spare. On top of that, I was inside the lap record on the second day of the test. I'd been in good form during the Grand Prix, finishing second behind Pedrosa and ahead of Stoner. My dad gave me his usual warning. I spoke with him on the phone at the end of the second day and he said, "Keep your feet on the ground because whenever you change bikes you need a period of adaptation. The lap times are good but be careful." On the third day, before the track had even warmed up properly I was already matching my times from the previous day. I thought "This is going to work out great!" but I was too confident. I went into the corner before the rise up to Curvone … and I can't remember anything else. I woke up in the ambulance with Juanito saying, "Calm down, calm down!" I was furious and shouting,

"It's happened again!" I still don't know what happened and that's the worst thing for a rider. That's why I went into a crisis.'

Jorge was nervous for a long time. He was slow, he didn't dare lean the bike over and he started to think that he was risking too much for the sake of a tenth of a second here or there. 'I was holding a good 10 per cent back. I didn't want to crash and hurt myself again and during the pre-season tests I was so slow, until we got to the IRTA test at Montmeló, just a few weeks before the start of the 2006 season. That is when I started to conquer my fear, thanks to the help of the psychologist Joaquín Dosil. He told me to try and understand whether fear was logical or illogical, if this fear I had in me was useful or not.'

Injury has been the only factor that has ever made Chicho doubt whether a career in motorcycles was the right thing for Jorge. Whenever he crashed the question of whether they were doing the right thing would come up. 'I never thought about quitting. I never considered throwing in the towel, but my father did. At least that's what he said in the hospital after I broke my collarbone during the IRTA tests at Montmeló in 2001. I don't know if he said it to see what my reaction would be or whether he really meant it. Either way, I told him to forget it, no chance. But if he was serious we would have had to quit, because at that time I was only 14 years old and he was the boss. But I wanted to make it and if we packed it in before I made my debut I would never have got anywhere. I wanted to give it a shot.'

BAD TIMES

Bike problems for a winner like Jorge lead to more than bad lap times, they create bad times in general. They say that when Jorge has a problem, when he's struggling with something, it has a negative effect on his riding. He continues going about his daily life, playing on his PlayStation, chatting online, downloading music and spending time with friends ... but you can tell things aren't right when he gets on his bike. For this reason Juan Llansá reckons you can identify the most difficult moments in his life by looking through his results. 'There was a time I remember in particular, on the Derbi, in Malaysia 2004. He'd won in Holland, Brno and Qatar and we got to Sepang, a circuit that he likes. The first day went well, he was third or fourth, but we had problems with the electronics on the second day and he ended up fifth or sixth. That hurt him! Then the bike broke down in the race and he couldn't finish. You should have seen him when he got back to the box. I have never seen Jorge so pissed off, not with a crash or anything. He got off the bike and I had to grab hold of it because he tried to push it to the ground. Dani got hold of him and took him to the back of the box for him to cool down … for a rider who is a true winner the most difficult thing to accept is not having the chance to get a good result. When a good rider crashes, he finds it difficult to accept that it's his fault. That's why he explodes if there's a mechanical fault.'

To a born winner, second place is for the first loser. When things were going badly for Jorge everybody would know about it. He'd come back into the pit box, take his helmet and gloves off and throw them onto the mechanics' work bench. 'He'd storm out and then a little later, once he'd calmed down, he'd come back and sit down. But he didn't bother picking the helmet and gloves up!' Juanito decided to teach him a lesson. 'One day I picked up the helmet and gloves and shoved them in the rubbish bin. A couple of hours later Jorge came and asked where his helmet and gloves were. I said I didn't know and he spent the next hour looking for them! When he got desperate I pointed to the bin. I said, "Next time I won't tell you where they are." That was in 2003, when he was really wild.'

In 2005 Jorge had a lot of things to work through and fight against: racing a 250, a new category for him; a rival in the shape of 125cc World Champion Dani Pedrosa; and a motorcycle, the Honda, that wasn't ideally suited to his riding style. 'The 250cc Honda was built with Pedrosa in mind,' says Juanito. 'Jorge had to ride it at 110 per cent and that's why there were crashes and clashes. None of it was intentional but when you are on the limit, these things happen. That's why in 2006, when he changed from Honda to Aprilia, he improved so much. With a bike set up just how he wanted it he was able to show that he could win races, and if he'd had an Aprilia in 2005 I think it would have been a different story – although we'll never know.'

Jorge wanted to be where Pedrosa was in 2005. He wanted to be up at the front, doing what Dani was doing, but even though he had the same bike he had to push beyond his own limitations. 'Sooner or later, you get caught out,' smiles Juanito. 'Because in reality we didn't have the same bike as Dani Pedrosa. The evidence was at Mugello, when the Aprilias were taking 15km/h out of our bike on the straights. They were quicker than Pedrosa's bike too, but not by as much – maybe only 5–6km/h. When you see yourself being passed so easily down the straights, you really have to go for it in the corners.'

Jordi Pérez worked with Jorge throughout his 250cc career and experienced many of the 'bad times' alongside him. 'He came with a reputation as a bad boy who produced moments of genius,' says Jordi. 'But it wasn't anything out of the ordinary. He was an aggressive rider but he didn't deserve that bad reputation. That should be reserved for riders who get off the bike looking sorry for themselves, telling lies about their bike to justify a bad result, when the only thing that let them down was their own performance. Instead of recognising that fact, they send their mechanics crazy by getting them to take the engine to pieces seven times. Which is worse? That? Or kicking and breaking a 50 euro wall panel like Jorge did? They also used to call him a killer when he was in 125cc but just look at the racing now. It is full combat!'

In 2005, at the Grand Prix of Japan, Jorge was given a one-race suspension to be served at the next round in Malaysia. It was without doubt the worst moment of his season and probably of his career. He was 17 years old and very angry – but so were the team, who felt Jorge was not at fault for the collision with de Angelis. They set the garage up as usual in Malaysia and on Jorge's seat they left a sign which read: 'I've just popped out for a while. Back in Qatar.' 'He was surprised and outraged about what had happened in Japan,' recalls Jordi Perez. 'It is very difficult to react well in situations like that. The way Dani

[Amatriaín] looked after him in the hours and days that followed was really important. He took him to Malaysia hoping it would cheer him up. He didn't break anything, he wasn't angry. Just sad.'

THE RAIN

Racing in the wet is a thorny subject with Jorge. In 2001, riding an Aprilia in the European Championship, he went well in the wet, but in the 250cc class, on the world stage, it was a different matter. 'When it rains you have to ride with respect but if you don't feel confident you'll go backwards or crash,' explains Juanito. 'We've worked hard to help him improve, training on a supermoto, small bikes, wet tyres, wet tracks ... but at the end of the day it's down to the rider. However much he works at it, riding in the wet is still very much in his head.'

Lorenzo is undoubtedly a hard worker: if every race was in the wet he knows he'd make progress, a theory finally proved in 2008 – the wettest season since the millennium and one that saw Jorge finally master the rain. 'I don't improve because I never have the opportunity to practise,' he said in 2007. 'There are so few races in the wet each year ... the problem is that I'm too cautious. The riders who are fast in the wet don't think about whether they're going to crash or not. I do, or at least I used to. I have always been scared of crashing in the wet because I had a history of doing so. Every time I got myself together and started going fast in the wet I crashed. The thing that annoys me about riding in the wet is that you crash and you don't know why. The difference between going through a corner quickly in the wet and then crashing at the same speed on the following lap is so small that you can't work it out. It is a very fine line.'

Jorge even used to crash in the wet on the PlayStation. 'I've just never gone well in the rain. The first wet race I had in the World Championship was in Portugal, on the Derbi. I was doing really well, riding really fast ... and then I crashed. So the next time I went slower. Then you get your confidence back, try to go fast again and you crash again! So then you say, I need to go even slower than that! It's like a spiral.'

They say that wet-weather riding is similar to riding dirt-track, which is why Jorge decided to spend the 2006 Christmas holidays with Kenny Roberts at his ranch in California.

Extracts from a text written by Jorge Lorenzo entitled:
'TO AMERICA WITH THE ROBERTS CLAN'

We arrived on a Friday night and the following morning we were up at the crack of dawn, desperate to get up to the ranch and start training as soon as possible. I ate a fantastic cheese and ham omelette for breakfast and then we jumped into the hire car. It would be a half-hour drive from our hotel to Kenny's place.

It was amazing. I couldn't believe my eyes as we pulled up to the ranch. The rolling hills looked like they were out of a Disney film and the tracks ... the tracks were like heaven on earth! Heaven on dirt! There were four tracks: a small U-shaped one, an oval that they call 'Short Track', and two motocross circuits. Kenny's stunning wood cabin, which includes a swimming pool and gym, is surrounded by thousands of square metres of open land.

I was in a hurry. I wanted to get on a bike and start sliding it straight away! I changed into my 'work' clothes as quickly as I could. I quickly encountered the first thing that was new to me. As I put the left boot on I realised that it had a steel shoe covering the bottom.

I was told that it was to help my left foot slide along the ground (dirt-track is always run on an anti-clockwise oval) and that I should take care for the first few laps because if you put too much weight on it you could slip and end up falling with the bike on top of you. That steel shoe was 25 years old! They told me Kenny Roberts himself used to use it before going to race in the World Championship. Well I suppose it was a little worn...

Before starting to ride we had a little snack that Kenny's Japanese girlfriend made for us. After that he gave me four main tips for riding in the wet and told me what aspects of my riding we would try to correct. Sir Roberts, 'El marciano' [The Martian], as we still call him in Spain, is a very special guy. He's got a very strong personality, he feels like an American and he acts that way. When you analyse his body language, you can see that he possesses overwhelming self-confidence, he is very much the Macho Alfa. His movements are slow but firm, and when he stands still he always has his legs slightly open and his chin raised.

His voice is deep and loud, and when he looks at you his eyes never wander from yours. He has a 'Yankee' sense of humour – a little arrogant but at the same time very funny. If you try and poke fun at him he will usually come back with something better, but if he doesn't have anything interesting to say he simply doesn't answer or he plays deaf. He loves cigars and you'll see him with one in his mouth most of the time, like Hannibal from the 'A-Team'. He could be a cross between John Wayne and Clint Eastwood, who knows…

When he gets on a motorcycle his movements are similarly slow. Watching him from the outside you'd be tempted to think that he's not going fast, that he's taking it easy, but when you look at the stopwatch you realise that he is going, as they would say, 'fucking fast!' Roberts Jnr has the same quality. But the thing I noticed about Senior was his energy and his vitality, more typical of a 15-year-old kid who is just starting out. He doesn't mind spending all day riding with us – what's more, he enjoys it, even though he must have covered millions of kilometres with his bike crossed over around this track.

I can still remember the little battle we had on my second to last day there, when I had got to the point where I was almost as fast as him. We started to pass one another in every corner, elbow to elbow. In one of them I was in front but I crossed the bike over too much as we entered the turn. He was planning to pass me on the inside but no, suddenly the gap was gone. His front wheel touched my rear wheel and he went flying into the air, landing heavily on his head … Massimo and I thought he'd really hurt himself and we were fearing the worst. Five minutes later he was back out there, throttle wide open…

'I never play to be second'
THE FULFILMENT OF A DREAM:
WORLD CHAMPION AT LAST

'I realised that to win championships I had to change. I couldn't keep taking so many risks. I had to quit being this daredevil rider and focus on improving my corner speed, on being more smooth with the Aprilia.'

The 2006 season arrived. Jorge had signed for Aprilia as their leading rider and he began the season in dominant style: pole and victory at Jerez, pole and victory in Qatar, pole in Turkey. No other rider had won the first three races of a 250 season since Daijiro Kato in 2001, and it proved a step too far for Jorge, but that electrifying start to the season was certainly an eye-opener. 'A lot of people were telling me I'd do it, that I'd be World Champion. But it was only after Jerez, after my first victory in 250, that I thought it myself for the first time.'

However, bad luck was waiting just around the corner – the first corner at Istanbul Park to be precise, where a collision with Shuhei Aoyama sent him into free fall. Jorge finished fourth at Shanghai and hit rock bottom in Le Mans. That weekend at the French Grand Prix saw him crash five times in three days, one of them in the race after making contact with Roberto Locatelli. He was unable to restart.

Jorge's morale was so low he felt he'd fallen into a bottomless pit. He needed somebody to throw him a rope and it was his manager, Dani Amatriaín, and his physical trainer, Marcos Hirsch, who initially came to the rescue. At Mugello Alex Debón joined them and the Italian Grand Prix proved to be the turning point, 'The Return of the King'. Jorge took victory from pole and repeated the feat at Assen, Donington, Brno and Phillip Island, as well as winning in Sepang. His first world title was in touching distance, he could feel it with the tips of his fingers, but in Portugal, his first bite at the cherry, he could only manage fifth – his worst race finish of the season – and victory for Andrea Dovizioso brought the Italian to within 13 points of Jorge, with one race remaining.

However, in spite of a stressful finale at the Ricardo Tormo circuit in Valencia, on 29 October 2006 fourth place for Jorge combined with seventh for his great rival made Lorenzo only the tenth Spanish rider in history to be crowned World Champion. The icing on the cake was a record-equalling ten pole positions in one season, a record that had been held by Antón Mang since 1981. The only thing that didn't work out well at Valencia was the wheelie Jorge pulled in celebration of his well-deserved title.

2007: THE DEFINING SEASON

'The biggest lesson I learnt from 2006 was that I realised that you don't have to win every race if you want to be World Champion. What's more, this year I plan to ride with more intelligence and more patience. The thing I'm most looking forward to is seeing the number 1 on my bike. I want to know what it feels like to defend a title.'

In 2007 Jorge had his cake with icing and a cherry on top. With his second world title, more records would fall. After starting out with victory in two of the opening three rounds, victory at Shanghai would equal Sito Pons's career record of 15 wins to make him the sixth most successful Spanish rider of all time, while his 20th pole would equal the achievements of two legends in the shape of Barry Sheene and Wayne Gardner. His 250cc record read 16 pole positions from 33 races but he made it 50 per cent in China, adding victory and fastest race lap to his weekend's work.

That made it three wins from the opening four races, which combined with a second place added up to 95 points, the best start to a season since Kato won the opening four rounds in 2001. Before that only six other riders had taken three out of the first four: Max Biaggi in 1996, Tetsuya Harada in 1993, Luca Cadalora in 1991, Carlos Lavado in 1986, Kork Ballington in 1979 and Dario Ambrosini in 1950. Unsurprisingly, all of them ended the season as World Champion.

Text written by Jorge Lorenzo entitled:
'LIVE FOR THE MOMENT'

I've left writing this column until late – the last possible day and the last possible hour. Why do we always leave things until the last minute? We let time slip by, saying we'll do it later, and end up doing anything else that we find more fun, whether it's watching the TV, surfing the net … But even then we don't learn and the lure of instant gratification gets the better of us, even though we know we shouldn't, even though we know that the only way to make life easy and comfortable is to do the things that are difficult and uncomfortable. It is like when you're going on a trip and you have to be at the airport at nine o'clock the next morning. Instead of packing your suitcase right there and then, you prefer to do it an hour and a half before you're due to take off, without a second to spare…

Personally I have to admit that laziness sometimes gets the better of me in certain aspects of my life but in others it doesn't even dare to try. For example, I'm a disaster around the house. I've still got bachelor-fever and I really struggle to stay on top of my clothes, keeping them tidy and putting them away. I hate washing-up too. However, if it is a matter of trying to improve myself as a person or as a rider, it's a different story. I have never taken a day off or skipped an English class. I have never said no to a test and I have never refused to do one more sit-up in the gym.

I actually like all that stuff and I'm really motivated by it (actually, if I'm totally honest maybe not so much by the English classes). If somebody were to ask me now what the secret to my success is I wouldn't say that it was my talent, or my courage, or even my experience. I honestly believe that the reason I am achieving things now (and don't anybody think I reckon I'm the best), if I am faster than everybody else on the track it is because I have put the most into the job, I have been the most dedicated to the task. I hope that this remains my main advantage, call it a weapon if you like, over the next few years.

I would also like to take this opportunity to briefly reflect on 20 fantastic years that life has blessed me with. I, or should I say we, have achieved great things on the track, things I never thought possible: 15 victories, 30 podiums, 20 pole positions, 5 fastest laps and a world title

… Yes, yes, that's all very well but what about the good times before and after each win? They are important too because nobody is going to change the world by winning or losing a race, or even a title. It can change your life, yes, but the world keeps turning without thought, continuing on its scary, mysterious and dangerous (thanks to us humans) journey. The only thing that counts is knowing to savour and not guzzle the good times that racing can bring, and knowing when you are lucky enough to do something you love.

Life as a rider goes by too fast. You arrive home on a Monday and by the following Wednesday you're on your way to the next race. It feels like yesterday when I made my debut at Jerez at 15 years of age, and now another five have gone by. That is why from now on and more than ever, I am going to try and stick to that most famous Latin phrase: 'Carpe diem' ['Live for the moment'].

With nine victories in a single season in 2007 he equalled the achievements of illustrious 250cc riders such as Max Biaggi, who won nine races in 1996, Valentino Rossi, who did it in 1999, and Marco Melandri in 2002. And with all of his nine wins coming from pole, he again equalled an Antón Mang record from 1981. As well as the victories he took a second place, two thirds, three fastest race laps and spent 183 of the 404 laps that season at the front of the pack.

Jorge missed out on his ultimate target of equalling Daijiro Kato's all-time record of 11 victories in a single season (in 2001), also falling ten points short of his all-time record of 322, but in a certain way he had outscored the Japanese legend because only Max Biaggi had scored eight wins or more in consecutive seasons. The victories at Misano and Australia took Jorge's overall 250cc winning tally to 17, two more than Sito Pons and Dani Pedrosa, to make him the most successful Spanish rider in the history of the quarter-litre category.

The people closest to him were able to enjoy the company of a completely different Jorge in 2007, like Cheni Martínez. 'That year things were much quieter because of the run of wins. In Germany, for example, things didn't go well but he took a positive attitude towards it, towards the set-up problems with the bike. He decided that he'd rather take fourth than throw everything away. He was much more settled at that time. In 2006 he used to do a lot of stretching in the box before the race. He used to watch the 125cc races on the television. There were so many things to distract him that he needed to do things that kept him focused. In 2007 that wasn't necessary.'

'Jorge had grown,' reflects Llansá. 'He had grown as a person, he was a more rounded man and that had given him the strength to tackle problems. When he had problems at that time he was able to resolve them without the same level of support that he had needed in the past. He was finally able to work things out for himself.'

6

ON THE PODIUM

Signing for Yamaha

*'**N**obody said that 2007 would be the year I'd move up to MotoGP. Maybe I'll stay in 250cc for another four years and try to win three or four titles more.'*

FIRST CONTACT

It all started on 23 March 2006. The 250cc World Championship was due to get under way in just a few hours' time and shortly after that Dani Pedrosa and Casey Stoner would be making their debuts in MotoGP. Jorge had taken over the role of title favourite, having left Honda to join Aprilia.

The negotiations with Yamaha came about through Dani Amatriaín's close friendship with Arnaldo Capellini, lawyer to Valentino Rossi and, as such, not only the best person to make the initial contact with Yamaha but the best person to give advice on getting the best contract. Dani met up with Davide Brivio, Yamaha's factory MotoGP team director and the man behind Rossi's sensational move from Honda, at Jerez. Dani listened as one of the most important men at Yamaha told him that Jorge could be a leading rider in MotoGP in the future and that, regardless of how long he was planning to spend in 250cc, Yamaha was the right team for him when he took that step up to the premier class. But Dani had known that from the start; Juan Llansá too. 'I'd been convinced that the Yamaha was the right MotoGP bike for Jorge since 2005,' says Juan. 'I'm not an engineer or a psychic but I know Jorge and I know how bikes work. And I could see that the Yamaha was perfect for Jorge! The chassis looked great and the cycle part of the bike was better than the Honda. Jorge has a higher corner speed than most riders so the Yamaha was just right for him.'

However, Yamaha was not the only factory to register their interest in Jorge. Amatriaín was also in contact with Ducati's MotoGP Project Director, Livio Suppo, although nothing much came of that. 'There were even talks with Honda,' reveals Lorenzo, 'but they already had Pedrosa and Hayden so that was always going to be unlikely.' Kawasaki was also a possibility, but Harald Eckl didn't make the call until October 2006. 'Can we speak?' 'It's a bit late for that!' came Dani's reply.

Negotiations with Yamaha dragged at the start, lasting all through 2006, but crucially they were kept alive. Not even Jorge's on-track crisis in May made Yamaha's interest waver, and before long Lin Jarvis, Managing Director of Yamaha Motor Racing, entered talks, which now turned to the technical staff Dani would like in place and a provisional plan for pre-season testing. Of course money came into it too, with an early clause set for how many titles Jorge would bring with him to MotoGP because, at that point, he wasn't yet a World Champion. To be fair, Jorge's wage was one of the areas that took least negotiation. 'The contract was 90 per cent agreed straight away,' recalls Pere Gurt. 'The main sticking point was the rider's image rights. It was important to define what things would belong to Yamaha and how much room for manoeuvre Jorge would have. It was a case of outlining the divide between his sporting and personal interests.'

Naturally the more races Jorge won, the more the interest grew and despite press reports to the contrary his future team-mate, Valentino Rossi, was not told about the negotiations until they were finalised. Dani's proposals for pre-season testing went down well at Yamaha and after the summer break he talked directly to YMC's MotoGP group leader, Masahiko Nakajima, who had always shown a keen interest and confidence in Jorge.

September 2006–July 2007
SEALING THE DEAL

A pre-contract agreement was signed at Motegi on 24 September 2006 during the Japanese Grand Prix. It was a binding agreement and the usual release clauses were significant by their absence. 'If the contract was broken by either side there'd have been one hell of a mess,' recalls Pere Gurt.

A deadline of 30 June 2007 was set for working out the definitive contract, giving Dani Amatriaín the opportunity to stipulate some important conditions before re-signing with Aprilia – notably that he would be allowed to test for Yamaha before the end of the season. 'With the MotoGP testing ban imposed between 1 December and the end of the January it was important to give him some testing time,' says Dani. The only clause inserted by Aprilia was that if Jorge subsequently signed for an Italian factory, in other words Ducati, he would not be free to test until January 2008. 'The deal was that if it was a Japanese factory there was no problem. That was fine for us, but we weren't allowed to say anything about it until July 2007.'

By the time the Dutch TT came around at the end of June 2007 the deal was practically done, and Jorge's cover was almost blown two weeks later at the Sachsenring. 'We almost got caught going in the back door of the Yamaha truck for a meeting with Lin Jarvis,' smiles Pere Gurt. The meeting was to discuss, among other things, how they were going to announce the signing, and if there would be an official presentation in Barcelona. 'I'd known I was going to be a factory MotoGP rider for a while but I didn't know anything about the team structure,' says Jorge. 'On the one hand I would have liked to be in my own team, for sponsorship reasons. Being egotistical, we could have got a personal sponsor for the team but in terms of media coverage the distinction of sharing a garage with Valentino was more attractive than being on my own. I knew we'd make a good team. Not a perfect team, but a competitive one.'

Two secret test sessions were written into the contract with Yamaha – one at the beginning of August at Almería, which only Jorge, Amatriaín, Gurt and Massimo Capanna, Jorge's chief mechanic at the time, were told about (as well as Esther Serra, who had to book the flights). Then, just five days before the test, Ricky Cardús and Pol Espargaró were invited along to keep Jorge company, along with three mechanics who had no idea where they were going.

Dainese were asked to make a white set of leathers, but weren't told what for, while Nolan were asked for a bunch of white helmets in Lorenzo's size. Even the owners of the Almería circuit weren't told what it had been booked for until the last second.

Everything looked to be going smoothly. Then came a brief period of panic: Yamaha were insisting that if the contract wasn't signed before the end of July they would not be sending their test team to Almería. The problem was that even though there was an understanding in place that the contract would be made official on 30 June, Yamaha had taken a step back. The USGP was just around the corner and the announcement of Lorenzo's signing would be a huge blow to Yamaha stalwart Colin Edwards in the build-up to his home race.

'The Hog's Breath Inn', Carmel, California
THE WORLD'S WORST KEPT SECRET

Laguna Seca turned into one mad rush – either the contract was signed or there'd be no test in Almería. Jorge had been enjoying his holiday and was preparing to do the Camino de Santiago, an annual Christian pilgrimage in the north of Spain, with Alex Debón, when he was asked by TVE to be the guest commentator for the MotoGP race at Laguna Seca. It was by sheer coincidence, then, that he ended up in the centre of the action and that the deal was finally sealed in the USA.

The truth is that everything happened at the last possible minute. Jorge and Pere read through the final version of the contract, which had been approved by the lawyers, at Munich airport, moments before they boarded for San Francisco. Their plane landed on the evening of Thursday, 19 July, and Pere made a beeline for their hotel in Monterey, where he had a meeting with Lin Jarvis early the next morning. Unfortunately, despite the help of a Sat Nav, the pair got lost. 'We got in the car and Jorge went straight to sleep,' recalls Pere. 'I was driving pretty fast, to be honest, because I wanted to get there and get to bed so that I'd be wide awake when it came to crossing the t's, dotting the i's and signing the contract the next morning. But we got lost! We covered at least an extra 250km and when we were almost there, in the middle of the night, flashing lights and sirens appeared out of nowhere. It was just like in the movies. This 4x4 police car pulled us over and I had to explain that we were looking for Laguna Seca, that we were here for the MotoGP and that the kid fast asleep next to me was a World Champion ... nothing! The policeman wasn't in the mood for a chat. He had a torch in one hand and a pistol in the other. We got fined at gunpoint!'

At eight o'clock the next morning Pere Gurt met Lin Jarvis at his hotel in Carmel and handed over their final alterations to the contract. 'I don't imagine there'll be any problems, but let me check,' said Jarvis. 'There we were, Lin and I, in a hotel room in California,' says Gurt, remembering a moment of great tension, but with the composure afforded by hindsight. 'I was on the phone to Dani in Spain, where they were nine hours ahead. It was five in the evening in Europe but Jarvis was speaking with his colleagues in Japan, and it was already the next day there! All the changes were sent by fax to Japan, who sent their version back to the US and then I had to forward it to Europe. It was stressful! In Europe they were getting ready to close shop for the weekend and in Japan it was Saturday already. We couldn't finalise everything but it was a done deal.'

With his contract 99.9 per cent in place, Jorge went to the same hotel that evening to meet up with his new boss. His first words? 'Nice room!' Jarvis was planning to stay on for a holiday with his family and his suite even had a piano in it.

That same night Jorge and Pere Gurt went to the 'Hog's Breath Inn', Clint Eastwood's restaurant in Carmel, to have dinner with a group of TVE staff. Emilio Pérez de Rozas, sports editor for leading Spanish daily newspaper *El Periódico* had already referred to Jorge Lorenzo signing for Yamaha as 'the world's worst kept secret'.

'Emilio was right!' said Jorge. 'It was the world's worst kept secret!'

Everybody was laughing, except Pere Gurt. 'Jorge, don't say that. If I remember rightly we signed the [initial] contract in October 2006 in Japan and nobody has found out about it until now. Lots of people suspected it but nobody published anything until *Solo Moto* revealed it on their front cover in July. In other words, nine months is a long time for the world's worst kept secret.'

'We could possibly have done more to keep it a secret,' says Jorge now. 'Some of the people who knew got caught out by the odd question and people started to guess. Maybe I even hinted at it with some of my answers, but the thing that bothered me most was my mechanics. I wanted to know who my crew chief was going to be in MotoGP. The three names we discussed were Juan Martínez, Santi Mulero and Ramón Forcada. Juan was working for Puig, although in the end he went to Kawasaki, Mulero is with Sito and we decided the best option was Ramón. I was convinced he was the right man and now I've worked with him I've had the opportunity to see how good he really is.'

The final version of the contract was signed on their return from the US on 25 July 2007 and the announcement was made two days later

27 July 2007
YAMAHA PRESS RELEASE

Yamaha Motor Co., Ltd announces that it has concluded a two-year agreement with 250cc World Champion Jorge Lorenzo. The 20-year-old Spaniard will make his MotoGP in 2008 debut aboard a YZR-M1, with direct factory support.

Lorenzo, who won the 250 title in 2006, is currently leading the championship with 191 points, after winning six out of the first ten races this season.

'Yamaha has been watching Jorge's career with interest for some time and we are delighted that he will be joining our MotoGP line-up from next season,' commented Lin Jarvis, Managing Director of Yamaha Motor Racing. 'We are sure that he will be a valuable asset for the future and we look forward to the commencement of his MotoGP career with Yamaha.'

For now, though, the hard work was only just starting and the first big challenge was already on the horizon – time was marching on and Yamaha's test team were sent to Almería, a secret that was kept better than the signing. In fact it was only a few days later, at Brno, that Andrew Pitt, Yamaha's Michelin test rider, let it slip that Jorge had been at the test and gone faster than him after just ten laps. Jorge Lorenzo had already begun to make his mark in MotoGP.

7 November 2007

Text written by Jorge Lorenzo entitled:

'THE DEBUT'

The alarm sounds. It is 10.15am. I sit up, pick up my mobile from the bedside table and hit the snooze button. Just because this is one of the most special days in my life does not mean I'm going to drop one of my favourite vices – that extra five minutes in bed. Two 'snoozes' later and I finally get out of bed, walk around the bedroom a couple of times and head for the bathroom. I look in the mirror and imagine what is going to happen over the next few hours.

After six seasons in Grand Prix and two titles it is time to make the step up to the premier class and to the Yamaha factory team, no less. Oh, and if you didn't already know, alongside Valentino Rossi! I know it and I don't want to be late for anything in this world, so I have a quick breakfast and head off to Cheste with Dani.

No sooner do I arrive at the circuit than I encounter the first perk of being a MotoGP rider. A fan gives me a leg of Jabugo ham (mmm ... I can't wait to try some with toast for my next breakfast!) as a gift. If all of my fans were that kind I'd no doubt weigh about 90 kilos! I say 'thank you' and head for box number 6, my new box.

When I walk in I'm amazed by what I see. This is another level. Everything: the bikes, the carpet, the television screens, the chairs, the toolboxes, the mechanics' uniforms ... and to think I didn't expect much of a difference! To give you a better idea of what it's like, I'd compare it to changing from a three-star hotel to a five-star. It is like being used to a Second Division football ground and then going to the Bernabéu or the

Camp Nou ... Everything is bigger and more glamorous. There are also a lot more people working for me than at Aprilia.

I'm introduced to my new crew chief, Ramón Forcada, and the rest of the mechanics, who fill me in on the basics of the bike. I'm already raring to go – my leathers on, helmet and gloves on standby. They have to weigh me first and I hit the scales at 70.5kg. Edwards, for example, weighed 78kg. The mechanics finally open the garage door. I look out and have to rub my eyes – there are fifty people out there, cameras at the ready! There weren't even a third of that number when I was fighting for the title here last year ... now that is what I call anticipation!

They fire up my bike and I head onto the track. I open the throttle. I'd forgotten how powerful this bike is...

'I could retire right now,' Jorge tells me. 'I am already a World Champion and that was my objective so I am satisfied. I've done it twice! That is not a submission, because I never submit, although I am looking at it from the outside. Because inside I'm thinking that I've got to have these guys for breakfast! I wouldn't be unhappy if I was forced to quit now, but the reality is that this is only the beginning.'

Marcos Hirsch had been telling Jorge the same thing for a long time. 'This is where the real story starts, Jorge; 125cc and 250cc are stepping stones but be careful because luxury and money can cause a man to loosen his belt and lose his will to fight. But for you the fight starts now. If you want to make history, this is your time. You are a nobody yet, you've done nothing. The only place for you to do your talking is on the track. The rest is bullshit. So far your career has been a winding, rocky path but now it is time to be a Spartan, to sleep on straw, to focus on the goal and to forget about hot chicks and fast cars. I believe this is your natural environment, this is your place. You made a huge sacrifice to stay small enough to ride a 250 considering how big you are. You have the heart for a fight, you are a warrior. Now it is your turn to make history. And Valentino had better not retire yet because to truly be victorious, you have to beat him.'

7

MotoGP 2008

Rookie of the Year

At precisely one o'clock on 4 November 2007 Jorge Lorenzo took the step up from being a 250cc rider and joined the big league. Over the previous two seasons he had won back-to-back quarter-litre world titles and had 17 250cc Grand Prix victories to his name, a record that established him as the second most successful rider in Aprilia history. Only Max Biaggi, with 23 wins, had done more for the Noale factory.

As the full complement of MotoGP riders lined up for the official pre-season photograph on 17 February 2008, at the Jerez IRTA test, Jorge Lorenzo was the last to arrive. 'It wasn't premeditated, I just got distracted,' Jorge insists. Either way, Lorenzo sat and smiled for the cameras – a genuine smile at the fulfilment of a dream. He was a factory rider, with Fiat Yamaha. 'I can remember seeing the happiness on his face the first time he came into the garage,' recalls Javi Ullate, an experienced mechanic who previously worked with Colin Edwards and was a member of Alex Crivillé's title-winning crew in 1999. 'I'll always have an image in my head of him sitting down in his seat, looking around and saying to himself, "I've done it, I'm a factory MotoGP rider." Most riders have started out in satellite teams and then moved on to a factory ride. It's not easy to enter MotoGP through the front door.'

9 March 2008, midnight

Losail Circuit, Qatar

A SHINING LIGHT

On his debut with the Yamaha M1 at Valencia, following the final GP of the 2007 season, Jorge Lorenzo set a very similar lap time to

Casey Stoner's race-winning pace from the previous day. 'Although it was with a soft qualifying tyre,' admits Jorge. After further test sessions at Sepang and Jerez he went on holiday in a satisfied mood. Despite a crash in the Crivillé corner at Jerez he had completed a stunning race simulation at the Spanish circuit that was actually quicker than Valentino Rossi's race-winning performance in March. It was at the same circuit that he would later sit for that pre-season photo, but he already knew that he would be taking a front-row seat in every sense of the word in 2008 – and for somebody who places as much importance on mental strength as Lorenzo, that feeling was the best companion he could wish to be taking on holiday with him. If it were up to him he would have carried on riding right through the winter, learning as much as humanly possible before the start of the season. But in MotoGP the most important test comes when the racing starts.

The new year held plenty of promise, and when the riders returned to action in Malaysia following the winter break, Jorge turned his focus to improving his riding style, above all his braking and corner entry. He also spent time adjusting to the carbon brakes and running in Yamaha's new pneumatic valve engine. By the third day he was closing in on the circuit record and lapping quicker than his new team-mate, Valentino Rossi.

'A few things surprised me over the course of the season,' says Lorenzo. 'When I tried the bike for the very first time at Almería in the summer of 2007, I was quick but at the same time well aware that any competitive MotoGP rider would have been a second quicker, so I didn't get carried away. Then in pre-season tests I was also quick but the lap times weren't exactly out of this world, and nobody had been too surprised. So I never thought for a second that I would start the season with pole positions and podiums, never mind taking my first victory in Portugal. That was something I never imagined! I dreamt of doing it but dreaming about it and actually doing it are two very different things. I remember that we got to the first IRTA test and I began to "show my cards". Then, at Qatar, a circuit I've always adapted well to, I set the fastest time on qualifying tyres. That's when my dreams began to turn into reality, with pole position.'

In the entire history of MotoGP, only Tadayuki Okada (Malaysia 1996) and Max Biaggi (Suzuka '98) had set pole position for their premier-class debuts. On Saturday 8 March 2008 Jorge Lorenzo added his name to the record books at Losail, one of his favourite circuits and a track that had seen him celebrate three victories, four podiums and four pole positions over the previous four seasons. In effect, this was his fifth consecutive pole position at the desert track.

The MotoGP World Championship was being turned upside down and Jorge was looking like anything but a rookie. 'Every rider is different but in all my experience I had never seen anything like this, somebody with such natural ability,' says Ullate. 'Jorge is a rider who never seemed to be in his first season. It didn't seem that way at all. The way testing went, the way he approached the season, the way he worked – it felt like he already had four seasons under his belt at this level. He got faster and faster, session after session, and it surprised us all. The ease with which he was able to get on the pace surprised everybody.' Of course, there was still plenty for him to learn. 'In 250cc he'd never used earplugs to block out the noise but in MotoGP it's impossible to ride without them! At the start he kept having to come back and take his helmet off because he'd forgotten to put his earplugs in!' laughs Ullate.

'I couldn't really understand why I was going so well,' explains Jorge. 'I didn't know if it was simply because we had a good package or maybe because the other riders were off the pace or still sleeping. Or maybe the level isn't as high as I'd thought! That's what I was telling myself. Maybe it's because the Yamaha is going really well, or maybe it's a bike that just adapts perfectly to my riding style, I still don't really know. The point is that I didn't know why it was happening but it was. Stoner seemed to be a step ahead of everybody in terms of race pace, but on a soft tyre I was able to go a second and a half or more faster than on race tyres. 'And I kept improving. On the Saturday I set pole and on the Sunday I finished second in the race. As with many of the occasions when I've been on pole, I struggled at the start of the race and thought it was going to be tough. But I also thought that it was simply a question of laps, of getting into a rhythm and allowing the fuel to lighten up. I was worried because I was passed by Valentino, who'd been slower than me in practice, and then Pedrosa came past and he'd been two seconds off the pace. I was concerned but I knew I would get faster as the race went on so I relaxed. I started to pass people, I can't remember if it was Edwards or Toseland first, then Pedrosa, and then Rossi. I didn't expect MotoGP to be so crazy over the opening laps. I didn't expect such a hectic start, with guys overtaking each other on the limit. I thought it would all be much calmer because the bikes are heavy, and they're dangerous. They're not a toy like a 125, which you can mess around on because if you crash it doesn't hurt much – the inertia isn't the same and they're not as powerful.' In the end, Jorge safely navigated his way to the podium. 'I was happy even though I'd been hoping for a win. It was still fantastic to finish second on my debut.'

At the age of 20 years and 310 days, Jorge Lorenzo became the ninth-youngest rider ever to stand on the premier-class rostrum. It was the first ever MotoGP night race and the Losail floodlights had cast their beams over an area the size of 70 soccer pitches. There was enough power to light a street from Doha to Moscow, some 3500 kilometres away. But the light that shone brightest on that night in the desert was undoubtedly Jorge Lorenzo.

From 30 March to 13 April
TWO CRAZY WEEKS

'When you look at it from the outside all you can see is that the level of riding is extremely high, but what you don't know is how well he will work. "What will he be like?" you wonder. The truth is that Jorge has great ability to ride a motorcycle and he works himself into the ground.' That comment comes from Ramón Forcada, and he should know. Forcada has worked in Grand Prix since 1989, when he was employed by JJ Cobas to make engines for Alex Crivillé, and he has twice been chief mechanic in a factory team – at HRC with Alex Barros and now at Yamaha with Jorge. He has also worked with Loris Capirossi, Max Biaggi, John Kocinski and Casey Stoner.

'I would say that Jorge is a rider who needs to make few changes to a motorcycle and who can adapt to what he has available. He is better at adapting to a bike than he is at setting it up. There is an advantage to this in that, while he is not very sensitive, at the same time he is not obsessive. He doesn't spend all day wanting to change things. Jorge is capable of riding fast even when the bike isn't set up.'

At Fiat Yamaha they have come to the conclusion that Lorenzo has a natural ability to adapt to any bike. 'I believe that he could get on any machine on the grid and go fast,' says Ramón. 'He races motorcycles, not a motorcycle.' From the beginning Forcada has always said that Jorge's riding style reminds him of Kocinski, the former 250cc and Superbike World Champion and 500cc Grand Prix winner. 'He rides with his backside pushed to the rear of the seat and in terms of balance under weight transfer, he is affected by this a little. We have to give him a stable bike. He doesn't put much weight on the front so his front tyre and front suspension have to be a little different to other riders. He also likes to keep his corner speed high but everybody has to adapt to new things. After spending a year with him I've realised that we've played with the bike too much. We wanted to adapt it to him and we haven't given him enough opportunity to adapt to the bike. Now we know what he needs, what he wants, and in 2009 we will do better.'

At his opening race in Qatar Jorge had already demonstrated that he could beat his new team-mate, Valentino Rossi, and even Masao Furusawa, Executive Officer of Engineering Operations at Yamaha Motor Company, admitted that this early form could cause a 'small problem' for the factory. 'Yamaha have treated me really well and I wasn't pulled up for anything at all last year,' reflects Jorge. 'They never had a go at me for crashing so much, for taking too many risks. As far as I know they have total confidence in my capacity to improve and to be the factory's rider for the future. I feel well loved and supported at Yamaha and I was surprised by what they said at the start of the season; that if I continued like that it wouldn't be clear who the factory's number one rider would be. It is gratifying that they should say things like that, although I knew that Valentino would still be number one, without any doubt.' Furusawa-san would later clarify that any updates for the M1 would initially be handed to

Rossi, adding at the end of the 2008 season: 'I am sure that Jorge Lorenzo will dominate MotoGP in the future. I like him a lot – he is a great boy and a great rider. He is very different from what I expected before he came to Yamaha. I have been impressed by his maturity. He is very intelligent, more than I could have imagined, and he has a huge talent for racing motorcycles.'

The month or so after Qatar was a crazy time for Jorge. Even though he was a double World Champion, he was still only 20 years old. There was the controversy with Dani Pedrosa, and the question of whether they should shake hands and make up became a national debate. In the Spanish Grand Prix at Jerez Jorge picked up his second pole position in as many premier-class races, the first rookie rider ever to do so, and just to add extra spice Pedrosa qualified second. Despite setting an excellent rhythm in practice Lorenzo could 'only' manage third in the race, equalling Max Biaggi's record as the only previous rookie to score podiums in his first two races. On the rostrum King Juan Carlos joined Jorge's hand with Pedrosa's in a reluctant handshake. Things don't get much crazier than that.

Then came Portugal. Estoril was a circuit that hadn't been kind to Jorge in the past and he had never won there in any category. It is the slowest and most technical circuit on the calendar, with its famous 'parabolica' corner that leads into the start-finish straight, and its unusual contrast between long, fast straights and tight, twisty corners, which put rare demands on the compromise between horsepower and chassis balance. Then there's that magical chicane…

'In Portugal I changed my routine. I set pole position again wearing my red helmet and Juanito (Llansá) said, "It looks like your red helmet is the fast one. Why don't you wear it in the race?" So I did and my luck changed. But that was just a coincidence because the real change came on the day after the race at Jerez. We had a test and I improved more than any other rider, knocking half a second off my best time from the race. That made me go to Portugal with real self-confidence. When I arrived at Estoril I rode well in practice and then went on to set pole again! In the race I got a good start. I remember being in third place and seeing Valentino and Pedrosa touch, giving me the chance to dive up the inside and take the lead.

Valentino passed me back in Turn 3 but coming out of the same turn – I don't know if it was a moment of bravery but I didn't think about it twice – I passed him back on the inside of the fifth-gear bend. I still don't know how I did it!'

Listening to Jorge recall his first MotoGP victory is an engaging experience. He doesn't stop talking, remembering every detail as clearly as if it were yesterday. 'The pass on Rossi came off and I was in the lead but suddenly he came back at me and four laps later I lost another place to Pedrosa. I gave myself a few laps to study the race and then it started to rain. It was a strange race and I realised that I was finding it easy to follow them. I told myself, "This is my moment!" I passed Pedrosa on the inside at the end of the straight and then decided to wait for one or two laps before trying to pass Valentino, to see how things went. Valentino brakes really well and he was sure to try and escape but I found it easy to close the gap. A few corners before the chicane I was right on him but there was no way past. Then we got to the chicane and it seemed so easy that I saw no reason to wait. I couldn't hold myself back – I had to go for it! It was the kind of impatience that sometimes shows through in my character. Even though I knew there were 15 laps left I went for it and I pulled it off. We were close, hard on the gas – it was a risky move but a clean one and it will stay in the hearts and minds of many people for a long time to come. I could see that he was having problems with the tyre and I didn't really have anything to lose. My experience told me that if I was decisive there would be no problem. I wanted to get past Valentino because I thought he was having more trouble than Pedrosa. It was a good chance to get past him and put him between myself and Pedrosa, slowing Dani down and giving me the chance to escape.'

With his victory at Estoril, Jorge Lorenzo began to rewrite the record books. He was now one of a select few to have won races in all three categories and the youngest rider in MotoGP history to chalk up three podium finishes, taking the record from Dani Pedrosa by a single day. He had become the 100th rider to win a premier-class race and, at the age of 20 years and 345 days, he was the fifth youngest. Furthermore, he'd won for Yamaha. Since the beginning of the four-stroke MotoGP era in 2002 only Max Biaggi and Valentino Rossi had scored wins for the Japanese factory. Not only that, for the first time in his career Lorenzo was the leader of the MotoGP World Championship.

'Like any time when you achieve something big, something you have dreamed about for such a long time and yearned for so much, when you finally achieve it you think it's not such a big deal. You imagine that when you achieve it the feeling will be like ecstasy but the reality is that you're happy, but it's not a movie, it's not science fiction, it's reality and it's no big deal. It's exciting, you feel great, but it's like when you're desperate to hook up with a girl. You spend the whole day thinking about her, chasing her. And she starts to take more and more notice of you, but by the time you finally get there, you're over it! Sure, you have a good time with her but the chase is over. Especially if, in this case, it's only taken three races to win!' This is Lorenzo in reflective mood, with the benefit of hindsight and perspective. But there was a different kind of Lorenzo altogether immediately after that historic win at Estoril and this is what he wrote:

15 April 2008. Two days after the Grand Prix of Portugal, Estoril
Text written by Jorge Lorenzo entitled:
'YO, ADRIAN! I DID IT!'

I'm writing this just a few hours before undergoing surgery because I want to tell you about one of the keys to my victory. I believe in cinema as a means of learning about human nature. I know that the 'Rocky' films aren't of the same quality as many others but they contain the basics of self-motivation that a sportsperson needs in moments of doubt. Rocky has helped me a lot over the years and now I can shout out like he did after beating Apollo Creed. I did it!

At the moment I'm sitting on the floor of my motorhome with my legs stretched out, trying to warm up my hamstrings and calves. To my left, on the sofa, is Dani Amatriaín, and in front of me is my laptop, which has a message on it that reads: 'Remember where you came from, how much it took you to get here and, above all, what he did to you the last time. Now it is your turn ... it is your turn.' The third race of my MotoGP career will start in just 20 minutes' time but my mind is not thinking about it in the same way it thought about the previous two. Instead, it is absorbed in the meaning of these words. They are the words of Apollo Creed, Rocky Balboa's great rival in his first two films. When he hung up his gloves, Creed channelled his motivation through Rocky, in the belief that due to money, fame or the death of his former trainer, he had lost the 'eye of the tiger' – his hunger for victory.

As I have mentioned on a few occasions, I am a huge fan of the movies. I reckon I must watch around a hundred a year. The ones that get through to me the most I watch again, because at second glance you often pick up on important details that you missed first time around. I think you can learn a lot from watching films, especially about human relations, which is why I love comedies and dramas. Obviously, the quality of the 'Rocky' films cannot be compared with films by the likes of Scorsese, Woody Allen or George Lucas, but for me they have always possessed, and always will possess, the basics of self-motivation that a sportsperson needs in moments of doubt or worry.

I remember perfectly seeing those films for the first time, during my first World Championship season in 2002. My father and I were at Sachsenring in my motorhome (which at that time was the worst motorhome in the paddock!), and Dani came over with some videotapes. He told me I should watch them of an evening before going to bed. At that time I was only a 15 year old, out of my comfort zone and scared, and I didn't really understand many of the things I understand now, so I didn't pay much attention to the message Dani was trying to get across. The results didn't improve instantly...

Four years later, at the start of 2006, we found ourselves in the middle of a crisis because after winning the opening two races of the season we only managed a further 13 points from the next three: Turkey, China and France. We'd hit rock bottom, nobody believed in us and, most importantly of all, I didn't believe in myself. With the help of Marcos (my physical trainer, who introduced Dani to the magic of Balboa when Dani was a rider and they trained together) and Dani himself, we set about working on digging ourselves out of the hole we had put ourselves in. We sat down together, I told them about my concerns and we discussed them. The evenings were taken up by Rocky and other big-screen heroes. We watched the first four films of the saga (we didn't have 'Rocky V', and 'Rocky Balboa' still wasn't out). We watched them in order, day after day. A year and a half later, with one world title already in the bag and with us well on the way to a successful defence, we were disappointed to miss our first chance to seal the double in Japan, where I finished 11th in a wet race. Our main rival Andrea Dovizioso had pulled back a stack of points and significantly closed the gap in the standings. When we arrived at Phillip Island I turned on my laptop and watched 'Rocky' again, this time on my own. You already know the result; I won the race by nearly 20 seconds...

The thing is that Apollo Creed's words were left imprinted on my mind. 'Now it's your turn ... it's your turn.' So I think: 'Okay, Qatar was my first race in MotoGP, fair enough. I made a soft start at Jerez and got beaten. But if we get beaten again in Portugal it won't be because we didn't fight until the end, it won't be because we doubted our own ability in this race.' Now I know that within a few hours I'll be going under the surgeon's knife and just thinking about that brings me back to earth from the clouds. However, before that I am going to shout at the top of my voice: 'Yo, Adrian! I did it!'

GP of China, Shanghai circuit
THE HARDER THE FALL

Valentino Rossi scored his first premier-class podium in his fourth race among the world's elite. At the same stage of his rookie season Jorge was leading the championship but, despite moving to the top of the standings with his victory in Portugal, his approach remained the same: I am not here to win the title. 'Did I mean what I said? For sure, I never thought I could win the championship. Among other things because the older I get the more cautious I become. I'm not as much of a dreamer any more; my feet are planted on the ground. Also, I know that a championship is long and a lot of things happen. You can win two races, get knocked off in the third and hit a career low. I knew anything could happen.'

China proved to be the place where his feet would come into contact with the ground, although not as literally or as forcefully as he had planned. 'My father always told me when I was on a run of victories or when things were going really well, not to get too confident or let my guard drop because bad things have always happened to me when my confidence has got too high. He said it to me again before the Grand Prix of China. Sure enough, I crashed! Crashes like that one have been virtually unheard of since the 500cc era, although in those days riders would crash as they opened the gas on their way through the corner, not when decelerating like I was. The truth is that I felt really confident coming from Portugal. I'd undergone surgery for the compartmental syndrome on both arms and I thought, "If I can win a race with two bad arms things should be even better now!" '

Jorge arrived in Shanghai planning his next victory celebration. Portugal had taken him a little bit by surprise and he hadn't had anything prepared other than the usual 'Lorenzo's Land' flag. For China he had even planned to pull out a Tibetan flag and drive it into Chinese soil in honour of the Dalai Lama and in a show of solidarity with the demonstrations against Chinese oppression in Tibet. The idea was dropped, not because he didn't want to do it but because it wasn't the time or the place to be making such political statements. 'Don't get involved in politics, Jorge,' Marcos Hirsch told him. There were other reasons why Jorge's mind might be better employed focusing on the Grand Prix. 'I was struggling to get on the pace in the first session in China. I was eighth fastest, two seconds off the quickest time and even though there was a long way to go I started to worry. I was trying hard but the times weren't coming. So I said to myself, "Come on, let's get going a bit here, we can't be this far back." As soon as I pushed a bit harder, forcing the direction change a little more than usual, with a bit more throttle, the front of the bike lifted and got out of shape. The tyre didn't have enough grip to make the turn and it started to slide with the most incredible force, throwing me off at such a speed that it didn't feel real. It was like I was in a PlayStation game! I felt so hot in my leathers at that point that as I flew through the air I started to think

I was dreaming. When I hit the tarmac I saw stars. I think I was in the air for more than a second and a half so I had time to think, "Madre mía! This is going to hurt!" It was a sickening impact, really hard. I bit my lip. It was like when you're running and you trip over and smash your mouth on the ground – your whole face hurts. And my mouth was the least of my problems! I started to feel a terrible pain in my ankles. I grabbed hold of them and started screaming, hoping it was just a dream because I knew if it was real my championship was ruined. And with how well everything had been going too! I was in so much pain in the ambulance, they gave me painkillers and I just prayed that it wasn't too serious. I was angry with myself too because I'd screwed up again by getting ahead of myself. My fucking head had let me down again!'

Jorge crashed during first free practice for the Grand Prix of China, between the second and third corners, in a downhill chicane. They say that the most important thing for a rider is to know why he crashed, so that he can recover his confidence as quickly as possible. 'Obviously it was my fault because I was going too fast, even though we were never able to work out from the telemetry exactly what happened,' reflects Jorge. 'I just kept asking what time the second session started because the only thing I wanted was to get back out on the track. But it was clear that it would be impossible because we had to get to Shanghai, go to the hospital and then return to the track and with the traffic there was no way we could. The hospital itself was a dump, I couldn't see a single person who wasn't Chinese, and that just made the whole experience even more surreal. Nobody wanted me to go back and race and nobody was forcing me to. On the contrary, everybody was telling me that I couldn't. But when you are leading the championship, you never know how much you're going to need those points. Did I say I wasn't thinking about winning the title? Of course I wasn't – but you never know. So I said, "Come on, let's try!" I remember being back in the hotel with my laptop and I couldn't even put my feet on the ground. I had to sit in a wheelchair, using only my arms and moving around really slowly. All I wanted was to wake up and see that everything was better, but it was the opposite. The swelling just got worse and worse, in fact it got to the point that I was in more pain and discomfort two weeks after the crash than I had been on the day it happened. But I was so desperate to get back on my bike that I spent the whole evening imagining it – I honestly think that is what enabled me to get back on my Yamaha the next day and ride so hard. I don't regret it because I went fourth fastest and I demonstrated things that not many people have shown before. From that point on, even my own team had more respect for me – they could see that here was a kid with balls who wasn't daunted by anything. I don't regret going out, although obviously if I'd have known that I'd end the championship in fourth place anyway and that I'd still be suffering from the after-effects in my ankles several months later then maybe I wouldn't have raced.'

The diagnosis was irrefutable: a re-fracture to the top of the malleolar bone in the middle of his left ankle as well as a severe impact oedema to the right heel, the astragalus [ankle] bone and the tibia. On his return to Barcelona, a 3D CAT scan carried out by Dr Xavier Mir confirmed the initial diagnosis and also picked up a fracture to his right astragalus and a torn lateral internal ligament in his left ankle. Yet in China there were still people at the track who refused to believe he was really injured. 'They can ask me, I spent the whole three days with him!' an indignant Héctor Martín interjects. 'Or tell them to ask the Clinica Mobile doctors who probably recall it as their worst moment of the year. The rider who claimed that the wheelchair was a joke should have seen Jorge shouting when he was given the injection. I spent several hours with him in the Clinica, watching him suffer, watching him scream every time he was injected in his ankle. The needle they use for the injection is huge and they push it in deep and hold it there for at least 20 or 30 seconds. He kept shouting "Madre de Dios!" ['Mother of God']. There was the odd swear word too! It was the worst state I've ever seen him in, because at Catalunya we gave up on any hope of racing but in China we had to push because he was leading the championship and he was only a fucking rookie!'

Jorge laughs at the vehemence of Héctor's defence. 'All right, I was injured, I can assure you of that. And I did scream when I put weight on my feet. Well, not when I put weight on them because I couldn't but when I touched the ground with them! I honestly couldn't take a single step. Fair enough, if I were a track and field athlete I would have been out for four months. But in motorcycle racing you are sitting on a bike … obviously it is still going to hurt, it's going to bloody hurt a lot! In the direction changes, with a 200+bhp motorcycle, with the way you need to move your weight around, you're fucked, basically. But you can manage! What is astounding is that certain people in the paddock can doubt you, although it didn't bother me really because it made me realise how bad we are as human beings to gratuitously criticise others. I thought about myself, about the times I have criticised others. I thought how easy it is to have a go at somebody without having been in their shoes. But in this case to criticise somebody who is left with long-term damage to their ankles is uncalled for. On the Saturday I had a huge moment on the bike and if I'd have crashed again they'd have had to chop my legs off!' Jorge can laugh about it now but at the time his face told a very different story. 'On top of everything the bike cut out on me during practice – the first time it had happened to me in six seasons of Grand Prix racing – and I had to support myself with my feet while I turned the bike around and waited for a push. Luckily, between the injection and the stiffness of the boots I was able to hold it up. It was a little bit like a Rambo movie. Everything goes wrong but in the end John Rambo gets up and shoots everybody!'

The crash in China had been his biggest so far, but there had been others during pre-season testing in Malaysia and at Jerez. 'In the next round, at Le Mans, he crashed a few times during practice and gave us goosebumps when he ran straight across the gravel at Turn 1,' recalls Ramón Forcada. 'But in the race, when it started to rain, instead of holding onto his position he started to push and take risks! He really made us suffer, going from fourth place to second like that, playing with fire. When you are on a bike, fear is not the right word for what you need to have but you do need to have respect. If you gamble on a motorcycle it can easily deal you a bad hand and Jorge was not showing the bike respect.' However, for the first time in the four-stroke MotoGP era there was an all-Yamaha podium at Le Mans, with Jorge crossing the line between race winner Rossi and third-placed Colin Edwards. He needed a chair to take the weight off his ankles during the podium ceremony and as he sat on the second step Jorge savoured the fact that he had surpassed his great idol, Max Biaggi, with the highest points tally by a rookie after five rounds.

From Montmeló to Brno
HERE COMES THE FEAR

Jorge escaped without further injury from another crash in the Italian Grand Prix at Mugello, where he lost the front when attempting an impatient pass on Andrea Dovizioso. It proved a disappointing end to his 100th GP appearance, when he became the youngest rider ever to reach the ton-up landmark, taking a record set only a couple of hours earlier in the 250cc race by his old nemesis, Héctor Barberá, who is 183 days older than Jorge. There was no time to celebrate his accomplishment or lament his disappointment, with just seven days until the next race at Montmeló. However, the fear finally set in at the Catalunya GP and everything changed as a result.

The weekend started well. On the Thursday the circuit organisers unveiled a plaque in Jorge's honour on the 'Avenida de los Campeones', alongside similar tributes to the likes of Mick Doohan and Alex Crivillé. Jorge was delighted to be back at his 'home' circuit and proud to form part of their 'Hall of Fame'. Everything was in place for a great weekend, but the optimism didn't last long. In the second free practice session, on Friday, Jorge crashed at Turn 11. He was immediately transferred to hospital and ruled out of the race. He had taken a hard blow to the head and was suffering from reactionary amnesia. He also needed an operation to his hand, having lost skin and suffered an abrasion to the extensor tendon of his fourth and fifth fingers, requiring a skin graft from his wrist. His ring finger also needed reconstruction work.

'I will never forget the image of Jorge in tears as they put him into the ambulance – it was heartbreaking,' recalls Héctor Martín. 'Crashing became normal because he was so desperate to do well,' adds Juanito Llansá. 'He recovers pretty well from injury but the one where he did the most damage was definitely Montmeló. It was a bit like Valencia in 2005 [at a post-race test] when he was knocked out and couldn't remember how he crashed.' Javi Ullate agrees: 'The crash that defined the season was the one at Montmeló,' he says. 'Psychologically I don't think the one in China was as major. The one at Catalunya wasn't even his fault – the telemetry doesn't lie. He'd taken the corner exactly the same way as he had in the morning and the very fact that he didn't know why he crashed and couldn't even remember how it happened because of the blow to his head affected him.'

'I'm getting overtaken because I am scared and when you ride scared anybody can pass you.'

'The bike is not giving me confidence, I'm scared of crashing and even though I'm improving I'm still looking for the light at the end of the tunnel.'

'Am I the first rider to admit being scared? Maybe so, but when you crash five times in five races and do yourself a lot of damage, like I have, you don't have much option other than to admit that when you get back on the bike you get butterflies, and a fear that you could crash again.'

The above statements were made by Jorge around that time, but the most insightful came following a visit to a bookshop in Barcelona airport, when his attention was caught by a title on understanding and overcoming fear by the renowned Indian spiritual self-help writer, Osho. He bought it straight away. 'I am not trying to overcome my fear, simply understand it,' he explained.

'Jorge began to admit that he was scared during a series of interviews following the Catalunya GP and a lot of journalists asked me what it was all about, all this talk of fear,' says Héctor Martín. "He needs to stop saying he's scared!" they told me, but to me it made sense for a guy who had crashed five times in five races to feel that way. Those kind of statements make you realise that Jorge is a normal person and an honest one at that. The fact he finished last in practice shows how scared he really was.'

'At Montmeló I started to think that I was crashing a lot and I thought it was my fault,' recalls Jorge, closing his eyes as if to block out the pain of the memory. 'There were two weeks between Montmeló and Donington – too much time to think, for things to go round in your head, to think things you shouldn't. When I eventually did get back out on track I decided to go slower, more carefully. On the one hand it was necessary because I didn't want to crash again, so it was good to go slow, but it was also dangerous because sometimes the slower you ride the more tense you are and the more chance there is of a crash. Also, of course, I then found it difficult to pick up the pace again. I managed more poles and podiums before the end of the season but I never recovered the confidence I had in Portugal or at Jerez. I'd crashed before, like when I broke my collarbone at Valencia in 2005, and I'd been knocked unconscious before – I couldn't even remember that crash at Valencia, for instance – but the problem at Montmeló was that the memory loss was longer term. On top of that, they initially told me that I had one pupil smaller than the other and said that it was very worrying, potentially problematical because after an accident like that the brain is often damaged and there are after-effects.'

Lorenzo can look back and laugh, even joke about it now, but only he knows how much he really suffered. 'I woke up in the hospital. I remember I looked at my finger and started swearing! I was saying that I wanted to pack it all in, retire. I couldn't see the point in suffering so much for this. At Montmeló I started to see everything in a bad light. Before that I hadn't placed too much importance on the crashes.' The truth is that Jorge has not traditionally been a crasher, despite the reputation he picked up in 2008, a reputation he refutes with indignation. 'If I were to crash a dozen times in a year, fair enough. If I were to spend that much time sliding across the floor, feel free to call me a mop! But check the statistics first. All some people want to see is that I've crashed five or six times – they can only remember the injured Lorenzo. But what about the poles? What about the podiums? How do they expect me to achieve those things in my first season? By cruising around? Especially considering we spent the majority of the season at a disadvantage.'

10 June 2008. Out of the Catalunya GP
Text written by Jorge Lorenzo entitled:
'MY LEFT HAND WRITES'

My left hand writes, my right is asleep. I crashed again. Whether it was my fault, the tyres, the track, a snail that got in the way – none of that matters. It would matter if we had a 'rewind' button, but we don't. What matters is that I hurt myself and I have undergone surgery. Over the past few days, spent in bed attached to a drip, I haven't wanted to think about why, or feel sorry for myself and my … bad luck? Bad luck is a relative concept. I only need to take a walk around this hospital to feel lucky. By the way, if any of the people in here are reading this, I want you to know I am with you. Don't let it get the better of you, it will pass and that which does not kill you can only make you stronger.

And so it is from within a [hospital] room that I begin to write this column with my left hand. What can I tell you? Having already asked for your forgiveness in my last column, I can now say that this latest mistake has made me take a different view on life. They tell me that after the crash I kept asking the same questions: 'Which corner did I crash in? What was it like? Have I ever won a race?' Every two minutes, the same thing over and over. I understand why people were worried; it must have been a real scare. I have been in similar situations during my short professional career and I have been lucky to have always come through the other side.

This is only the second race I have missed since I made my debut as a 15 year old. The first was in Malaysia in 2005, through suspension. This time it is Barcelona, my home, and it is through injury. Both of them are hard to swallow, very hard. Having watched the race from my room I would like to congratulate Dani Pedrosa for a great race. He rode the best from the start and had a perfect race. I also thought it was a nice touch that Dani showed his support for the anti-guardrail campaign. I had also planned to support the initiative because it is a great cause. Valentino also deserves congratulations for such a great fight back. I'm keen to fight for victory with both of them and if I manage to beat them one day, 'mano a mano', I will feel very proud. The pair of them are as different as they are difficult to beat.

Thank you Pol! Thank you team! I couldn't watch anything on Saturday because I was in the ICU but just as I entered my room on Sunday morning I saw Pol Espargaró holding up a sign with a message of support for me. You have no idea how much words like this can help. Pol is a rider who reminds me a lot of myself when I started, and the early part of our careers have been similar. Later I saw my two bikes with a sign written half in Italian and half in Spanish by my team-mates. Thank you all of you! There is no such thing as failure, simply things that are done well and things that are done badly. Oh, and I'm happy that the Tito Rabat[1] thing turned out to be nothing. I was worried about him.

They have given me painkillers and I feel very comfortable. I want to say thanks to the people who have been to visit me, especially my good friend Jonathan, who has been here practically the whole time, my mother, Marcos Hirsch, Dani Amatriaín, Doctor Mir, Sebastián Salvadó (President of the RACC) and Héctor Martín. The truth is that if I had been on my own the days would have been sad and boring.

I have recently received hundreds of letters from fans, which has made me think about how important it is to set a good example to young people. I will always try to transmit good values, something I hadn't really thought about in the past.

Jorge had just two weeks to recover from the effects of the Catalunya crash. He used them to put in some sessions with Miguel Ángel Violán. 'We spent the time practising interviews in English, trying to get him more fluent and widening his vocabulary. Languages come easily to Jorge – he picks them up quickly. If he put his mind to it he could be the best non-native English speaker on the grid,' affirms Violán. It was in England that Lorenzo smiled for the first time since leaving hospital. As the paddock opened its gates to the Day of Champions in aid of Riders for Health, on the Thursday before the British Grand Prix at Donington Park, Jorge took great comfort from the support of the British public. At the auction a fan paid £5700 for a set of his racing leathers. He started the race second to last on the grid and finished sixth.

[1] Esteve 'Tito' Rabat is a 125cc rider who crashed on the same day as Jorge and was put into an induced coma. He was woken on the Saturday and given the all-clear to leave hospital on the Monday.

Before travelling to Holland he paid a visit to Centre Court at Wimbledon, where he had hoped to see his fellow Mallorcan, Rafa Nadal, in action. Unfortunately the match schedule denied him that opportunity, but it was from the spiritual home of tennis that he travelled to the spiritual home of motorcycle racing: Assen. 'The Cathedral', as it is called, has always been good to Jorge and over the previous four seasons he had celebrated victory on three occasions – in the 125cc class in 2004, and in the 250cc class in 2006 and 2007. In 2005 he was recovering from an operation on his collarbone yet still finished third. Jorge felt at home and had little trouble repeating his sixth-place finish from Donington. The days ran into each other, Jorge travelling from Assen to the next race at Sachsenring via Misano for the Yamaha Fest. Even though he crashed again in Germany, this time it was because of the rain and he had no reason to blame himself. He was finding his feet again.

'After China we put more traction control on the bike,' explains Juanito Llansá. 'But when he was back to full physical fitness there was clearly too much because he was opening the throttle and the bike wasn't pulling in a progressive manner. That's when his nervous side started to come out again because the results weren't coming and he couldn't understand why things weren't working like they had at the start of the season. When we started to gradually remove the traction control after Montmeló and he started to ride it as he knew how again, we got back on our original path, where his wrist had more of an influence than the electronics.'

Extracts from a text written by Jorge Lorenzo entitled:
'I HAVE BEATEN THE FEAR'

The last few weeks have been a difficult period for me; a time of reflection, with many hours spent in hospital, not wanting to crash and hurt myself again. I have taken time to consider my profession, seeing it in a bad light, and that makes you exaggerate the risks it involves and makes you more cautious. Now I think that in a way this injury has been good for me and I would compare this period to a similar situation in 2005, when

I was punished for an incident at Motegi and suspended from the following race in Malaysia. It was a turning point for me because it made me realise that you have to plan every step you take to make sure it is not the wrong one. Now, like three years ago, I've been given a warning shot. Back then it was because I had been too aggressive, this time it is because I believed too much in my own ability. It led me to try things without considering the consequences. It has served as a reminder that, without losing my self-confidence or belief, I can still achieve a lot in the sport, but I still have to bear in mind the need to take care…

I never believed for a second that I would arrive at Donington having lost the 'eye of the tiger'. That is something that can only happen when you have achieved everything you were chasing and your motivation drops. My situation was different. I had hurt myself badly at Montmeló and I was scared it could happen again. I don't hide from fear. In the past I might have been embarrassed to admit that I was scared but I think it is a positive thing to let people see that we are human, and like anybody else we feel scared from time to time. I was scared and I have had to learn to respect my bike, but at least now I can say I have overcome the fear.

However, there was yet another heavy blow to come. It was time to travel to Laguna Seca for the USGP. It had already proved to be a nightmare circuit for Michelin, but Jorge managed to qualify fourth and after a good start in the race he immediately found himself in the leading group. He felt confident, he felt calm, until suddenly he took flight again – just as he had in China – and highsided out of his debut appearance at the legendary track on the first lap. This time the medical report revealed fractures to the third, fourth and fifth metatarsals in his left foot but, thankfully, no further damage to his ankle.

'Laguna Seca was my biggest crash and my lowest point of the season,' reflects Jorge. 'But it was my mistake and I knew why I had crashed – not like at Le Mans or Montmeló. Even so I was still pretty fucked. My ankles again … I thought I had broken the lot this time. It was so painful I thought I'd broken my leg – tibia and fibula. My leg was on fire! Luckily it was more spectacular than it was anything else. The worst thing was I missed my holiday! I spent a month in a cast and couldn't even take a bath. It was one too many injuries for a single season.'

Juanito Llansá has been at Jorge's side for as long as either of them care to remember and there is not much he hasn't seen, but at Laguna Seca he was concerned. 'His morale was extremely low in America,' he recalls. 'He wanted to quit. I was taking him by scooter to the helicopter that was going to transport him from the circuit and Jorge was sitting behind me in tears, with his head resting on my back. He didn't want to hurt himself any more. He'd had enough of crashing and he wanted to quit racing. I told him: "Jorge, that is the last time you ever tell me you're going to quit racing. You are a winner and this is your life." He said that was all very nice and easy for me to say but the one getting hurt was him. He was right, but I had to try and motivate him somehow.'

Luckily the fear never returned and the only way for him to recover his confidence on the bike was by racking up the laps. First of all, a month away from it all did him good, and by the time the paddock reconvened at Brno for the Czech Republic GP his mindset had changed. 'I realised that I just had to start out more relaxed in practice, take it easier basically. That is what I learnt, to take it step by step. Because the reality was that I didn't know the bike, not even 60 per cent. So I began to see that if I did things properly and gradually I was less likely to come across risky situations, on the limit. Sometimes as riders we don't think about the risks, but you do know that however happy you are when you go out onto the track you can quickly find yourself in a situation like Montmeló – waking up in hospital!'

'I think the real change didn't take place in the race at Brno but in the post-race tests on Monday and Tuesday,' reckons Javi Ullate. 'On the Monday everything changed. Jorge was a new man, keen to work and able to do it well. He still wasn't quite the same as he had been at the start of the season but you could see he was much better. At Brno I saw a change in his attitude, he was much more positive. He realised that we were having problems with the tyres but that we had to work with what we had. We worked to fit the geometry and the electronics to the tyres. The rest of the Michelin riders went home because they claimed the tyres were no good but we worked hard. It paid off two weeks later at Misano.'

'At Misano, Rossi's home track, I returned to the podium,' remembers Jorge. 'We went there from Brno, where we'd had a terrible time and I'd had to see my name at the bottom of the timesheets. I'd had to race on tyres that, exaggerating the point a little bit here, could have blown up at any time. Basically, we went there on the back of being barely competitive – two seconds slower than the Bridgestone guys – but the Michelins weren't too bad at Misano, I felt strong in the race and I saw my chance. Stoner crashed and I moved up to second. I tried to catch Valentino but I soon realised that he was out of reach.'

September 2008
A BREAK FOR FREEDOM

During the month of September 2008 Jorge's relationship with his lifelong manager, Dani Amatriaín, began to splinter. Once again, people associated his problems on the track with his personal circumstances off it, allegations Jorge denies. 'My problems away from the track had nothing to do with my crashes,' he insists. 'From a sentimental point of view I wasn't affected at all by what was happening. I had started to see things I didn't like, strange things, but I had so much confidence in this person that I never imagined the things that were going on could happen. Practically right up until the split, until the final month, I still had complete faith in him. I wasn't worried. The crashes were simply a result of me trying to do more than I could with what I had underneath me rather than my concerns about what was going on around me.'

ER: Haven't you ever asked yourself why these things always seem to happen to you?

JL: I don't feel like an unfortunate person, a person who has suffered, in any way. I have toughened up over the years and I don't lose sleep over anything any more. Every night I sleep the eight hours I have to sleep. I don't have any trouble. I don't know if in the future there will be something that keeps me awake but right now there's nothing. Yes, certain things have happened to me that other people, if they were to happen to them, would spend every day worried and depressed about. But, you know, first of all I had to separate from my father and put all of my trust into a person I have now had to separate from. Right now I am with somebody else, somebody who knows both of them and has been with me through all of it. I trust that it won't happen again.

Not everybody who was aware of what was going on at the time subscribes to Jorge's version of it. At the end of the day, we are all human. 'I think that the split with Dani has made Jorge more relaxed,' says Héctor Martín. 'In my opinion, the crash at Laguna Seca was related to problems that were going on off the track. I am convinced of it. The ones at China, Le Mans and Catalunya weren't, but Laguna Seca was. There came a moment, 5 September to be exact, when he split from Dani, face to face in Alella, and he changed his "chip". By the tenth of that month, when he was sent a fax from Las Vegas legally confirming the end of their professional relationship, he was completely liberated.'

'If a man like Valentino Rossi's performances were affected when he had problems with the tax authorities in 2007, how could Jorge's not be?' agrees Javi Ullate. 'What happened to him was like a break-up in a marriage. That would affect anybody.' But the person who was most surprised by what happened, and by Jorge's reaction, despite his vast experience, was Ramón Forcada. 'In real terms he aged a year over the course of 2008 but in terms of maturity he aged a decade. Considering the problems he's had this year he has shown an incredible capacity to shut it all out and concentrate on riding. It was like a thought bypass! Shortly before he would get on the bike you could see that he was troubled, but he would put on his leathers and it was as if he didn't have a care in the world. When the session finished we would chat about what we had to change for the next practice or for the race, and then you saw the worry creep back onto his face. But he came through it, he rose above it. Indianapolis was the clearest example of that, and the clearest example of him making the bike his own. He had never finished on the podium in a wet race before and he finished third. Plus it would have been second if they hadn't stopped the race!'

Throughout the weekend in Indianapolis, Jorge barely moved from his motorhome. 'We had a 100 per cent record in the United States,' smiles Héctor Martín. 'We'd been there twice before and got pulled over by the police both times! So he just kept himself to himself, watching videos on YouTube and the movie *Karate Kid*, which he'd never seen before.'

Even though the Indianapolis Motor Speedway, a temple to racing in the USA, is most famously home to the Indy500 and NASCAR events, the first event that ever took place there was, in fact, a motorcycle race. In 1909 Erwin 'Cannonball' Baker took victory on an Indian. Just short of a full century later, Jorge Lorenzo made his own little piece of history at the Brickyard with the first wet-weather podium of his life – and that includes his amateur junior career. 'Riding in the wet is simply a matter of faith,' says Forcada. 'But since Indianapolis it has become something normal for Jorge. Previously it was abnormal!'

15 September 2008, shortly after the Indianapolis GP
Text written by Jorge Lorenzo entitled:
'RAIN MAN'

I've just had to come out of my hotel room at Indianapolis in my underpants. A fire warning is blaring out from the speakers in the halls, telling people not to use the lifts. Luckily it's a false alarm but what a fright! Coincidentally it is the weapon used to combat fires that takes the starring role in this very column. In fact, alongside 'Ike' (the hurricane that was supposed to be brushing past the circuit on Sunday) it has been the main character in this weekend's entire story. The only day water wasn't falling on Indy was Saturday and on Sunday it reached ridiculous levels, it was literally blowing a gale and at midday in my motorhome we were convinced that Race Direction would suspend our race, set to take place at 3pm local time, 9pm in Spain.

If I'm honest with you, I didn't fancy this race much. Simply imagining myself going through a corner at over 200km/h in three or four centimetres of water removed any desire I had to get on my bike (the thing I care most about in my life). Looking at the images on the television you could see the sorry state the track was in so I came out of my motorhome, looked at the sky and prayed for 'Rain Man' (Dustin Hoffman, 1988) to keep up his work and force the race to be cancelled or postponed. My prayers were answered but not in the way I had hoped because right at that very moment the rain stopped and the circuit was gripped by a strong wind. Four trucks were sent out to sweep and dry the new section of the track, which was the slipperiest and most dangerous part. There was no question about it now, the race was going ahead.

When the red lights finally went out I got a good start but I was passed by three riders into the first turn. It was one of those occasions where you need to be alert and ride with care, using the pace set by others as a marker before pushing to find your own limit. I saw the first few 'moments' take place ahead of me and within a few corners I had latched onto Pedrosa, who was running fifth. It was already clear that if I could stay upright then this was not going to turn into one of my usual disastrous wet races.

I passed Pedrosa and caught up with Valentino, who I didn't have much trouble getting past either. However, the Italian, wily old fox that he is, latched onto my wheel and got into a position where he could pass me back at any opportunity. I think he knew that if he couldn't get past me quickly he would have more difficulty doing so later in the race because I always tend to get stronger. As it turned out, my Fiat Yamaha team-mate used the slippery section of track to make his move.

Rossi then passed Dovizioso and went after Hayden, who held a three-second lead at the front. I also passed Andrea although it took me three laps to do so, enough time for me to lose touch with Valentino. My mission was simple: keep up a good rhythm to maintain the gap over Dovi and Stoner and see if it brought me any closer to the front. When it really started to rain I made up the gap that separated me from Hayden but the red flag came out, leaving the third step of the podium as the only available option.

Jorge celebrated his 'new-found freedom' on the podium. 'Up to that point, Jorge had not been the man in charge of his own things – not his life or his money,' says Marcos Hirsch, his new manager. 'A manager without a termination clause!' jokes the Brazilian. 'Jorge was a slave in a golden cage. Even though it was made of gold, it was still a cage! The first change we wanted to make with him was to open the cage. At Valencia, in the final Grand Prix of the year, Jorge was already doing things he'd never done before. He was free to do things his way. He was still surrounded by sharks and leeches, but he was able to hold his hand out to whomever he chose, which he couldn't do before. I said to him, "Jorge, say what you like, do what you like. The old regime is over!" I think it has been a huge weight off his shoulders and I think that he is smiling now because he is having fun, he is happy.'

MotoGP Rookie of the Year
A WORLD CHAMPION IN WAITING

Motegi is one of Jorge's worst circuits. His only podium there was a third-place finish in the 250cc race in 2006. In the 125cc class, in 2003, he came off at the chicane before the start-finish straight when he was fighting at the front, and in 2005, during his rookie season in the 250cc class, he crashed out in an incident that also earned him a one-race suspension. But in 2008 things changed for the better: he picked up the fourth pole position of his debut season among the world's elite. 'I felt I bounced back with that pole at Motegi, I recovered my confidence and I felt it was all coming back to me and that I was riding really well again,' says Jorge. 'Unfortunately, in the race, the tyres never gave me the opportunity to finish off what had been an otherwise positive weekend. I had problems with grip and with my starts. I hadn't had a good start since Portugal and I was continually losing positions that were then impossible to make back. That is something I definitely have to improve for 2009. After Catalunya I never recovered the confidence to ride like I had at the start of the season. I felt safer, perhaps, but I never had total confidence in the bike and tyres. That is why I didn't win again. Although the level had been raised as well and that made everything even harder.'

Valentino Rossi won the race at Motegi and with it the title of World Champion for the eighth time in all classes, his sixth in MotoGP.

Additionally, and thanks to Jorge's contribution, Yamaha clinched their eleventh constructors' title with a points tally that would eventually reach 402 by Valencia, breaking their previous record of 381 from the 2005 season. And despite the wall down the middle of the garage, Fiat Yamaha proved to be the world's strongest team, finishing with an advantage of 159 points over their nearest rivals, Repsol Honda.

On a personal level Jorge finished the year fourth in the championship on 190 points, making him the most successful debutant of the four-stroke MotoGP era and comfortably securing him the 'Rookie of the Year' title. 'Doing as well as he did at circuits that were so new to him like Misano, which was only being used for the second time, or Indianapolis, are sure signs that when he gains experience Jorge is a World Champion in waiting,' asserts Forcada. 'Jorge is capable of producing really strong finishes to races on spent tyres, but he has to improve in the early part of the race. When Jorge sets a fast lap he knows how he has done it. There are other riders who occasionally surprise themselves with a fast lap or who can set a time by following somebody else, but with Jorge he knows why his time was so quick and as such he's able to do it again. He never takes a backward step. He only moves forward, constantly consolidating his progress. Watch out for him in the future!'

My chat with Javi Ullate ends with a comparison between Jorge Lorenzo and the only Spaniard to have won the premier-class title, Alex Crivillé, a man Ullate knows very well. 'Does Jorge have a bit of "Crivi" in him? Definitely! They both go fast immediately. They are not like Biaggi or Cadalora, who can't ride if the bike isn't right, or like other riders who can't race if they're not at the front. They both go quick straight away and they know how to adapt to different situations – a bit like Stoner. The most important thing is that when it came down to the last lap I would always make Alex the favourite. It is the same with Jorge. Whoever he is fighting with, he is the favourite on the last lap and he will beat whoever dares to compete with him. His potential at the end of a race is huge, his limits unknown. There is no doubt, he has what it takes to be World Champion.'

Jorge Lorenzo Guerrero
Results and statistics

Date of birth	4 May 1987
Place of birth	Palma de Mallorca (Spain)
Height	1.73m
Weight	62kg
Place of residence	London
Marital status	Single
Favourite holiday destination	Palma de Mallorca
Hero	Max Biaggi
Favourite actors	Brad Pitt, Tom Cruise
Favourite fictional character	Bart Simpson
Favourite books	*Scar Tissue* by Anthony Kiedis
	It's Not About the Bike: My Journey Back to Life by Lance Armstrong
	The Warrior Athlete: Body, Mind and Spirit by Dan Millman
	The Game by Neil Strauss
	How to Win Friends and Influence People by Dale Carnegie.
Favourite films	*The Beach* and *The Notebook*
Favourite actress	Angelina Jolie
Favourite music	Red Hot Chili Peppers, Linkin Park
Favourite car	Aston Martin
First bike	Puch 50
Favourite food	Paella and pasta

Favourite animal	Lion
Main strength	Willingness to improve
Main defect	Sometimes too bad-tempered and vain
Things I would take to a desert island…	A motorcycle, a television, a fishing rod and a boat to come back Jorge later says 'a buddy and two chicks!'
Dislikes	Losing, laziness
Likes	Honesty, a solid personality, being a good person
Dream	To get close to absolute happiness
Motorcycle	Yamaha M1
Number	99
Favourite circuit	Assen
Hobbies	Video games, football (soccer), music, friends
Best moment	My first victory (Brazil 2003)
Best races	Assen 2004; Italy 2006; Australia 2007; Portugal 2008; Indianapolis 2008
Worst races	Malaysia 2002; Catalunya 2005; Japan 2007
If I wasn't a rider I would like to be…	An actor
Website	www.lorenzo99.com

Track record

125cc

GP appearances (2002–2004)	46
First GP	Spanish GP 2002
Pole positions	3
First pole position	Malaysian GP 2003
Victories	4
First victory	Brazilian GP 2003
2nd place	1
3rd places	4
Total podiums	9
Fastest laps	3
Points	279
Titles	0

250cc

GP appearances (2005–2007)	48
First GP	Spanish GP 2005
Pole positions	23
First pole position	Italian GP 2005
Victories	17
First victory	Spanish GP 2006
2nd places	6
3rd places	6
Total podiums	29
Fastest laps	4
Points	768
Titles	2

MotoGP

GP appearances (2008)	17
First GP	GP of Qatar 2008
Pole positions	4
First pole position	GP of Qatar 2008
Victories	1
First victory	Portuguese GP 2008
2nd places	3
3rd places	2
Total podiums	6
Fastest laps	1
Points	190

TOTAL

GP appearances (until 2009)	111
Pole positions	30
Victories	22
2nd places	10
3rd places	12
Total podiums	44
Fastest laps	8
Points	1237
Titles	2

Season by season

2008
4th in MotoGP World Championship (Yamaha). 190 points
* 1 victory: Portugal
* 4 poles: Qatar, Spain, Portugal, Japan
* 1 fastest lap: Portugal
* 3 second places: Qatar, France, San Marino
* 2 third places: Spain, Indianapolis

2007
250cc World Champion (Aprilia). 312 points
* 9 victories: Qatar, Spain, China, France, Catalunya, Netherlands, Czech Republic, San Marino, Australia
* 9 poles: Qatar, Spain, China, France, Catalunya, Netherlands, Czech Republic, San Marino, Australia
* 3 fastest laps: China, Czech Republic, Australia
* 1 second place: Turkey
* 2 third places: Portugal, Malaysia

2006
250cc World Champion (Aprilia). 289 points
* 8 victories: Spain, Qatar, Italy, Netherlands, Great Britain, Czech Republic, Malaysia, Australia
* 10 poles: Spain, Qatar, Turkey, Italy, Netherlands, Great Britain, Germany, Czech Republic, Australia, Japan
* 1 fastest lap: Netherlands
* 1 second place: Catalunya
* 2 third places: Germany, Japan

2005
5th in 250cc World Championship (Honda). 167 points
* 4 poles: Italy, Netherlands, Czech Republic, Qatar
* 4 second places: Italy, Czech Republic, Qatar, Valencia
* 2 third places: Netherlands, Australia

2004

4th in 125cc World Championship (Derbi). 179 points

* 3 victories: Netherlands, Czech Republic, Qatar

* 2 poles: Catalunya, Qatar

* 2 fastest laps: Netherlands, Qatar

2003

12th in 125cc World Championship (Derbi). 79 points

Takes first pole in Malaysia, first fastest lap at Motegi and first victory in Brazil

Becomes youngest Spanish rider ever to win a GP at 16 years and 139 days

* 1 victory in CEV: Jarama

2002

21st in 125cc World Championship (Derbi). 21 points

Becomes youngest rider ever to make GP debut (15 years and 1 day) and youngest to score points (15 years and 43 days)

2001

4th in CEV. 69 points

6th in 125cc European Championship

*1 victory: Braga, Portugal

2000

18th in CEV

1999

125cc Copa Aprilia Champion

1998

50cc Copa Aprilia Champion

INDEX

AC/DC 205
Alella 23, 112, 305
Alméria circuit 276-277, 280, 283
Alonso, Fernando17, 31, 61
Alonso, Javier 101
Alzamora, Emilio 50-51, 242, 254, 256
Amatriaín, Dani 21, 39, 46, 55, 57, 102, 111, 165, 174, 290
  becomes JL's manager 139-141
  and Dani Palau 23-24
  first sees JL 18-20, 139, 238, 240
  and incident with police in US 56
  and JL's early races 244
  and JL's education 112
  and JL's father 78-79, 82, 149, 150, 161, 168-169
  and JL's first world title 151
  and JL's maturity 154-155
  and JL's nervousness 150
  and JL's professional development 20-21, 26, 142-143, 144-145
  and JL's respect for team 36
  motivating JL 290-291
  and negotiations for MotoGP contract 92, 274, 275, 276, 278
  recruits Alex Debón 147, 175, 193-194
  splits with JL 83, 84-85, 304, 305
  2005 season 100, 265-266
  2006 season 269
  2007 season 193, 219, 220, 224, 262
  2008 season 300
  and victory celebrations 222, 223
Ambrosini, Dario 270
Amsterdam 55-56
Angeloni, Mattia 256
Aoyama, Hiroshi 99
Aoyama, Shuhei 160, 161, 269
Aprilia 37-38, 78, 86, 92, 172, 176, 193, 246, 262, 264-265, 269, 274, 276, 282 see also Fortuna Aprilia Team
Aprilia Cup see Copa Aprilia
Aprilia RSA 206
Aprilia RSW250 210, 235

Armani, Giorgio 68
Armengol, Carme 235, 237
Armstrong, Lance 61, 102
AS (sports daily) 41, 95
As Good As It Gets 227
Assen circuit 96, 132, 231-232, 244, 301

Baker, Erwin 'Cannonball' 306
Baldolini, Alex 244
Balearic Motocross Championship 131
Ballerini, Andrea 244-245
Ballington, Kork 270
Barberá, Héctor 95, 96, 97, 162-163, 172, 174, 251, 257, 296
Barcelona 21, 22-24, 34-35, 139
  Calle Numancia 27
  Calle Vilamarí 27
  Flash-Flash restaurant 46
  Hotel Barceló-Sants fitness centre 46, 216-217, 236
  Las Ramblas 166
  Monlau mechanics' school 19, 34, 111-112, 140, 141, 143, 240-241
  Port Olímpic 43-44
Barcelona Business Administration School conference 210-211
Bautista, Álvaro 46, 95, 96, 198, 204, 249, 250
Beatles, the 17
Biaggi, Max 29, 86, 87, 90, 213, 243, 249, 270, 272, 282, 284, 287, 288-289, 296, 309
Bianco, Stefan 249
Bonci, Luciano 38
Brazil, 125cc Grand Prix, 2003 40
Bridgestone 88, 107
British GP, 125cc, 2003 49
British GP, 250cc, 2007 231
Brivio, Davide 274
Brno circuit 96-97
Bush, George W 17
Butler, Paul 101

Cadalora, Luca 203, 270, 309
Camino de Santiago pilgrimage 277
Cantona, Eric 17, 59, 70

Capanna, Massimo 162, 276-277
Capellini, Arnaldo 274
Capirossi, Loris 242
Cardús, Carlos 41
Cardús, Ricky 44, 45, 57, 61, 70, 111, 230, 277
Carmel, California, 'The Hog's Breath Inn' 278
Cartagena circuit 259
Casanova, Giacomo 17
Casas, Rosa 235, 237
Catalunya circuit 17, 230, 259-260, 296-297
Catalunya College for Journalists 25
Cervantes, Miguel de 170
Chercoles, Mela 101
Chinese GP, 250cc, 2006 177
Chinese MotoGP, 2008 292-293
Chupa Chups 58, 215
Cinderella Man 167
Clinica Mobile 170-171, 172, 197, 260, 294
Clooney, George 17
Coduras, Oscar 211
Coleman, Ronnie 47
Conte, Loris 38
Copa Aprilia 18, 22, 231
Copa Aprilia, 50cc 135, 137, 140, 141
  1997 238-239
  Caja Madrid race 18-19, 20, 137
  1998 35-36, 241-242
  Montmeló race 215
Copa Aprilia, 125cc, 1999 35-36, 242
Crippa, Walter 36
Crivillé, Alex 90, 103, 109, 239, 309
Crowe, Russell 167, 226
Cruise, Tom 228
Cruyff, Johan 215
'Cycling Manager 08' game 58
Czech Republic 125cc GP, 2004 96-97

D'Antin, Luis 41, 132
Dailymotos.com 79-80
Dainese 277
Dall'Igna, Gigi 176
Danis, Claude 101

316

de Angelis, Alex 97-98, 99, 100-102, 172, 173, 193, 202, 203, 218, 250, 252, 255, 260
Debón, Alex 17, 28-29, 147, 157, 158, 204, 205, 209, 277
    email to JL after Italian GP 2007 practice 198-200
    factory ride 207-208
    in Italian 250cc GP, 2006 172, 173
    letters to JL 158-159, 160, 194-196, 202-203
    relationship with JL 158-159, 160, 169-172, 173-174, 175-176, 193, 196, 198-203, 204-205, 206-207, 208
        in Spanish GPs 193, 205-207
    2006 season 172, 173, 269
Derbi 35, 38, 39, 40, 42, 54, 132, 138, 229, 246, 251, 252, 254, 266, 267
Di Giacomo, Lucas 210
Diario de Mallorca (newspaper) 77-79, 147-148
Disney films 227
Doha, Hotel Ritz-Carlton 219, 220
Dominican Republic 43, 44-45, 113
Donington Park circuit 29, 231, 300, 301
Doohan, Mick 87, 239, 251
Dosil, Joaquín 147, 148, 163, 164, 263
Dovizioso, Andrea 75, 97, 159, 160, 161, 163, 172, 176, 199, 202, 203, 204, 206, 229, 232, 233-234, 244, 245-246, 291
    JL's mask 225
    2008 season 296, 307
Ducati 275, 276
Dutch MotoGP, 2008 300
Dutch TT, 125cc, 2004 96
Dutch TT, 250cc, 2007 231-232
Dutch TT, 500cc, 1998 132

E.T. 227
Eckl, Harald 275
Edwards, Colin 91, 92, 94, 105, 277, 281, 295-296
Einstein, Albert 17, 62
El País (newspaper) 119-122
Elías, Tony 197-198, 244
Ericksonian Therapy 167-168
Espargaró, Aleix 57
Espargaró, Pol 57, 193, 206, 277, 300
Estoril circuit 283, 287-288
Eto'o, Samuel 15
Europe (band) 210
European Championship, 125cc, 2001 244-245, 254
Eva (girlfriend) 113, 114, 148, 164-165, 166
'Eye of the Tiger' 220

Facebook 59
family relationships in racing 127-129
Fiat Yamaha Team 36, 42, 92, 278, 286, 309 see also Yamaha
'Final Countdown' 210
Flores, Javier Menéndez 64, 66
'Football Manager 08' game 58
Forcada, Ramón 36, 42-43, 279, 281, 283-284, 295, 305-306, 309
Forés, Javier 242
Fortuna 176
Fortuna Aprilia Team 210, 218 see also Aprilia
French GP, 250cc, 2006 163, 164
French GP, 250cc, 2007 223, 224, 225, 260-262
French MotoGP, 2008 295-296
Furusawa, Masao 286-287

Game, The 44, 114
Gandhi, Mahatma 17
García, David 44, 45
García, José María 28
Gardner, Wayne 270
Garibaldi 218
Gates, Bill 16-17
Gaudí, Antoni 17
German GP, 250cc, 2007 88-89, 204
Gibernau, Sete 242
Gladiator 167, 226, 228
GQ magazine 217
Guerrero, María see Lorenzo, María
Gurt, Pere 18, 19, 25, 57, 169, 224, 226, 235, 236, 257, 275, 276, 277-278, 279

Harada, Tetsuya 242, 270
Harrison, George 65
Hayden, Nicky 197, 307
Heidolf, Dirk 225
Hirsch, Marcos 46, 61, 66, 95, 146, 150, 157-158, 164, 165, 169, 174, 209, 269, 300
    and films 218, 229-230
    and JL's arrival in MotoGP 281
    and JL's father 81, 82, 146-147
    JL's mental training 48-52, 53-54, 229-230
    as JL's new manager 307-308
    JL's physical fitness training 46-48, 52, 53, 216, 217, 219
    and JL's poor form 165-166
    and JL's victory celebrations 217, 218, 222, 234-235, 292
        motivation of JL 165-166, 167-168, 169, 290
Hola (magazine) 247
Honda 55, 75, 86, 245, 256, 257, 262, 264, 275
Honda XR70 126
Honduras 43, 44-45, 113
How to Win Friends and Influence People 70-71
Hungaroring circuit 244
Hurricane, The 230

Indianapolis MotoGP, 2008 197, 306
Interviú (magazine) 117
Istanbul Park circuit 160, 161, 269
Italian GP, 250cc, 2006 170, 172-173
Italian GP, 250cc, 2007 95-96, 197-200
Italian MotoGP, 2008 296

Jacarepaguá circuit, Brazil 40, 250, 251-256, 257
Jackson, Michael 227
Japanese GP, 250cc, 2005 99-101, 265
Japanese GP, 500cc, 1998 87
Japanese MotoGP, 2008 107-108, 308
Jarvis, Lin 55, 275, 276, 277, 278, 279
Jerez circuit 18-19, 20, 105-106, 137, 142, 222, 241-242, 247-249, 287
Jesus Christ 17
Juan Carlos, HRH King 106, 287

Kallio, Mika 244
Karate Kid 306
Kato, Daijiro 269, 270, 272
Kawasaki 275
King, Don 235
Kocinski, John 286
Kuala Lumpur 56

La Voz de Galicia (newspaper) 84-85
Laguna Seca circuit 109, 116, 277, 278, 300-301, 305
Last Castle, The 230
Lavado, Carlos 270
Le Mans circuit 42, 43, 163, 164, 223, 224, 225, 260-262, 295-296
Ledesma, Xavi 231, 240
Legends of the Fall 228
Lewis, Carl 16, 71
Llansá, Juan 'Holly/Juanito' 30, 36, 37, 39-42, 43, 86, 95, 96, 159, 215, 224, 236-237, 244-245, 250, 251-252, 262-264, 265, 266, 273
    and JL's animosity with Dani Pedrosa 98-99
    and JL's move to Yamaha 274-275
    and pit boards 140
    2008 season 287, 296-297, 301, 303
Llansá, Zaida 42, 236
Locatelli, Roberto 163, 257, 269
lollipops see Chupa Chups
London, Laver Street apartment 154, 214
London, Mau Mau bar, Portobello Road 65-67, 83
Lorenzo, Chicho (father) 38, 76-77, 84, 262, 290
    in Barcelona 140, 141, 142

character 110
and Dani Amatriaín 18-19, 139, 149, 150, 161, 168-169
early life 129, 132
and JL's early races 239-240, 241, 245, 259
and JL's early years 109-110, 111, 126-127, 134
and JL's education 112, 143
and JL's first Grand Prix 248
and JL's fitness 46
and JL's injuries 136-137, 263
and Marcos Hirsch 146-147
newspaper article 84-85
and 125cc Grands Prix 248, 250
opinions on JL 83
relationship with JL 76-77, 84, 137-138
problems 77-82, 129, 132, 144, 145-146, 147, 148-149, 164-165
rebuilding 83, 155-156
separates from María 137
and use of sports psychologist 147-148, 163, 164
and Valentino Rossi 86, 146
training JL 130, 131-132, 133, 136, 138
Lorenzo, Jorge
and 'AC/DC' 205
accidents see Lorenzo, Jorge: injuries
acting classes 154, 213
admiration of Valentino Rossi 86-88, 89-93, 213-214
arrogance perceived by others 123-124
artistic talents 141
in Barcelona 34-35, 140, 141
and being called a 'crack' 73-74
and being himself in public 67-68
and bike problems 263-265
birth 129
and this book 66-67
and camel joke 42, 43
care about personal appearance 216
and charisma 69-70
Christian name variations 126, 132
coming back after Catalunya crash 297-300, 301-302
coming back after Laguna Seca crash 303-304
competitive modesty 117-119
crowned 250cc world champion (2006) 177, 270
crowned 250cc world champion (2007) 29, 30, 204, 205-206, 234, 236
desire to be different 85-86, 214
desires in life 16-17

and dividing wall in pit box 88, 94, 95, 309
early races 238-243, 258-259
early years 22, 76-77, 109-110, 126-127, 129, 130-135
and education 111-112, 144
emotional side 29-30, 159-160
and excuses 75-76
first Grand Prix 247-249
first MotoGP victory 283, 287-288
first motorcycle 130-131
first race 214-215
first world championship win 250, 251-256, 257
first world title 150-151
and films 57, 167, 217-218, 219, 227-228, 229, 235, 286, 290, 306
flag, 'Lorenzo's Land' 222, 225, 226, 233, 237
and friends 70-71, 110
and girls 43, 44-45, 113-117, 217-218, 289
and gladiators 167, 226, 228, 229, 230
hairstyle 19, 37, 126, 127, 135
and Héctor Barberá 162-163
and Héctor Martín 54-57
holiday in Dominican Republic ('Operation Honduras') 43, 44-45
and humility 118-119, 122
injuries 136-137, 224, 246-247, 258-263, 293-295, 296-297, 298, 302-303
joins Aprilia 269, 274
joins Derbi 246
joins Yamaha 87-88, 92, 151, 280-281
at Kenny Roberts' ranch 267-268
lack of 'social education' 111, 138
leads MotoGP World Championship 289
leaves Mallorca 21-22
leisure activities 58, 59
letter to his team 37-38
and Marcos Hirsch 165-166
maturity 154-155, 156, 273
medical staff 53
and mental training with Marcos Hirsch 48-52, 53-54, 263
and money 122-123
motivation techniques 167-168, 169, 219, 291
and motocross 131, 239
MotoGP 'Rookie of the Year' title 309
negotiations for MotoGP contract 274-279
nicknames 48
number one, being 72-73, 194-196

and physical fitness training 46-48, 52, 53, 74, 143, 216, 219-220, 223
and pit boards 140
pole position for MotoGP debut 284
and practising 62-63, 74-75, 126, 130, 131, 136
predicting results 251
public persona 124
public speaking training 24-28, 31-32, 210-211, 212
race number 21, 60, 210
and reading books 43-44, 61, 64, 65, 70, 143; 297
records 249, 251, 257, 270, 272, 284, 288, 294
relationship with Alex Debón 158-159, 160, 169-172, 173-174, 175-176, 193, 196, 198-204, 204-205, 206-207, 208
relationship with Dani Pedrosa 97-99, 101-102, 103, 104-105, 106-107, 145, 287
relationship with father 76-77, 84, 137-138
problems 77-82, 129, 132, 144, 145-146, 147, 148-149, 164-165
rebuilding 83, 155-156
relationship with mother 153-154
relationship with Valentino Rossi 93-95
reputation as risky rider 97-98
and respect for team 35, 36-39, 43
and responsibility 60-61
on retirement 125
riding qualities 238, 240
school days 21-22, 141
seeks recognition 211-213
and sister Laura 134
and sleeping 55-56, 109-110, 305
as Spanish hero 31
splits with Dani Amatriaín 304, 305
sponsorship 32-33, 215
suspension, one race 265, 301
texts
'Does practice make perfect?' 62-63
'Flying is not impossible' 261-262
'I have beaten the fear' 301-302
'If only I could...' 16-17
'In my free time' 58
'In search of glory' 197-198
'Let's talk cinema' 227-228
'Live for the moment' 271-272
'My first GP' 247
'My left hand writes' 299-300
'My moment' 252-256

INDEX

'Rain man' 306-307
'Sighting lap' 220-221
'The aliens have not yet
landed' 88-89
'The debut' 280-281
'The kid with the stars'
126-127
'To America with the Roberts
clan' 267-268
'To my successor' 208-209
'25 keys to being a number
one' 72-73
'Yo, Adrian, I did it!' 289-291
victory celebrations (the
'LorenShow') 210, 214, 215-217,
218, 221-222, 223-226, 229, 230,
231-232, 234-236, 292
visualisations 167, 168, 219,
220-221
wet races 266-267, 306-307
'X-fuera' ('around the
outside') moves 211, 254,
255, 256
Lorenzo, Laura (sister) 134,
137, 154
Lorenzo, María (mother) 65-66,
109, 132, 151, 237, 300
against JL's education
finishing 143
early life with husband
Chicho 129
guidance for JL 150, 152,
153, 154
and JL's childhood 129-130,
133-134, 135, 138-139, 141
and JL's diet 152-153
and JL's early races 215, 239
and JL's injuries 136-137
and JL's relationship with his
father 145, 147, 149-150, 155
pilgrimage to monastery 152
relationship with JL 153-154
separates from Chicho 137
and use of sports psychologist
148
and Valentino Rossi 214
and watching JL race
151-152
Losail circuit, Qatar 219, 221,
283, 284-285, 286
Luzzi, Carlo 36

Madrid, Auditorio de la Casa de
América de 210
Madrid, 'Charlie's' specialist
shop 235
Malaysian GP, 250cc, 2007 234,
236-237
Mallorca 21, 22, 122, 141, 155-156
see also Palma de Mallorca
Monasterio de Lluc 152
Muro circuit 258-259
Manciucca, Fabricio 36
Mancurti, Ivanno 37
Mandela, Nelson 17
Mang, Antón 270, 272
Maradona, Diego 17

Martín, Héctor 54-57, 58, 59-60,
94, 107, 294, 296, 297, 300,
305, 306
Martín, Marc 25, 225
Martínez, Eugenio 'Cheni' 15,
34, 35, 36, 47, 73, 77, 86, 118,
140, 143, 216, 217, 229, 236,
272-273
Martinez, Juan 279
Martorell, Gonzalo de 54
Maynard, Kyle 61
McEnroe, John 17, 70
Meda, Guido 226, 228, 229
Melandri, Marco 91, 132, 217,
251, 272
Meridius, Maximus Decimus
167, 226, 228
Messi, Lionel 17
Michelin 88, 107, 302, 304
Milan 32-33
Million Dollar Baby 235
Mir, Dr Xavier 294, 300
Misano circuit 228-229, 304
Mohammad Ali 17
Monterey, California 56-57, 116,
277-278
Montmeló circuit 215, 230, 296-297
Most circuit, Czech Republic
244-245
Motegi circuit, Japan
99-101, 308
Moto Salom 238
'MotoGP Club' (Spanish TV
programme) 30, 103-104
MotoGP 2008 282-309
Catalunya, practice 296-297
Chinese 292-293
Dutch 301
French 295-296
Indianapolis 306
Italian 296
Japanese 107-108, 308
Portuguese 283, 287-288
Qatar 283, 284-285, 286
San Marino 304
Spanish 105-106, 287
US 187, 302-303, 305
Motorsport48 24, 57,
221-222, 233
MotoViva magazine 54
Mugello circuit, Italy 46, 95-96,
170, 172-173, 197-200, 225-226,
257-258, 296
Mulero, Santi 279

Nadal, Rafa 17, 61, 135, 301
Nakajima, Masahiko 275
Negri, Valentino 36
Nieto, Ángel 243
No Excuses 61
Nolan 277

Okada, Tadayuki 284
Oliva, Jordi 226
Olivé, Joan 57, 102, 241-242
O'Neal, Shaquille 17
Osho 297

Palau, Dani 22-24, 44, 45, 115,
141, 153, 260
and JL's victory celebrations
217, 218, 221, 222, 223, 226, 230,
231, 232, 235
Palma de Mallorca 19, 21,
129, 246
Aquacity Waterpark 132,
133, 135
go-kart and minibike circuits
126-127, 130-131, 132, 133,
136, 213
Hotel Victoria 25, 26
La Milagrosa school 21-22,
36, 132, 135, 215
Son Dureta Hospital 129
Pedrosa, Dani 99, 100-102, 250,
252, 254, 258, 259, 260, 264, 265,
274, 288
animosity with JL 97-99,
101-102, 103, 104-105, 106-107,
145, 287
2008 season 285, 287,
288, 299
Peña, Ivan de la 48
Pérez, Jordi 21, 32, 33, 109, 118,
212, 229, 265-266
Pérez de Rozas, Emilio 278
Picasso, Pablo 17
Pitt, Andrew 280
Pitt, Brad 17, 228
Play It Again, Sam 228
PlayStation 22, 23, 34, 38, 57,
267, 292-293
Poggiali, Manuel 163, 249
Pons, Sito 270
Pope, the 17
Portugal, European
Championship, 125cc, 2001 256
Portugal, 125cc Grand Prix of,
2003 40
Portuguese MotoGP, 2008 283,
287-288
Presley, Elvis 17
'Prima' ketchup 32-33
Puig, Alberto 101, 102, 103,
106, 139

Qatar GP, 250cc, 2007 219, 221
Qatar MotoGP, 2008 283,
284-285, 286

Rainey, Wayne 243
'Rambo' films 295
Raúl, González 31
Red Hot Chili Peppers 67, 71, 76,
85, 95, 108, 113, 117, 220, 230
Repsol Honda 309 see also Honda
Requena, Valentín 242
Riders for Health Day of
Champions 300, 301
Rio de Janeiro GP, 125cc, 2003
250, 251-256, 257
Roberts, Kenny 267-268
Roberts Jnr, Kenny 268
'Rocky' films 57, 167, 219, 220,
221, 236, 237, 289, 290, 291

Rodriguez, Ángel 243-244, 250
Rodríguez, Valeriano 'Vale' 37
Romagnoli, Daniele 36
Ronaldinho 31, 70
Rossi, Valentino 16, 17, 56, 85,
105, 106, 213, 234, 242, 243, 272,
283, 288-289, 291
    Chicho Lorenzo's views on
86, 146
    JL's admiration of 86-88,
89-93, 213-214
    JL's relationship with 93-95
    move to Yamaha 274
    2008 season 284-285,
286-288, 295-296, 299, 307, 308
    victory celebrations 214,
215, 237
Rovira, Alex 119-122
Rozas, Emilio Pérez de 278
RSM 27
Rubén (friend) 132, 133,
136, 213

Sabbatani, Max 242
Sabina, Joaquín 64-65, 66
Sacchi, Giampiero 35, 165,
246, 258
Sachsenring circuit 204
Salgari, Emilio 234
Salom, David 238, 239
Salom, Toni 238, 239, 240
Salom family 238-239
Salvadó, Sebastián 300
San Marino GP, 250cc, 2007 202,
228-229
San Marino MotoGP, 2008 304
Sandi, Giovanni 37, 234, 249
Sanna, Simone 243
Saturday Night Fever 218, 228
Schwantz, Kevin 211, 243, 256
Sepang circuit, Malaysia 29, 30,
234, 236-237
Serra, Esther 233, 235, 277
Shanghai circuit 161, 292-293
Sheene, Barry 270
Silva, Iván 140
Silva, Tony 84
Simón, Julián 36, 102-103,
249, 250
Sinatra, Frank 17
Smets, Joel 239
Solo Moto (magazine) 279
Spanish Boxing Federation 235
Spanish Championship, 125cc
(CEV), 2000 243-244
Spanish Championship, 125cc,
2001 244
Spanish GP
    125cc, 2002 247-249
    250cc, 2005 259-260, 262-263
    250cc, 2006 176-193, 217,218,
269-270
    250cc, 2007 43, 205-207, 222
Spanish Motocross
Championship, 80cc 239
Spanish MotoGP, 2008
106-106, 287

sponsors 58
Stallone, Sylvester 220
'Staying Alive' 218
Stoner, Casey 91, 107, 250-251,
252, 254, 255, 258, 274, 282-283,
304, 309
Strauss, Neil 44, 114
Studio 54 228
Suárez, Carlos 'Carlitos' 37-38,
44, 45
Suppo, Livio 275
Survivor 220
Susmozas, Jonathan 44-45, 300
Suzuka circuit, Japan 87,
107-108

Takahashi, Yuki 163, 172
Televisión Española see TVE
Thailand holiday 59
300 (film) 167, 226, 228
Top Gun 228
Toseland, James 55
Travolta, John 218, 227-228
Turkish GP, 250cc, 2006 160,
161, 269
TVE 30, 90, 103-104, 116, 129,
130, 220, 221, 242, 277, 278
Tyson, Mike 17

Uccio (Valentino Rossi's buddy) 23
Ullate, Javier 36, 43, 94, 105,
282, 284, 297, 303, 305, 309
US MotoGP, 2008 197,
302-303, 305

Valencia circuit (Cheste) 43,
176, 193, 205-207, 217, 218, 244,
262-263, 269-270
Violán, Miguel Ángel 25, 26-28,
29, 31, 60, 69, 87, 98, 115,
118-119, 122, 210, 211, 300

Waldmann, Ralf 86
website 22, 23
Wimbledon, Centre Court 301
World Championship, 125cc,
2002 39, 246-250
    Spanish GP 247-249
World Championship, 125cc,
2003 40, 250, 251-252
    British GP 49
    Rio GP 250, 251-256, 257
World Championship, 125cc,
2004 257, 264
    Czech Republic GP 96-97
    Dutch TT 96
World Championship, 250cc,
2005 145, 257-258, 264, 265
    Italian GP 257-258
    Japanese GP 99-101, 265
    Spanish GP 259-260, 262-263
World Championship, 250cc,
2006 150, 160-161, 269-270, 290
    Chinese GP 161
    French GP 163, 164
    Italian GP 170, 172-173

    Spanish GP 176, 193, 217,
218, 269-270
    Turkish GP 160, 161, 269
World Championship, 250cc,
2007 43, 200-207, 219-237, 222,
225-226, 270, 272-273
    British GP 29, 231
    Catalunya GP 230
    Dutch TT 215-232
    French GP 223, 224, 225,
260-262
    German GP 204
    Italian GP 46, 95-96, 197-200,
225-226
    Malaysian GP 29, 30, 234,
236-237
    Qatar GP 219, 221
    San Marino GP 202, 228-229
    Spanish GP 17, 205-207
World Championship, MotoGP,
2008 see MotoGP 2008

Yamaha 91, 146, 288-289, 309
see also Fiat Yamaha Team
    dividing wall in pit box 88,
94, 95, 309
    JL signs for 87-88, 92, 151,
279, 280-281
    JL's arrival at 280-281
    JL's negotiations with
274-279
    'sofa of champions' 55-56
Yamaha M1 41, 92-93, 282-283,
284, 286-287
Young, Angus 205
YouTube 59, 230, 306

Zidane, Zinedine 17